# MAINLY MURDER

Thomas White, Midshipman at the Bar of the high Court of Justiciary for the Murder of William Jones, Seaman on the Shore of Leith, on the 15th of June, 1814. —

Mr. Midshipman Whyte at the Bar

*(From an etching by Kay)*

# MAINLY MURDER

BY

## WILLIAM ROUGHEAD

"Yes," murmured the magistrate, "yes, M. Tabaret,
you have discovered the criminal. The evidence is
palpable, even to the blind."

EMILE GABORIAU: *The Widow Lerouge.*

WITH FOUR HALF-TONE ILLUSTRATIONS

CASSELL AND COMPANY LTD.
London, Toronto, Melbourne and Sydney

*First published* . . 1937

Printed in Great Britain by T. and A. CONSTABLE LTD.
at the University Press, Edinburgh
F. 337

# PREFACE

"IF people must murder in the byways of an immense world,"
says the hero of that fantastic fiction, *The Inheritors*, "they
must do murder and pay the price. But that I should have
been mixed up in such was not what I wanted." I have
pleasure in seconding that sentiment. As a person compara-
tively respectable, averse from taking—save only in the case
of wasps—the life of any living creature, and with hands
wholly free from innocent blood, it is hard that Fate should
have allotted to me the rôle of an historian of homicide.

My personal bent is all for the portrayal of quaint and
curious characters of past times, preferably in regard to their
reactions to the law of the land, and of such it has been my
happy fortune to resuscitate a round dozen. For wrongdoers
in general I have always had a weakness; but how one who
shudders at a cut finger and flees from the sight of a street
accident, should come, professionally, to be steeped in gore
is, as Miss Knagg would say, to me a mystery indeed.

It began, I suppose, in my taste for attending criminal
trials, reports of which in the fulness of time I was led on to
edit. But my interest in crime *qua* crime was academic; what
appealed to me was the human element, the dramatic quality
of the facts; so that each case, howsoever in itself horrid and
repellent, became merely an abstract problem, inviting investigation and calling for treatment.

In my reading of other writers' studies in murder I had
noted that there were two disparate methods employed: the
solid, dry, and technical manner of the serious inquirer, whose
aim was educative and his style severe; and the brightly-
written, unreliable accounts of the irresponsible relator, concerned only to tell a rousing tale with scant regard to accuracy.
It occurred to me that to combine the exactitude of the one

with the readableness of the other, and as in the matter of Mr. Stiggins's moral pocket-handkerchiefs, to blend amusement with instruction, might give some fresh value to the criminological essay. To this end my literary labours have been, not I trust unfruitfully, directed.

The first "murder" paper I ever wrote, that on Philip Stanfield (reprinted in the present volume), grew out of a suggestion all generously made to me by Andrew Lang, that we should collaborate in a book of Scots crime. He did not care for Stanfield, whom he esteemed but a dull dog (although I am bold to think that Philip has his points); but he was genially enthusiastic as to my second venture, Katharine Nairn (also here reprinted), which he was good enough to characterize as "ripping." But alas, in the exigency of his manifold literary engagements, the scheme fell through, and I had to carry on by myself without his inestimable aid. The result was *Twelve Scots Trials*, published in 1913, now (for what it is worth) one of the world's lost books, long out of print and practically unobtainable. From that forgotten volume I have been persuaded to revive a third favourite of mine, Keith of Northfield, which I hope may be held to warrant resurrection.

So much for the old stagers. The recent Perth murder, Death in Cuddies Strip, is the only one of these cases I personally heard, although I have been asked whether I attended that of Madeleine Smith! Of all the murder trials with which it has been my lot to deal none is more strange and startling. The clue afforded by the handkerchief of the Indian trader, leading as it so amazingly does to the deed done in the Perthshire wood, is unique in the annals of crime; and might well have furnished Sherlock Holmes with one of his inimitable "cases." The persistent impression that there is something that we do not know, something that the evidence has withheld from us, increases the interest of the story.

The murders respectively staged at Whinny Park and upon the Pier of Leith really owe their inclusion (as I have confessed in recounting them) to the admirable illustrations available.

But I venture to think that on their merits both are worthy of record.

Time and again have I been asked why I have never written of Madeleine Smith, hers being the most famous of Scots murder trials. My answer was, hitherto, that she had already been so often and so ably "done" that there seemed to be nothing new to say about her. And now, after all, I have been moved to contribute to her monument my small memorial tribute. The sole excuse for so doing resides in perennial fascination of the subject.

For fear that my collection be deemed by the southern reader too exclusively Scots, I have qualified the contents by the inclusion of two alien crimes: one English, the other Irish. Although Mistress Pleasant Rawlins was not physically murdered, yet she was the victim of a moral outrage scantly less flagitious, and so is entitled to her place. Further, she is a creature of that delightful period, the eighteenth century, to which it is always for me a pleasure to return. Dr. Cross calls neither for introduction nor excuse. His is the most celebrated of Irish poisoning cases; in view of his years, it is a palmary example of the class of crime so tenderly regarded by our friends across the English Channel; and its resemblance to that of my earliest experiment in criminous biography, Dr. Pritchard, peculiarly appeals to me.

So I commend to your kindly consideration this handful of malefactors, believing that they will serve as a timely warning to such of my readers as might otherwise be tempted to provide material for my insatiable pen.

WILLIAM ROUGHEAD.

12 BELGRAVE CRESCENT, EDINBURGH,
*March* 1937.

# CONTENTS

DEATH IN CUDDIES STRIP: A TALE OF THREE HANDKERCHIEFS . . . . . . . 1 PAGE

THE INTEMPERATE MIDSHIPMAN; OR, TROUBLE ON LEITH PIER . . . . . . . 45

THE WEAVER'S HAND: A TALE OF TWO GRAVES . 71

THE PLIGHT OF PLEASANT RAWLINS; OR, THE PRE-TENDED BROTHER . . . . . . 103

THE ORDEAL OF PHILIP STANFIELD . . . . 137

THE SHADOW ON SHANDY HALL; OR, "WHAT LOVE COSTS AN OLD MAN" . . . . . 161

KATHARINE NAIRN . . . . . . . 199

KEITH OF NORTHFIELD . . . . . . 231

TO MEET MISS MADELEINE SMITH: A GOSSIP ON A WONDER HEROINE OF THE 'FIFTIES . . . 257

INDEX . . . . . . . . . 295

# LIST OF ILLUSTRATIONS

Mr. Midshipman Whyte at the Bar .     *Frontispiece*

View of Whinny Park . . .     *facing page* 80

Dr. Cross and Miss Skinner . .     "    176

Katharine Nairn . . . .     "    208

# DEATH IN CUDDIES STRIP:
## A TALE OF THREE HANDKERCHIEFS

A

# DEATH IN CUDDIES STRIP:
## A TALE OF THREE HANDKERCHIEFS

Sure, there's some wonder in this handkerchief.
*Othello*, Act III. Sc. iv.

NEITHER the bold M. du Boisgobey, who loves to begin his novels with a bang, nor the ingenious M. Gaboriau, his rival in sensation, whose very first page always provides the makings of a mystery, ever conceived or executed a situation more arresting than the opening scene of the Perth murder, or furnished a stranger clue than the far-travelled handkerchief which figures in the forefront of that tragedy. Two other handkerchiefs, green and blue, play surprisingly their minor parts; but the rôle of the principal indefinite one is unique, and fraught with consequences as unlooked for as was the fateful napkin of Desdemona.

On a quiet summer evening of mid-August a courting couple, boy and girl, are walking homeward in the gloaming, his arm around her waist, along the narrow, shady pathway which winds amid the trees, whins, broom, and bushes of the Cuddies Strip, a popular Lovers' Lane of amorous Perth. They are approaching the stile, whence by the fields lies the way to the Buckie Braes, a public park or Happy Valley, and so down to Cherrybank, a suburb of the city. Suddenly from the wood a shot rings out behind them and the girl feels something whiz through her hair. Alarmed, they turn apart, each facing the other, and the boy tells her not to faint. Immediately there is a second shot, and without a cry he falls dead at her feet. She, distracted, bends over him, calling his name, and is aware of a stranger standing above her in the dusk. Apparently she does not deem him the assassin, for she asks him to stay by the boy while she goes for help. As she hastens towards the stile, the sinister figure runs silently beside her. Arrived there, he throws her to the ground, drags her into the bushes, strips off all her clothes, and criminally assaults her. He leaves her, going back in the direction of the body. Clad only in her coat, which she has cast about her nakedness, and with the handkerchief that bound her hands still tied about her wrist, the girl flies sobbing down the field. She finds aid; and on returning with others to the spot, sees the dead boy lying as she had left him, with one remarkable exception. His face is now decently covered with his own green handkerchief, tucked in carefully beneath the chin. No explanation of this singular fact was offered by the evidence given at the trial. It is astounding that the murderer, having, as we shall see, rifled the body, should shew such respect for the dead as to cover the face of his victim. But I am informed that the solution is simple: it is an inveterate custom of members of the tinker class so to do by the dead.

Some time before the crime a burglary had been committed at the neighbouring mansion-house of Aberdalgie, and divers articles were stolen. These included the very handkerchief found that night upon the girl's wrist! Nay, more; by one of those curious oversights to which criminals are fortunately prone, the thief had left behind him at the scene of the burglary his own blue handkerchief—later to be an important factor in the detection of his guilt, literally, in the premises. So there you have my three handkerchiefs, of which two will prove very formidable links in the chain of circumstances welded by the Crown. These, I submit, are facts that, as a starting-point, have not been bettered even by the resourceful French fictionists to whom I have referred.

Apart from them, to me the case is rendered attractive by the admirable quality of its place-names. What could be more euphonious than these: Hill Farm of Pitheavlis (the accent on the second syllable), Kirkton of Mailer, Callerfountain Hill, and Aberdalgie (the "l" being silent)? What more attaching than Cherrybank, Necessity Brae (which savours of *The Pilgrim's Progress*), Buckie Braes, and Cuddies Strip? What, in this connection, more appropriate than Gallow's-park Wood? In comparison with such, a murder done in an ordinary numbered house of a commonplace street is at a sad disadvantage. But leaving aside these æsthetic considerations, let us resume our tale.

Within a few hours of the occurrence the girl is medically examined at the Police Station, and the fact that she had suffered an assault definitely established. The only garments she had brought away from the scene were the "swagger" coat before mentioned and a suspender belt, which yet hung around her neck. It had been placed over her mouth by her assailant, but had slipped down. The rest of her clothes had vanished. Next day there are found, by the police and by certain amateur detectives, at the spot indicated by her as the scene of the outrage, an india-rubber band, used by her as a garter to supplement the faulty suspender; part of a silk shoulder-strap, which had sustained her shift; and a glass pendant, belonging to a bead necklace worn by her that night. I point this out thus early in the tale, because there is a false but widespread and persistent rumour that this young girl of seventeen, when she left home that evening for a three-hours' walk with her lover, had on no stitch of clothing other than her outer coat, that being, as is alleged, on such occasions a common practice among the modern Fair Maids of Perth! If it indeed be so, then their disregard of propriety is only equalled in effrontery by their defiance of the local climate. Be that as it may, it is certain that at least she had on shoes and stockings, *and these were never found.*

Now at the time of the tragedy there was living in a little tent in a wood near Kirkton of Mailer a young man, otherwise homeless. His mother and stepfather, who shared his rural retreat, were then absent at Essendie, near Blairgowrie, engaged in what was picturesquely termed "at the berries," *i.e.* peripatetic employment as pickers in that fruit-growing district. His sole visible means of support was what he

5

earned as a casual labourer on an adjacent farm, but he possessed, as we shall hear, an additional resource in a double-barrelled shot-gun, a rifle, and an assortment of snares for game, all which doubtless unlawfully contributed to the replenishing of the family pot. Further, had the police taken the trouble to inquire into his antecedents, there were on record against him no less than five recent convictions for assault, robbery, and housebreaking. Yet despite the sojourning of this undesirable and suspicious stranger within their gates, encamped within $1\frac{1}{3}$ miles of the scene of the burglary and but 1 mile from that of the murder, the local authorities, though vainly hunting high and low for the perpetrator, apparently did not think it worth while even to give him a call. Nor, indeed, until the Glasgow police, summoned in consultation, had traced through a laundry mark the original ownership and subsequent theft of the famous handkerchief, and a witness had volunteered a most significant conversation held by him with the tent-dweller on the very day of the crime, did the Perth police request the man to walk into their official parlour, where, being identified by the girl as her assailant, and by two other witnesses as the man seen by them near Cuddies Strip on the afternoon and evening of the murder, he was arrested and charged. An examination of his tent disclosed sundry articles, the proceeds of the burglary above mentioned; but as ten days had been allowed to elapse since the shooting of the boy and the attack upon the girl, it is not surprising that neither the pocket-book stolen from the body nor the girl's clothes—assuming these had been there—nor the double-barrelled shot-gun were recovered.

Of the dead boy, Danny Kerrigan, the evidence tells us next to nothing. I have often noted in a murder trial how little is said about the victim, whose personality is quite eclipsed in interest and importance by that of his alleged destroyer. Designed in the indictment as an apprentice glazier, his uncles, who identified the body, bore witness that the lad had plenty of friends, both male and female, and that his interests included football and billiards. That is all.

At the date of his death he was but nineteen. From his photograph it appears that he was a good-looking, bright-faced boy, well groomed and turned out, as his clothes produced at the trial shewed, and somewhat superior to his class.

Marjory Fenwick proved to be a pretty and attractive girl of modest demeanour. Looking much younger than her age, seventeen, and of very slight build—what the reporters dreadfully termed *petite*—she was actually, by the first person to see her fleeing from the wood, taken for a child that had lost her way! She lived with her parents in the charmingly named neighbourhood of Dovecotland, and was employed in a local "sweetie" factory. She and Danny had been friends since she was fourteen, and about New Year, 1935, she began to walk out with him twice a week.

The accused, John M'Guigan, an Irishman aged twenty-four, was of the tinclarian persuasion. On his mother's remarriage he had assumed the name of his stepfather. Squat, sallow, and swarthy, he was manifestly of a low type, and he looked, as Marjory Fenwick described her assailant, very strong. His previous criminal experiences embraced an assault upon a girl. His other recreations were poaching and the Pictures; but he specialized in the disgusting game locally known as "spying," *i.e.* scouting with telescope or glasses for courting couples, and playing the despicable part of a Peeping Tom.

I watched him during the five days of his trial and was impressed by his complete imperturbability. Hour after hour he sat in the dock with folded arms and immobile face, only his eyes following the question and answer of counsel and witness. But twice was the fashion of his countenance changed: when Marjory professed her failure to appreciate the art of Shirley Temple, and when the Foreman of the Jury announced upon the murder charge a verdict of acquittal. On each of these pronouncements the accused broadly smiled. He received sentence on the other charges with his wonted composure.

It has been my lot to listen to many murder trials, yet I recall few to which I have hearkened with greater interest than to this, by reason of the astonishing nature of the girl's story and the wondrous adventures of the incriminating handkerchief.

I

On Monday, 25th November, 1935, within the High Court of Justiciary at Edinburgh, the trial began before the Lord Justice-Clerk (the Right Hon. Lord Aitchison) and a jury consisting—scandalously, in my view—of eight women and but seven men. Mr. Albert Russell, K.C. (who before the end of the trial was to become Solicitor-General for Scotland), assisted by Mr. John Cameron and Mr. N. M. L. Walker, Advocates-Depute, represented the Crown. Mr. J. R. Wardlaw Burnet, K.C., with Mr. A. M. Prain and Mr. J. H. Gibson, advocates, appeared for the defence. The indictment, to which were appended lists of 71 witnesses and no less than 106 productions (exhibits), was in the following terms:—

JOHN M'GUIGAN *alias* JOHN MILLIGAN, prisoner in the Prison of Perth, you are Indicted at the instance of Thomas Mackay Cooper, Esquire, His Majesty's Advocate, and the charges against you are that (1) between 14th May 1935 and 14th August 1935, both days inclusive, you did break into the premises known as the Laundry, adjacent to Aberdalgie House, Parish of Aberdalgie, Perthshire, occupied by Lady Laura Mary Douglas, and did steal a handkerchief, a telescope, an alarm clock, a purse, a razor, and a football; (2) on 14th August 1935, in a strip of wood known as " Cuddies Strip," in the Parish of Forgandenny, Perthshire, situated about 400 yards or thereby south of the dwelling-house on the Hill Farm of Pitheavlis, in the Parish of Perth, Perthshire, lying said strip of wood immediately to the south of the fields on the said farm numbered 115 and 124 on the Ordnance Survey Sheet, Perthshire Sheet XCVII 12, which Ordnance Survey Sheet is number 29 of the productions lodged herewith, (*a*) you did assault Marjory Watson Fenwick, residing at 8 Longcauseway, Dovecotland, Perth, and Daniel Kerrigan, apprentice glazier, then residing at 18 Union Lane, Perth, and did discharge a loaded shotgun at said Marjory Watson Fenwick and said Daniel Kerrigan, and did shoot the said Daniel Kerrigan in the chest, neck, and face, and did murder him, and (*b*) from the pocket of the said Daniel Kerrigan you did steal a pocket-book or wallet; and (3) on said 14th August 1935, at a stile on the south side of said field numbered 124, adjoining the east end of said strip of wood, you did assault the said Marjory Watson Fenwick, and did seize hold of her, carry or drag her along the ground, throw her down, compress her throat with your hands, pull off her clothing, expose her private parts, tie her hands, lie on the top of her, and did ravish her; and you have been previously convicted of dishonest appropriation of property and of crime inferring personal violence.

The accused having adhered to his plea of Not Guilty, proof for the prosecution was led. Formal evidence having been given by two uncles of the deceased as to the identifying by them of the body, a Perth surveyor was examined at vast length regarding the topography of the district, with reference to the Ordnance Survey Sheets produced by the Crown. I doubt whether the jury were much the wiser; personally, all I gained was some acquaintance with the local names; but these matters have to be proved. It is difficult to visualize from descriptions and plans the lie of a countryside. Then two young men, M'Dougall and Wilkie, stated that, on the night in question, they were at work on the magneto of a motor-cycle, outside the barn at Hill Farm of Pitheavlis, some 400 yards across the fields from Cuddies Strip, when a few minutes after 10 p.m. they heard shots from the direction of the Strip. Wilkie heard two shots in quick succession; M'Dougall, who was hammering at the magneto, heard but one. Thinking that there were poachers about, they went up the steading to look and listen, but saw and heard nothing further. It was a fine, quiet night, and there was still light enough to see by when they resumed their work.

The girl Marjory Fenwick was then called. Smartly dressed in black and wonderfully composed, she told, in reply to Mr. Russell's questions, her amazing tale. On 14th August Danny Kerrigan called for her by arrangement at 7 o'clock. He proposed that they should go to the Pictures, but she said she did not like Shirley Temple, so they decided to go for a walk instead. (I note in passing

that as he was taking his girl out for the evening, he must
have had some money on him.) They went through
Buckie Braes and up the field to Cuddies Strip. They
passed another couple, going down, and the "chap" hailed
Danny by name. They crossed the stile into the Strip,
walked along the footpath, and sat down on the grass by
the wayside. While sitting there, Danny produced his
pocket-book and shewed her certain photographs; he also
spent some time in kissing and embracing her. When they
heard the Perth Academy clock strike ten in the valley
below, they rose to go home and retraced their steps along
the path, Danny having his right arm round her waist. A
shot was fired from the bushes behind them, something
whizzed past her ear, and Danny turned round in the direction of the shot, saying: "Don't faint here, Madge." As
he did so, a second shot was fired and he fell backwards
to the ground. She bent down to him, crying: "Danny,
Danny!" There was blood on his face and he was moan-
ing. She shouted: "Help!" and looking up, saw a strange
man standing beside her. He was of medium height, wore
dark clothes and a cap, and carried nothing in his hands.
He had a beard—a day's growth. She asked him to
wait there while she got help; he made no reply. As she
started to run to the stile she found the man was running at
her side, still saying no word. She had one foot on the
stile, when he pulled her off, held her down with his knee,
tied something over her mouth, and bound her hands behind
her. She was so frightened that she pretended to faint.
He dragged her into the bushes, unloosed her hands to get
her coat off, stripped off all her clothes, and tied her hands
again. He then criminally assaulted her. At this stage
the thing slipped from her mouth, and she shouted: "Help!"
He gripped her by the throat and nearly choked her. He
next tied her suspender belt over her mouth, bound her feet
with something soft, and went away in the direction of the
body. After a time she managed to free her hands and feet,
picked up her coat, and crawled to the stile. She was naked

save for the coat, the suspender belt round her neck, and the handkerchief, with which her hands had been bound, yet upon her wrist. She ran across the field towards Buckie Braes, where she met the witnesses Spence and Ewan, from whom we shall hear in what state they found her.

Witness next described how they took her down to Cherrybank, where they telephoned for the police, and how, having been furnished with a pair of shoes, she accompanied certain witnesses back to where Danny lay. His face was then covered by his own green handkerchief, which was not so when she left him. She was afterwards taken to the house of a Mrs. Drummond at Cherrybank, where she was provided with clothes, and later to the Police Station.

When she went out that night with Danny she was wearing a peach-coloured vest; a pink brassière; a green suspender belt; two pairs of knickers, green and pink; an underskirt, with straps over the shoulders; a skirt to match the "swagger" coat; and a green blouse. She also wore stockings and grey suede shoes, grey gloves, an elastic band as a garter, and a necklace of beads on a silver chain with a glass pendant. All these were removed from her person by her assailant. Witness was then shewn and identified the coat, the handkerchief with which her hands had been tied, Danny's own handkerchief, the belt, the band, the pendant, and the strap of her underskirt—the three last articles having been found at the scene of the assault, as before narrated. She further identified a small comb, found in Danny's pocket, as having been used by her that night. Until this tragic happening no man had ever interfered with her. She had been "unwell," and was just getting better. She then described how on 28th August she was shewn a number of men at the Police Station, and had identified one of them as her assailant. She had no doubt about it: "His face came back to me." Asked whether she now saw the man in Court, witness pointed to the accused and said, emphatically though ungrammatically: "That's him." On the day after the tragedy she pointed out to the police the several places mentioned in her story.

Mr. Wardlaw Burnet opened his cross-examination thus: "Marjory Fenwick, have you told us the whole truth about what happened the night that Danny Kerrigan was shot?" to which witness firmly replied: "Yes." Counsel then took her through her account of the fatal walk. When they met the couple before they reached the stile, she and Danny were "capering": jumping backwards and forwards over the ditch at the side of the path. They sat for more than half an hour in the Strip; she saw no one except the couple they had passed. She then, as requested by counsel, repeated her account of what happened. She had never said they were sitting when the first shot was fired. Danny let go of her and they turned towards each other. When the second shot was fired her back was to the direction from which it came and Danny was facing it. She was quite close to Danny all the time. Asked what the man looked like, witness pertinently replied: "He looked like the man sitting there in the dock." He had glaring eyes. With regard to the day's growth of beard, this was the first time she had mentioned it. His face was "reddish-like" and he was a young man; he looked about thirty. The man ran by her side all the way to the stile. (It is a very narrow path.) She cried out as loud as she could when he seized her; she was very frightened. He threw her to the ground and put his knee on her chest; she pretended she had fainted. He tied a handkerchief over her mouth and another round her wrists. She maintained that her hands were first bound behind her back. Having dragged her to the bushes, he untied her hands to remove her coat, tied them again, and took off all her clothes—"He just threw them about." She made no resistance—"It was no use struggling with a strong man like that." When the handkerchief slipped from her mouth, he tied the suspender belt over it with a knot at the back. He picked that up from the ground beside them. This was after he had effected his purpose. He then tied

12

her feet with something that stretched, like a stocking. When he had left her, she got her feet clear, pulled one hand free of the handkerchief which bound her wrists, put on her coat, and fled from the wood.

Marjory was next cross-examined as to the identification parade and her description of her assailant as having a beard, a reddish face, and glaring eyes. "Has the man you see in the dock got a red face?" asked Mr. Burnet. "No," replied the witness; "but perhaps the passion is not on him just now." "Was the passion on him at the identification parade?—Well, he was staring at me, anyway." When she identified him, the accused said: "Take another look. You are mistaken." She left her clothes lying where the man had thrown them; it never occurred to her to clothe herself more fully.

Re-examined—As she and Danny were walking homewards, her hands were in the pockets of her coat. The second shot passed her and hit Danny; none of it struck her. While the man was outraging her she did not see his face: she shut her eyes. She had just seen her boy shot down, had her clothes stripped off, and her person assaulted; she was frightened and very much upset. She felt powerless in the grip of this man.

By the Court—When she was given clothes at Mrs. Drummond's house she did not remove any blood from her person. As regards the assault, she did not resist, pretending that she had fainted; she was terrified. She could not say whether the man completed the act of connection. (It is plain, from her account of his proceedings, that he did not do so.) About three-quarters of an hour elapsed before she returned with the police to the scene. The first shot seemed to come from behind her right shoulder. Danny was not struck by it. He turned round as the second shot was fired. It was all a matter of two or three seconds. Anyone concealed in the bushes could have heard their conversation and seen him shewing her his pocket-book. Danny never said that anyone was jealous over their keeping com-

13

pany or bore him any ill-will. As to her use of the word "beard," she meant that the man was just dirty and unshaven. She described him as well as she could. She had been shewn other men at the Police Station, and had failed to identify the man, before she did so on 28th August. The man was a complete stranger to her; he was no one either she or Danny knew. "I suppose you realize that the accused is on trial for his life," said his Lordship. "Keeping that very solemnly before your mind, do you say that the accused is the man who assaulted you that night?" To which the witness gravely answered: "Yes." "And do you say that with a full sense of responsibility?" "Yes," was her last word.

From what I had previously learned of Marjory's remarkable story, I was prepared to regard it with strong suspicion as being well-nigh incredible. But having heard it from the girl's own lips, and found it unshaken by the very searching and skilful cross-examination of Mr. Burnet, I became persuaded that it was in substance true. That a young girl, having undergone such a dreadful ordeal, should not be perfectly clear as to every detail of her so terrific experience is hardly surprising. And when, as we shall find, on each point upon which corroboration was possible she *is* corroborated, I am satisfied that she told, so far as she could remember it, the truth. With one pardonable exception. She stated that prior to the outrage no man had ever taken advantage of her, a statement not supported by the medical evidence. As one of the doctors who examined her discreetly phrased it: the appearances presented "were not consistent with virginity." But how could she be expected *coram populo*, before that crowded audience, to admit the fact of her misfortune?

With respect to her failure accurately to describe her assailant, that is in the circumstances natural enough. Indeed, I myself have never, from a mere verbal description, been able to identify anybody. Even at leisure and with a quiet mind it is almost impossible to supply an adequate description; how much more difficult when in terror and under cloud of night! But the "jump," which it is proved she gave when in the Police Station her eyes first lighted upon the accused, is to me convincing. Only a consummate actress could have compassed that touch, and this was but a simple girl. Again, had she set out to fabricate a rape, is it likely she could have contrived the inconceivable features of this one, looking to the fact of her regrettable acquaintance with the sexual act?

## II

John Spence and Dorothy Ewan had spent an hour or so that evening at the Buckie Braes. They left for home at 10.40, and as they went down the path they heard someone running on the other side of the fence. It was a young girl who, on seeing them, cried out: "Can you help me, mister?" She was sobbing and terribly upset. She had on only a coat, a suspender belt was round her neck, and a handkerchief was tied upon her right wrist. Her bare feet were scratched, her hair was ruffled. She told them what had happened and begged them to "go and see to Danny." They helped her through the fence and took her down to Cherrybank, where Spence telephoned for the police. Miss Ewan then left them; when she first saw the girl, she says, "I thought that she was just a child of about thirteen who had lost her way." While sitting at the Braes they heard neither shots nor cries. The girl kept on repeating her tale: that a man had shot Danny Kerrigan in Cuddies Strip, and taken off her clothes and tied her up. Spence asked whether he had "interfered" with her and she said he had. She said he was a small man, thick-set and very strong, with large staring eyes. She drew attention to the things on her neck and wrist as those with which he had bound her, and said he had also hurt her mouth. He seemed to come out of the bushes. Spence then told how, along with a constable and a man named Drummond, he went back from Cherrybank to the Strip accompanied by the girl, for whom shoes had been obtained; how they found the

15

body lying with a handkerchief over the face, and how he went again to Cherrybank, returning with a police-sergeant. It was then 11.30 and quite dark. Leaving the police in charge, he and Drummond took the girl to the latter's house, where she was given clothing. They had to carry her across the fields as the shoes were hurting her. Both witnesses identified Marjory Fenwick as the girl, and stated in reply to the Court that it never occurred to them to doubt the truth of her story; she was obviously in real distress, greatly excited and upset.

P.C. Ptolmey, the officer who responded to Spence's call and accompanied the others to Cuddies Strip, described the position of the body. The handkerchief covering the face was carefully adjusted; it must have been deliberately so placed. Having seen that the boy was dead, he sent Spence to telephone to the County Police, and Sergeant M'Callum arrived at 11.40. There was blood on the right sleeve of the girl's coat; she said: "It must have been when I bent over Danny." She complained of being very cold and was sent away with Spence and Drummond. Witness and M'Callum searched the ground with a hand-torch for the girl's clothes, but found nothing. It was then dark. Several other officers came, also Dr. Moffat, who examined the body, which was taken to the ambulance about 3 a.m. He saw a cartridge wad lifted from the deceased's chest. Cross-examined—The girl was anxious to get back to the place and did not seem alarmed for her own safety. He did not examine the handkerchief on her wrist, but noticed that it was knotted. She gave him the same account of what had happened as that which we have already heard. She described her assailant as "about 5 feet 3 or 5 inches in height, stoutish build, dark clothes and cap well over the eyes, dark in the face, cheeks red and big eyes, staring." Re-examined—Although he saw from the first that the boy was dead, to "reassure" the girl he remarked to Drummond: "I'm afraid he is seriously hurt." Whereupon she began to cry. It is plain that till then she did not realize the injuries were fatal.

James Drummond, janitor of Perth Academy, stated that he saw at Cherrybank near his house two girls and a young man (Marjory, Miss Ewan, and Spence). They were joined by a policeman (Ptolmey), who asked him to go with them to Buckie Braes. The girl was barefooted and said she had no clothes on, so they borrowed a pair of shoes for her. She urged them to hurry, saying they would be quicker to go across the fields; they climbed a fence and reached the body. Witness felt the pulse and exclaimed: "My God, he's dead!" The girl started to sob. He saw M'Callum take the handkerchief off her right wrist; it was not tightly bound. She was shivering with cold, so Spence and he took her to his own house. Cross-examined—The handkerchief was tied in three knots; he could have got three fingers under it. By the Court—He thought a girl of her build could have pulled her left hand free with a struggle.

Mrs. Drummond described Marjory's condition when brought by her husband to her house. The girl had nothing on except a coat and shoes. She supplied her with some clothes. The death of the boy being mentioned, the girl wept. Witness made tea for her, but she could not drink it as her tongue was sore. She was taken away in the police car. Cross-examined—Asked why the suspender belt was not removed from the girl's neck when she helped her to dress herself, witness replied: "Well, usually, if you have to do with the police, you are supposed to touch nothing."

Robert Barrie went for a walk with a friend, Robert Stewart, on 14th August. About 8 p.m. they were going along the dyke that runs from the stile at Cuddies Strip in the direction of Kirkton of Mailer. It was a fine, clear evening. They noticed a man coming down the other side of the dyke towards the Strip. Witness said to Stewart: "Here's the keeper coming; we had better get down and not let him see us." They did so. Witness looked over the dyke to see whether he had passed, and saw him do so at four yards' distance, going towards the Strip. He disappeared in the whins; they watched, but he did not come out. They walked along the Strip, where they had a talk with two men, Speedie and another Stewart. Returning by the stile, they heard the Academy clock strike nine. The jacket produced was like that worn by the man. On 29th August witness attended a parade at the Central Police Office, was shewn seven men, and picked out one as the man he saw at the dyke. Accused was the man. He recognized him by his face. Cross-examined—He had neither dog, gun, nor snares with him that night, and knew nothing about them. He admitted that he knew a rabbit when he saw one. They were just out for a walk. He was not frightened when he thought it was the keeper: he was not poaching, but was trespassing. The Lord Justice-Clerk—"At any rate you don't like game-keepers." He remarked to his friend that it was not the keeper: it was a far younger man and of different build. Speedie and the other Stewart had a dog with them. They asked: "Was yon the keeper coming down the dyke?" Witness said it was not.

Robert Stewart gave similar evidence. He did not see the man close enough to be able to recognize him.

Speedie and Stewart *secundus* corroborated. While at the stile, they saw the man go down the dyke and the two others lie down behind it. As Stewart was going home at about 10.15 he heard two shots in quick succession from the direction of Cuddies Strip, half a mile away. He said to himself it was some lunatic shooting rabbits in the dark. Speedie deponed that when Barrie and friend "clappit doon ahint the dyke," the man "keeked over at them canny-like, and then went off like anything." Cross-examined by Mr. Burnet— "There was nothing furtive or secretive about the single man's action?—No." "Do you know what 'furtive' means?" asked Mr. Cameron. "No," was the frank reply, "I never heard it before." "Do you know what 'secretive' means?— No." "Do you know what 'canny-like' means?—Yes."

John Peddie said he was eighteen and a ploughman at Kirkton of Mailer. The accused was an occasional worker there; he lived with his parents in a tent half a mile westward of the farm, on the way to Aberdalgie. Some time in July, apropos of poaching, he told witness he had a gun. A fortnight later he shewed it to witness at his tent: a double-barrelled shot-gun. Peddie handled it; the gun was unloaded, and accused "took it down in two bits"; it was a hammer gun, with "dog heads" on it. He did not say where he got it. They were alone in the tent, the father and mother being "at the berries." On the evening of 14th August witness went for a walk with a friend, Mackenzie, who worked on the farm. They were up at the Cuddies Strip, and on their way home passed near accused's tent, but saw no sign of him. Next evening he and Mackenzie met M'Guigan at the steading. There was some talk about the murder. After Mackenzie had left them, witness suggested that, as the accused had a gun, he might have been out shooting "and accidentally shot the man." "I thought you would be thinking that," was M'Guigan's curious comment; and he told witness "*he had it* [his gun] *hidden*," but did not say where. Having no licence, "he was frightened for the police getting it." The following day accused told Peddie that on the night of the murder he had been "spying" on him and Mackenzie as they walked upon the hill. Peddie knew he had a "spy-glass" about two months before the murder. (Witness identified the large telescope found in accused's tent.) Peddie had exchanged with him a small telescope for a pair of field glasses, now produced. Shewn a blue handkerchief, he identified it as belonging to M'Guigan; it was the only one he had ever seen him with.

This young ploughman was a reluctant witness and gave the impression that, had he been so minded, he could have told us more about M'Guigan's doings. Cross-examined by Mr. Burnet, he was even more guarded in his answers. He admitted that he said nothing to anyone of these conversations with accused until questioned by the police on 29th August. It was on a Sunday morning that he was shewn the gun. His interest in glasses was due to admiration for the beauties of the local scenery.

19

Mrs. M'Guigan, the mother of the accused, was the type of old woman commonly associated with a clay pipe. Although unable to write her name, she gave her evidence with a distinctness which put to shame some of the less illiterate witnesses. She carefully abstained from looking at her son, and said her age was fifty-two, but it might well have been seventy. She identified as the accused's certain garments, in particular the blue handkerchief, and a shirt, of which half the lower front part had been torn off. She herself had taken that piece out for patching. As to her son's jacket, she had put a patch on the pocket, where it had a hole burnt in it, long before she went to Blairgowrie in July. Her son spent every week-end there.

This shirt, on examination, shewed little signs of wear and had scarcely reached the stage of being torn up for dusters or dishclouts. No *patched* shirt was produced. As regards the patched pocket, see the evidence of Gow, *infra*.

Ronald Mackenzie corroborated Peddie regarding their evening walk on 14th August, and meeting on the following night the accused, whose first words were: "Have you been away looking for the man with the glaring eyes?"—the girl's description of her assailant being then common knowledge. (Perhaps this was an echo of "The Man with the Glaring Eyes" in a contemporary case in England.) Witness left him and Peddie together. Next day, while working beside M'Guigan in a cornfield at the farm, they saw a policeman cycling along the road; he dismounted, and went up towards the accused's tent. "They need not bother going up now," remarked M'Guigan; "*I have my gun away*." He did not say where he had put it. A fortnight before the murder he told witness he had a double-barrelled gun, and a week before the murder he spoke of getting some cartridges. Witness had often seen him with both the large and the small tele- scopes. Cross-examined—Accused was quite open and un- concerned in discussing the murder. He did not seem nervous when he saw the policeman. Witness was positive he used the words: "a double-barrelled gun." For some curious reason there was no evidence by the Perth police as to tracing the purchase of cartridges by the accused.

Arthur Hill was walking with a girl in the Cuddies Strip on the evening of the 14th. They saw the man going down the dykeside, and the two men hiding behind it, one of whom looked over as he passed. This was about 8.30. They walked up Callerfountain Hill, and on their way back heard someone moving in the wood; witness remarked to his companion: "That is somebody laying snares." They reached the stile about 10 o'clock, and as they went down the field, heard two shots from the direction of Cuddies Strip. His lady friend was frightened, and he said: "That's some stupid devil shooting rabbits at this time of night!"

John Arnott lived at Kirkton of Mailer, near the accused's tent, and knew him well. They used to play draughts at witness's house. Last winter M'Guigan said he had a rifle. Arnott met him one evening by arrangement near the steading. He crossed the road and picked up a rifle out of the grass; they went down to the River Earn and had a shot at the ducks. On 15th August witness was talking to Elder, the grieve, about the murder when the accused came up to them. Elder said to him: "What's this you've been up to now, John?" M'Guigan replied that he had been up the hill with his glasses, but he was down at half-past nine. He looked disconcerted by the question. Charles Elder—who, it was explained to the Court, was deaf—corroborated, but said he did not hear the accused's reply. He changed colour when witness put the question. Witness asked him why he had not been at work all that week, but accused gave no explanation.

James Shepherd was with a girl at the Cuddies Strip on the night of 14th August. (It would seem that the young people of Perth were there in strength that evening.) Between half-past nine and a quarter to ten they passed Marjory with Danny Kerrigan, whom he knew; they were "capering" near the stile: jumping back and forward over the ditch and laughing. Witness said: "Hullo, Danny," and Danny suitably replied. Witness and friend got to the foot of Buckie Braes as the Academy clock struck ten.

## III

The evidence on the third day largely concerned the adventures of the famous handkerchief and the burglary at Aberdalgie House. Sergeant M'Callum told how he was summoned to the scene of the crime as already mentioned. He took the handkerchief off the girl's right wrist; it was "comfortably tight." There was room for about two fingers under it; he had to untie, the knots to get it off. Cross-examined—It seemed to him too tight for the girl to have got her left hand out of it. From the evidence of other police officers it appeared that a cartridge wad was found upon the left breast of the body as it lay in the wood, and next day three other wads were found on the path where the deceased had lain. Fifty feet from the spot, half of a pearl shirt-button was picked up on the stump of a small tree, upon which, at the foot, were some spots and a smear of blood. There was nothing on the body but a pocket-comb and a prize-draw ticket; the pocket-book, and such money as Danny may have had, were missing.

But the most intriguing discovery in the case was that of the laundry mark on the celebrated handkerchief and all that it led to. Not less striking is what happened at the identification parade. I shall dispose of the latter first. When, "in consequence of information received," M'Guigan was invited to call at the Police Station on 28th August, six men of similar age and size having been brought in from the street, he was told to take any position he liked among them, and elected to stand at the far end of the row. The girl was taken into the room in the presence of the Chief Constable and divers detective officers of Perth and Glasgow. "She looked down the line," says Inspector Davidson, "and whenever her eyes lighted on the accused *she gave a start, sort of jumped*, and said: 'What shall I do now?' Asked whether she identified any person, she said: 'I am nearly certain.' She took a second look, and said she was positive." Chief Constable Macpherson says: "I brought Miss Fenwick into the room, and as I did so she took what I describe as the head of the line, and ran her eyes down till she came to the end man. I was standing close beside her, and when she came to this man she seemed to be startled: *she sort of sprang up and got all of a tremble*, and her hand got up as if pointing, and she gave a slight nod of her head." For the rest, he concurs with the Inspector. When the girl pointed her finger at the accused, he said: "You have made a mistake; I may resemble the man."

Next day, under similar conditions, the accused was shewn to the witnesses Barrie and Gow. Barrie was the gentleman who disliked gamekeepers; Gow we have not yet heard, and it will be convenient now to do so. In common with many of his fellow-citizens, Mr. Gow chanced to take a walk by Cuddies Strip on the afternoon of 14th August. As he was crossing the field he saw a man near the wood, standing with "something cocked up at his eye," which witness thought was a gun. When they met at the stile, Gow saw it was a "spy-glass" (identified as the large telescope). He was looking at a couple lying some 45 yards up the field. Witness remarked: "Can't you see enough without glasses?" He himself had a look through the glass and could see the time on the Academy clock: 4 p.m. The man said he was working at Kirkton of Mailer. The conversation turned upon sport, the man said he killed a lot of partridges. "You will have a bird net?" inquired Gow. "No," said the other, "*but I have a gun and a rifle.*" He added that nobody knew about them. While talking to the man, Gow noticed that there was a hole burnt at the left corner of his jacket. When later shewn the same jacket by the police, he saw that the hole had been patched. Cross-examined—Witness told the man that he did a bit of hunting and poaching himself when he was not at work. He was positive that *two* weapons were mentioned: a gun and a rifle. He did not at first say anything about the incident: "I thought the police would get him."

Both Barrie and Gow positively identified the accused as the man they had seen that day at Cuddies Strip. Charged with the murder and the other crimes, accused said: "No; there is a mistake somewhere. I must resemble the man."

When on 23rd August the Glasgow detectives came upon the scene they saw the significance of the laundry mark : M 12 : sewn on the handkerchief. Intensive inquiries proved it to be a Kelso mark, used exclusively for the household of Lady Laura Douglas of Edenhall. The Douglas family had taken Aberdalgie House for the season, and Mr. David Douglas was at Essendie, where, by a curious chance, M'Guigan's parents were then "at the berries." The police shewed him the handkerchief, which he had no difficulty in recognizing as his property. He gave them his personal laundry book. Their next visit was to Kelso, where the mark was identified as that used for the Douglas washing.

The officers noticed that the handkerchief had a peculiar smell, described by them as "stick reek," *i.e.* the smoke of burnt sticks, commonly associated with the wood fire of a tinker's camp. When on the night of his arrest the police visited for the first time the accused's tent, a similar smell was at once perceived. Among the articles there found and taken possession of by them were the large telescope, a purse, a razor, a football, and an alarm clock.

When Inspector Davidson was being examined as to these, Mr. Wardlaw Burnet objected to the evidence as incompetent. The police, he maintained, had at the time no authority to search the accused's tent; they were not entitled to do so without a search warrant, which they only obtained the next day. The point was debated learnedly and at length, but as it led to nothing and my sands are running out, I shall not follow Mr. Burnet's ingenious argument and Mr. Russell's reply. Suffice it that the Lord Justice-Clerk held that, in the circumstances, the matter being in the view of Inspector Davidson one of urgency, the police were entitled to act without delay and without having obtained a warrant from a magistrate. In this case 13 articles had been put in evidence, bearing labels shewing where they were found, to which no objection had been taken. It was out of the question to exclude them now. His Lordship had no hesitation in repelling the objection and allowing the evidence.

Mr. David Douglas stated that when he came home for good from South Africa, reaching Perth on 3rd July, his heavy luggage was deposited in a separate building at Aberdalgie House, known as the "Laundry." It was not used as such, but as a lumber-room. His boxes were left open, the "Laundry" door being locked at night. He recognized the handkerchief as his from its colour and pattern, the laundry mark, and the special circumstances in which he originally acquired it. Before leaving for home on a visit in 1934 the handkerchief, with a tie to match, was presented to him in South Africa by an Indian trader with whom he had dealt. He gave the tie away but kept the handkerchief, which was still in his possession when he came back in July. He last stayed at Kelso in the winter of 1934-35; it was then that the handkerchief got the local laundry mark: "coloured hankies" was an entry in his laundry book of that date. Also in his luggage was a large telescope which had belonged to his grandfather. It was included in the inventory made for insurance purposes before he left South Africa. Witness identified it as the telescope found in accused's tent. He could not be certain that the alarm clock was his, but thought it very likely; he had three, and one was missing. On looking through his luggage to see whether anything else had gone, he found lying on a box in the "Laundry" a blue silk handkerchief which did not belong to him. Witness identified it as that already proved to be the accused's. A searching cross-examination by Mr. Burnet effected little more than the putting up of the witness's rather irritable back. He could not remember when he last saw the handkerchief, nor say quite definitely that he packed it before leaving South Africa. By the Court—"Look at the handkerchief again. To the best of your knowledge and belief is that the handkerchief that was given to you by the trader?—To the best of my knowledge and belief, yes." His Lordship then directed that the handkerchief be inspected by the jury, with reference to the peculiar pattern printed only on one side.

Mr. John Douglas stated that he was a lieutenant in the Seaforth's, home on leave. He came to Aberdalgie in July. When the family removed from Edenhall his luggage was put in the "Laundry." On 29th August he was shewn by the police certain articles in order to see whether they were his property. He could not be sure about the football, but had no difficulty in recognizing as his own the purse, which had his name written on it by himself. He also spoke to the finding of the blue handkerchief as above narrated. While examining his luggage to see if anything else had been stolen, he noticed that a razor case for two razors, which had belonged to his father, contained only one. He could not swear that he had seen the other; they were "cut-throats," which he never used. It had the makers' name impressed in red and the word "Saturday" engraved on the blade. He informed the police, who shewed him a razor in every respect identical with his, except that it bore the word "Friday." (This had been seen in the accused's possession and was found in his tent.) Witnesses from Kelso were called to prove the identity of the laundry mark. So ended the third day.

It was a relief to listen to the clear, cultured tones of the Messrs. Douglas after suffering the rustic mumblings of the country witnesses. I have long wondered how much of the evidence is actually heard by a jury in the High Court. The acoustic conditions are deplorable; and despite the repeated pleadings of counsel: "Please speak a little louder; these ladies and gentlemen have got to hear you"; and the admonitions of the Bench: "Do speak up; I can't hear a word you say," the witness, after a feeble and ineffectual effort to raise his or her voice—women are the worst offenders—relapses into the wonted inarticulate and inaudible murmur. Only an all-hearing Providence and the shorthand writer, who sits beside the box, are privileged to know the purport of the replies. In this case, indeed, things were so bad that Mr. Russell had frequently to repeat the answers to the jury. As most witnesses are in this regard beyond praying for, it is high time that amplifiers be introduced to mitigate the nuisance.

## IV

The fourth day opened with the evidence of the finger-print experts, of which, as it was very technical and given in great detail, I can only mention the results, the rather that these were not seriously impugned. Two warders from Perth Prison described the taking by them of impressions of the accused's finger-tips and thumbs, and explained the method adopted.

Detective-Sergeant Duncan, of the Glasgow police, told how, accompanied by Inspector Davidson, he visited Aberdalgie House on 9th September, and found finger-print impressions on one of the two casement windows of the "Laundry." He removed the window for further examination, and now identified it as produced in Court. He had made photographic enlargements of the impressions on the casement and of those made on paper by the accused. On comparing these he had no doubt whatever that they were made by the same hand. In each case there were 16 ridge characteristics which agreed. By the Court—No two persons have ever been found with identical finger-prints, although millions have been taken. There is no known example of error. Witness had examined over 300,000 impressions and never found two which agreed even in three or four ridge characteristics.

Detective-Lieutenant Hammond—who, by the way, was the expert employed in the Ruxton murder case at Lancaster —said he was in charge of the Finger Print and Photographic Department of the Headquarters Division of the Glasgow Police. He conducted, along with the last witness, the examinations and concurred in the results. He had no doubt whatever as to the respective impressions being made by the same hand. In the course of his twelve years' experience he had examined the impressions of some 400,000 fingers, and had never found two to be the same in the sequence of ridge characteristics.

Three local young men having told how, on 15th August, they found beside the footpath at Cuddies Strip, a couple of yards from the stile, the glass pendant of the bead necklace, Mrs. Fenwick, Marjory's mother, was called. She knew that her daughter walked out with Danny Kerrigan and that she was to do so on 14th August, though witness was not at home when they left the house. She identified as her daughter's the pendant and the suspender belt; also the rubber band and the shoulder-strap found respectively on 15th and 16th August by the police. Marjory wore her "swagger" coat and skirt that evening: witness laid them out for her. She had never seen the famous handkerchief before; there were no laundry marks on Marjory's things, which witness always washed herself.

Alexander Martin, gunmaker, Glasgow, identified certain wads and pellets as of the type used in loading the cheaper qualities of 12-bore cartridges. He had examined the post-mortem photographs of the deceased; there were 190 pellet-holes in the body. The average number in the ordinary 12-bore No. 5 cartridge is 234, so that approximately 40 pellets must have passed without finding a target in the body. (It is interesting to recall that, in the Ardlamont case, young Hambrough was killed by a 12-bore gun with No. 5 shot.) In his opinion the shot struck the deceased from the right at an oblique angle, and was fired from about 8 yards. He formed that opinion after carrying out certain tests, of which he produced diagrams. Cross-examined as to how, in his view and if her story were true, the girl could escape being hit, witness suggested that as the 30 to 40 pellets which were not in the victim's body would only occupy a space of about 3 by 4 inches over his shoulder, those that missed him were very close to his head and shoulder. Witness would not expect anyone to have been hit by them unless occupying the small space at the corner of his neck. The shot occupied an area of only 8 inches in diameter at the point where it struck the boy, and if the girl were not within at most 4 inches of his neck there would be no pellets to touch her. Of course, if she were between him and the assailant in the line of fire, she *must* have been hit.

Dr. Moffat, of Perth, stated that at 1.30 a.m. on Thursday, 15th August, he examined at the Police Station the person of Marjory Fenwick. She related to him how she had been assaulted by a man at Cuddies Strip between 10 and 11 p.m. the previous night. He had prepared, and now read, his medical report. Reduced to comprehensible terms, his findings were as follows. There were small superficial bruises over the edge of her shoulder-blades and scratches in the middle line of her back. There was one fairly large bruise on the right side of the neck and three smaller ones on the left side. There were multiple abrasions on the left foot, one on the left knee, scratches on the right knee, and on the left thigh and buttock. No marks were visible on the wrists or ankles. From his examination he was of opinion that the girl had been forcibly assaulted. The scratches down the back were quite fresh; they seemed to be due to the undergrowth, with little bits of stick sticking up. The marks on the neck represented the places where a right-handed man, seizing a victim by the throat, would put his thumb on one side and his fingers on the other. The girl was not a virgin; the conditions were quite consistent with penetration having taken place and leaving no sign.

Witness told how, at 2 a.m. the same day, he examined the body of Danny Kerrigan at Cuddies Strip, and described the state in which he found it. The jacket, cardigan, and shirt were thickly covered with blood and perforated with small round holes; the chest, neck, and face were in the same condition. Over the breast-bone was a felt wad from a shot-gun cartridge. Death was due to gun-shot wounds and was practically instantaneous. The gun was fired at close range by some person 10 yards away. That day at

10.35 a.m. witness, accompanied by Dr. Trotter, made a further examination of the girl at her own house. Their joint report concludes: "We are of opinion that the above person was forcibly attacked; that the marks on the throat were consistent with pressure of the thumb and fingers of an assailant; and that recent forcible penetration had not been successfully accomplished."

On the following day witness assisted Dr. John Anderson, of Glasgow, to perform a post-mortem on the boy's body. Their joint report states: "Multiple gun-shot wounds of pellet size were present, extending from a line drawn at the level of the nipples upwards over the front of the chest, neck, and face, to a line drawn across at the level of the nostrils. . . . The area of distribution of the shot wounds was $13\frac{1}{2}$ inches from above downwards and 14 inches from shoulder to shoulder. The wounds were more numerous on the left side of the chest than on the right, while in the case of the neck and face they were more numerous on the right side. . . . From the above examination we are of opinion that death was due to shock and haemorrhage into the left pleural cavity, the result of a gun-shot wound. The distribution of the pellets indicates that the shot was fired at close range and directly towards the front of the body of the deceased." By the Court—Witness could definitely say that the girl's injuries were not self-inflicted; he was satisfied that she was assaulted. Dr. Trotter and Dr. Anderson concurred.

Professor Allison, of Glasgow, stated that, along with Dr. Anderson, he made on 26th August an examination of the person of Marjory Fenwick. (It were as needless as unpleasant to go into details; the results were negative.) They also reported upon the clothing of the deceased. Of the shirt, they state: "One of the pearl buttons is broken, and a fragment of another broken button is present on the surface of the front of the shirt." Was this part of the half-button found upon the blood-stained tree stump? It looks likely, but we are not informed. By the Court—As a medico-legal expert witness was aware that young women sometimes pretend that they have been criminally assaulted. "Have you ever known a case, either in your experience or in your reading, of a young girl whose lover was shot dead making up a story that the murderer criminally assaulted her?—No, I have never known a parallel case."

The case for the Crown was then closed, and Mr. Wardlaw Burnet intimated that he did not propose to lead any evidence.

## V

The addresses of counsel and the charge of the learned Judge were on the high level of the occasion. But as Mr. Russell spoke for two hours and twenty, Mr. Burnet for two hours and seven minutes, and the Lord Justice-Clerk took exactly as long as Mr. Russell, the whole as reported in the typescript of the official shorthand notes filling 189 folio pages, it is manifest that in the space at my disposal I can only deal with them in briefest outline.

Mr. Russell opened with a striking picture of the tragedy: the young lad killed by a gun discharged by some lurking ruffian, who, as the boy's life was ebbing away, committed on his girl a most revolting outrage. The question was not: Who killed Kerrigan and assaulted Marjory Fenwick? but: Did the accused do it? That was for the Crown to prove. The first evidence to implicate the accused was that of the girl herself. Did they believe her story? If there were some discrepancies between it as told in the witness-box and to other people at the time, they would bear in mind the agitation and distress in which she then was and whether the recollection of the witnesses was infallible. They, the jury, were the judges of her credibility. They would see how her story was corroborated by other facts and circumstances.

The first people who saw her, at 10.40, found her terribly upset, sobbing and crying, naked except for her coat, the belt round her neck, and the handkerchief on her wrist. Her first words were: "Will you help me, mister?" At the time when she says the two shots were fired, shots were heard by four witnesses: M'Dougall, Wilkie, Stewart, and Hill. She says the shots were fired at close range; experts, both medical and mechanical, said that they must have been fired from about 8 yards. They could see from the photographs of the *locus* that there was excellent cover. The injuries found by the doctors on the girl's body were just what they would expect if she were lying naked on that rough ground with her assailant above her. The marks of the throttling to which she spoke were seen upon her throat. Her garter was afterwards found at the place which she had pointed out to the police next morning as that where she was outraged; so, severally, were her pendant and the strap of her underskirt. The account which she gave to Spence and Ewan did not differ in substance from that which she had given in the box. Had her story been false, it would always have been the same in word and phrase; that it was not so went to prove its truth. Sergeant M'Callum, who thought she could not have got one hand out of the handkerchief as tied, admitted he never tried how far it would stretch. Drummond, the janitor, who was long in her company that night, said that she could have withdrawn one hand. The first persons to see her all thought her story absolutely true.

If this were proved, was the accused the man that committed these crimes? The girl swore on oath that he was; she described him to the best of her ability, and she positively identified him. Was it not significant that the accused, while as yet not charged with any crime, should say: "You have made a mistake. I may resemble the man"?

Then there was that most extraordinary history of the handkerchief found upon her wrist, as disclosed by the evidence. About the telescope and the purse there could be no question; they found their way from the "Laundry" at Aberdalgie to the accused's tent. The blue handkerchief found in the

"Laundry" was proved to be his. If there were any doubt as to how these articles came into his possession, they had the finger-print evidence, which shewed clearly that the impressions on the casement window could only have been made by his hand. It was proved that he left behind him there his own handkerchief and finger-prints, and took away with him the telescope, the purse, and the handkerchief, which, apart altogether from the girl's story, formed a link between the crime and the accused. In considering the house-breaking charge they might lay aside the alarm clock, the razor, and the football, the evidence not being clear that these were in fact in the "Laundry" at the time. The precise date was immaterial, if they were satisfied that he did steal the other articles.

Counsel then reviewed the evidence of the Messrs. Douglas as to their ownership of the handkerchief, the telescope, and the purse, and that of Peddie, Mackenzie, and Gow regarding the accused's possession of the telescope. His own handkerchief was identified by his mother and by Peddie. After dealing in detail with the expert evidence as to the finger-prints, which he held were conclusive of the accused's guilt, counsel passed to the question of the weapon.

No gun belonging to the accused had been found. From the closeness of the shots, they were fired from a double-barrelled shot-gun. That the accused possessed such a gun was proved by Peddie, who saw and handled it. The day after the murder he told Peddie he had it hidden; on the following day he made the remark to Mackenzie, apropos of the policeman's visiting his tent: "I have my gun away." A fortnight earlier he had told Mackenzie he had a double-barrelled gun, and a week later, that he was going to buy some cartridges. On the afternoon of the murder he told Gow he had a gun and a rifle, and that he had a rifle was proved by Arnott.

Being possessed of a gun, was he likely to be in the vicinity of the crime that night? At 4 o'clock he was seen with his "spy-glass" by Gow, who had a conversation with him at the stile. At 8 o'clock Barrie saw him go by the dyke towards the Cuddies Strip and disappear among the whins. The accused told Peddie he had been "spying" on him and Mackenzie that night; he told Arnott he had been "up the hill," but was down by 9.30.

Was the accused, if proved to have been the man who assaulted the girl, the man who fired the shot? He appeared beside her within a second or two after the boy fell. The shot was fired from about 8 yards away. The girl had seen no one near them: where did he come from, if not from the hidden place in the bushes whence the gun was fired? Had they any reasonable doubt that the same man who outraged the girl fired the shot?

Of the broken shirt-button and the blood-stains round the tree stump, counsel offered an ingenious explanation. The girl's assailant desisted from his act before it was finally consummated. When she freed her mouth and screamed, he got up, tied the suspender belt over her mouth, bound her feet, and went off in the direction of the body. In handling it he gets some blood and the fragment of the button on his hand; these he shakes and wipes off at the stump, before going back to collect the girl's clothes.

The Lord Justice-Clerk here pointed out that there was no legal evidence of the theft of the pocket-book, and he would direct the jury accordingly. Mr. Russell agreed; the only evidence was that of the girl herself.

There remained the charges of house-breaking, murder, and rape. Having examined the medical evidence respecting the last, counsel explained that if they were not satisfied that it was established, they might find the accused guilty of indecent assault. They could have no hesitation in finding that the assailant was also the murderer. He asked for a verdict of Guilty on charges (1), (2), and (3), as modified.

It was a fine address, dignified and impressive, in the best tradition of the Crown, and calculated, one would have thought, to secure a verdict on all the issues.

# VI

Mr. Burnet's speech for the defence was at once forceful and effective—inasmuch as it saved his client's neck. He began with a telling reference to the Court-room as the scene of so many famous trials, notably those of Madeleine Smith, who was acquitted, and of Oscar Slater, who was convicted, the verdict being overturned some twenty years later. But he doubted whether it had ever heard so strange and inexplicable a story as that told by Marjory Fenwick.

The three charges were interrelated; they must consider each upon its own merits, and find whether there was sufficient evidence bearing upon each and all of them to warrant a verdict of Guilty. Suspicion would not do; they were not there to speculate or to conjecture. The sole question was: Had the Crown satisfied them beyond reasonable doubt that the accused was the man who committed these crimes, particularly the murder of Kerrigan?

The story told by the girl was so frightful that, if it were true, it was incredible that any sane human being should have behaved as she says this man did. None but a madman could have been guilty of such horrible and revolting conduct, and there was no suggestion that the accused was insane. A singular feature of the case was that, apart from sheer bestial, brutal lust, absolutely no motive was alleged. Robbery was not now suggested—the pocket-book had been given up—and there was no question of jealousy.

Two things were clear: the boy was killed by a shot fired at close range; and about 10.40 the girl was seen by Spence and Ewan in the condition which they described. None of her clothing—with the possible exception of the band, the tape, and the bead—had been discovered. The Crown, when they charged the stealing of the pocket-book, did not charge the theft of the clothes. While he did not say the girl's story was entirely false—something very terrible indeed must have happened that night which resulted in Kerrigan's death—

35

when she first told it she was in an hysterical condition, and they must not make allowances for her to the prejudice of the accused. "The opinion you form of the reliability of the girl as a witness," said Mr. Burnet, "is absolutely crucial in this case, so far as the charges of murder and rape are concerned." Were they satisfied that she had told the whole truth and nothing but the truth?

I cannot follow counsel throughout his lengthy and able criticism of her tale. If her account of the manner of the shooting were true, she must herself have been hit. She did not connect the man who appeared at her side with the man who fired the shot. She asked them to believe that he ran beside her along that narrow path without touching her, for 200 yards to the stile. It was impossible for them to accept her account of the alleged rape, and its improbabilities were greatly increased by the medical evidence. Of the several descriptions which she had given of her assailant, none in the least resembled that man in the dock. On the accused's clothing no marks were found to substantiate her description of his actings. They must accept Sergeant M'Callum's statement that she could not have got her left hand out of the handkerchief. There was no sign that the suspender belt had been forcibly torn off. Nobody heard her cries for help, though there were people in the vicinity.

Counsel then reviewed the evidence of the witnesses who were said to corroborate her story, and maintained that it fell far short of doing so. Gow, for example, identified in August the accused's jacket by a burnt hole which Mrs. M'Guigan had patched in July. Peddie alleged that he saw the gun at the accused's tent on a Sunday, whereas his mother proved that the accused spent every week-end at Blairgowrie.

Mr. Burnet devoted much attention to Peddie, whose evidence, if true, was very damning to the accused; but it is difficult to see what object this young farm-hand, a decent-looking lad, could have in falsely swearing away the life of his friend and fellow-worker, whom, on the contrary, he plainly seemed disposed to shield.

Counsel then turned to what he well called the most dramatic element in the whole case, namely, that afforded by the wondrous handkerchief. "This," said he, "is a sordid and terrible case; but one cannot help feeling intrigued by the fact that this handkerchief, which was given to Mr. Douglas by an Indian trader abroad, should now be a clue of the utmost importance, from the Crown point of view, in this murder which happened in Perth." After recounting the evidence relative thereto, he challenged the Crown to shew that it, the handkerchief, was ever in the "Laundry" at all. As regards the telescope and the purse, the accused at once told the police that he got them from a man at the cross-roads at Meikleour. There was no clear evidence that either of these articles was in the "Laundry." As for the blue hand-kerchief found there being the accused's, the only evidence was the doubtful recognition of his mother and the unreliable testimony of Peddie. Counsel invited the jury to be their own experts in deciding upon the alleged correspondence of the finger-prints, as shewn in the enlarged photographs.

In conclusion, he asked the jury to return on the first charge (house-breaking and theft) a verdict of Not Guilty, or at least Not Proven. On the second and third charges (murder and rape) he asked, with confidence as regards the former, a verdict of Not Guilty.

## VII

The jury had listened to two very powerful addresses, the one demonstrative, the other subversive of the Crown case. They were now to hear the commentary of the learned Judge, by whose wisdom they should be guided into the right way.

His Lordship began by referring to the great gravity of the main issue they had to try, and explained the relative bearing of the several charges. It was for the Crown to prove guilt, not for the accused to prove innocence. Only by considering the cumulative weight of proved facts and circumstances was it possible to say that the case had passed from the region of reasonable doubt into that of reasonable certainty. It was not necessary for the Crown to prove motive. The most vital question in the case was this: What weight was to be given to the evidence of Marjory Fenwick? First, was she an honest witness? Second, was she a reliable witness? Unless they were satisfied on these points it would not be safe to convict upon so grave a charge as murder.

His Lordship then reviewed what he justly termed her very remarkable story. What impression did she make in the witness-box? Did she strike them as telling the truth? She was not a glib or plausible witness; she was rather cautious and reserved. It was said that her story was incredible. "Don't forget that when you are in the region of crime of this gravity you are quite definitely in the region of the abnormal. People who commit crimes of this kind are not to be measured by ordinary standards. Also don't forget that the man who was capable of shooting Kerrigan dead in the presence of that young girl when they were sweethearting together, was a man capable of any crime. . . . There is no doubt that whoever committed this crime was a man of low and degraded mentality." Was her story a pure invention? Kerrigan was certainly shot dead; she was found naked but for her coat, and her clothes were never discovered. Did she take them off herself and conceal them? If so, why? What conceivable motive could this girl, whose lover had just been brutally murdered, have to strip herself naked and pretend that the murderer had ravished her? His Lordship, after the most anxious consideration, could find nothing that would account for her doing so. If she knew the murderer and wanted to screen him, all she had to say was that she did not know the man and could not recognize him.

But then consider the probabilities: was it likely that her story was a mere pretence? Three articles belonging to her were found at the place where she said she was assaulted; did she put them there as part of a false story? She was not to be discredited because she said she was a virgin and the doctors said she was not. No single act of unchastity was put to her in cross-examination. Was her story corroborated by the medical evidence? That this young girl was physically assaulted was clear beyond all doubt; her injuries were recent and were not self-inflicted. As regards the sexual assault, her account of what happened derived in the most amazing way corroboration from the medical reports. No girl inventing a rape would have described it as she did. Having dealt with Mr. Burnet's criticism of her story, his Lordship observed of the handkerchief, as tied round her wrist, that M'Callum admitted he could get two fingers under it. The two fingers of a police-sergeant might not be much less than the hand of a slim young girl. The jury could have it if they wished and make their own experiments.

The first three or four witnesses who saw her had not the least doubt the girl's story was true. But she might be honest and yet unreliable. After narrating the several descriptions given by her of her assailant, his Lordship observed that it was extremely difficult to give an accurate verbal description of any person; the important thing was her identification of the man at the Police Station and in Court. Mistakes had unquestionably occurred in certain celebrated cases; but they must consider whether here there was not in the evidence corroboration of the girl's oath. Peddie proved that the accused had a double-barrelled shot-gun. On the very day of the crime he told Gow that he had a gun. Gow saw him "spying" there with his telescope, and whoever shot Kerrigan was someone who was lurking in Cuddies Strip, spying out what he could see, someone—if they wanted a motive—who wished the lad out of the way in order to take advantage of the girl. Then the day after the murder the accused told Peddie he had hidden his gun because he had no licence. Was that the real reason? He also said to Mackenzie when the policeman was going to his tent: "They need not bother going up now. I have my gun away." It was impossible to say there was no corroboration of the girl, if her identification were reliable.

But the most formidable part of the Crown case in the matter of identification was the handkerchief found upon the girl's wrist. If that handkerchief was stolen from Aberdalgie House by the accused—well, they had just got to face up to it. So they must most anxiously consider the evidence relating to the first charge. They had only now to deal with the telescope, the purse, and the handkerchief. There was no doubt whatever as to the theft of the two first articles, as proved by the Messrs. Douglas, and they were found in the accused's possession. If Aberdalgie House was broken into and things were stolen, was it not a reasonable inference that the handkerchief reached Cuddies Strip by way of Aberdalgie? Could they have any doubt who committed the burglary and the theft? The evidence of the finger-print experts was of the greatest possible importance. If the accused's own handkerchief was found in the "Laundry," and something from the "Laundry" was found in his possession, that was very curious cross evidence, which was always of the greatest value. If they thought the first charge proved, his Lordship directed them as to the form of their verdict. If they were satisfied that the handkerchief found on the girl's wrist was that given by the Indian trader to Mr. Douglas and that it was stolen by the accused from Aberdalgie House, it went a very long way to corroborate his identification by Marjory Fenwick.

If the accused was the man who stole the handkerchief from Aberdalgie and tied it on her wrist, then the inference that he was the man who fired the shot became inevitable. It was circumstantial evidence; but they had the direct evidence of Marjory Fenwick that though she did not see him pull the trigger, the accused was there at the time. If, as reasonable men and women, they were satisfied that the charge of murder was proved, they must not shrink from their plain duty of finding a verdict against him.

His Lordship then directed the jury on charge (2) (*b*)— the theft of the pocket-book—to find a verdict of Not Guilty. On (*a*)—the murder—there were three possible verdicts:

Guilty, Not Guilty, or Not Proven. On charge (3)—the rape—if they thought him guilty of house-breaking, they must not take that into consideration, except as regards the theft of the handkerchief, if they held that proved. His Lordship explained the nature of the third crime, as laid down in the text-books. If they believed the girl was so terrified as to be incapable of resistance, that would not prevent the commission of the crime. Whether or not the victim were a virgin was immaterial. Unless there was sufficient evidence to satisfy the jury on the vital question of identification, they could not convict on charge (3). It was open to them in law, on a charge of rape, to find a verdict: guilty of indecent assault. Here again they had the choice of three verdicts. His Lordship concluded by reminding the jury of the solemn words of their oath: "You will truth say, and no truth conceal."

This strongly reasoned and admirable charge ought surely to have carried "conviction" to the minds of the jury; but the ways of juries—especially since the introduction of the feminine element—are mysterious and past finding out.

## VIII

The jury retired at 12.30, and after an interval asked to see the accused's jacket, the handkerchief, and the suspender belt. Having considered these and other matters for two hours and ten minutes, they returned to Court with the following verdict: On charge (1) as modified, GUILTY, unanimously; on charge (2) (a), NOT PROVEN, by a majority, and (b), NOT GUILTY; on charge (3), GUILTY, unanimously. I understand that on the murder charge, the only one on which they disagreed, the vote was 9 for Not Proven and 6 for Guilty.

The Lord Justice-Clerk, addressing the accused, said he had been found guilty by the unanimous verdict of a jury on the grave charges of house-breaking and theft, and of the very

41

grave crime of rape. In 1929 he had been convicted of assault, of theft by house-breaking, and again of theft; in 1932 of theft by house-breaking; and in 1934 on four charges of theft. It appeared from his record that he was a dangerous criminal. In considering what sentence to impose, his Lordship left completely out of account the grave suspicion that attached to him in connection with the murder, of which he had been acquitted. But having regard to the gravity of the other offences and to his record, the sentence was that he be detained in penal servitude for ten years.

In thanking and discharging the jury, the Justice-Clerk referred to their finding as a "discriminating" verdict. I know not whether this was only courtesy, but it humbly seems to me that the term "illogical" would have been more appropriate. One would think that the man unanimously pronounced guilty of the rape, must necessarily be the per-petrator of the murder by which it was immediately preceded, there being no evidence that any third person was present, although I have been told, extra-judicially, that the accused was accompanied that night by a friend, who was sharing his tent in the absence of his parents, and assisted him in the burglary at Aberdalgie. If this man shot the boy to enable M'Guigan to attack the girl, he was singularly altruistic. Both crimes must stand or fall together. Had I served on that jury, my finding as regards the rape would have been: Guilty—of indecent assault. On the other hand, as regards the murder—but perhaps it were as well to keep my verdict to myself: I may perchance survive the convict's liberation.

When discussing the case with others, I have found a very general opinion that in this mysterious crime we have not got the whole facts. That, of course, holds good of almost every murder trial. Yet here, especially, one has a feeling there is something lacking, something that we ought to know, some-thing that perhaps the girl might have told us, although as I have said I believe her story to be in substance true. In an interview, published in *The People's Journal* on 7th December, she says: "I spoke nothing but the truth. There was, however, much more I could have said, but somehow or other I never got the chance to say it. Indeed, when Mr. Burnet was addressing the jury I felt like jumping up and requesting to be allowed to go into the witness-box again. With another half-hour there I believe I could have cleared up a number of hazy points." For myself, I have no theory to offer, none at least that squares with the proved facts. All we can be sure of is that Danny Kerrigan was foully slain, that Marjory Fenwick was criminally assaulted, and that the accused is to be congratulated on his acquittal of the major charge.

## IX

Apropos of this curious verdict, so much in keeping with the mysterious features of the case, it is interesting to note that Lord Cockburn, in his *Circuit Journeys*, that delightful book which is, I fear, less read than it deserves to be, records a singular instance of the peculiar workings of the jury-mind. Writing of the Glasgow Winter Circuit in January, 1850, his Lordship says:—

It was an unusually black tribunal, there being 79 cases, involving about 125 culprits; among whom seven were charged with murder, and many with other serious crimes. Of the murderers, one, a female poisoner, was doomed to die; two were transported for life, and one for seven years; one was acquitted, one escaped, and one was imprisoned. The poisoner had first stolen a bank deposit-receipt, and then finding that she could not get the money without the owner's signature, she forged it, and then, having committed these two offences, she murdered the victim in order to hide them. She was tried for the whole three crimes. The forgery, and the administration of arsenic were very clearly proved. But there was a doubt about the theft, and therefore the jury found it *not proved*. Yet upon this fact a majority of them grounded by far the most nonsensical recommendation to mercy that any jury, known to me, ever made themselves ludicrous by. They first recommended without stating any reason, and on being asked what their reason was, they retired, and after consultation, returned with these written words, viz.: that they gave the recommendation " in consequence of the first charge, of theft, not having been proved, which they believe in a great measure led to the commission of the subsequent crime"! Grammatically, this means that it was their *acquittal* of the theft that did the mischief, but what they *meant* was, that the murder was caused by a theft *not proved to have existed*. It is the most Hibernian recommendation I have ever seen.

Lord Cockburn would doubtless have admired the logical faculty exhibited by these later assizers. The case to which his Lordship refers is that of Margaret Lennox or Hamilton, who suffered at Glasgow for the murder of her sister-in-law, the paltry consideration being but £20. The report of her trial which I happen to have bears the certificate by a former owner: "I saw her hanged."

# THE INTEMPERATE MIDSHIPMAN;
## OR, TROUBLE ON LEITH PIER

# THE INTEMPERATE MIDSHIPMAN;
## OR, TROUBLE ON LEITH PIER

"'All flag officers and all persons in or belonging to His Majesty's sloops or vessels of war, being guilty of profane oaths, execration, drunkenness, uncleanness, or other scandalous actions, in derogation of God's honour and corruption of good manners, shall incur such punishment as——'"

"Damnation!" cried the master, who was mad with rage, hearing that the whole ship's company were laughing.

"No, Sir, not damnation," replied Jack, "that's when he's tried above."

CAPTAIN MARRYAT: *Mr. Midshipman Easy.*

"IT chanced in the year 1813 that Archie strayed one day into the Justiciary Court"—the supreme criminal tribunal of the College of Justice in Edinburgh. The business in hand was the trial of one Duncan Jopp, and lovers of *Weir of Hermiston* well know how that conjunction has provided entertainment for the posterities.

It also chanced in the following year that one Mr. John Kay—caricaturist, engraver, and miniature painter, as he describes himself—strayed into the same Court, before which a young naval officer was then on trial for his life. Struck by the appearance of the accused and the peculiar circumstances of the case, and having about him the materials of his art, Kay made a drawing of the prisoner as he stood at the bar, between two veterans of the City Guard, later to be included among his inimitable *Portraits*. The fact was fraught with happy results for my present purpose.

By a coincidence, for me equally fortunate, Kay had drawn and published a similar sketch in 1796, when he witnessed the trial before Lord Braxfield of James M'Kean in the same Court, for the murder of the Lanark carrier.[1] In both plates the same two soldiers of the Guard are shewn as warding the respective "pannels" (prisoners).

[1] Cf. "The Hanging of James M'Kean: Lord Braxfield's Last Case," in my *Glengarry's Way* (Edinburgh: 1922).

It may be that for the artist the case had a further attraction in that the *locus* or scene of the tragedy was the Pier of Leith, with which his own early days had unpleasant associations. Born in Dalkeith in 1742, on the death of his father some six years later, the boy was boarded by his mother with certain relatives in Leith. By these unconscionable kinsmen, he tells us, he was used extremely ill, for not only did they neglect, but they beat and starved him.

> While he lived with these savages in Leith, he run various risks of his life from accidents without doors, as well as from bad usage within; and there is every reason to believe that they really wished his death and took every method to accomplish it except downright murder. On one occasion he was blown into the sea from the Ferryboat Stairs, and on another he fell into the water on stepping across the joists below the Wooden Pier, but recovered himself both times, by grasping the steps on the one occasion and the joists on the other.
>
> But he ran a still greater risk of drowning upon a third occasion, when, happening to be seated on the side of a ship in the harbour, he was accidentally pushed overboard, and being taken up for dead, remained in that condition for some time, till one of the sailors, anxious to see him, in his hurry trampled upon his belly, which immediately excited a groan, and produced respiration and articulation. He might have died, however, that same evening, had not other people taken more care of him than his barbarous relations did.

*Pace* his obvious prejudice, it would seem that these misfortunes were due rather to his own carelessness than to the contrivance of his unnatural enemies. The manner of his resuscitation provides a novelty in life-saving methods.

From his earliest years John was possessed by a passion for drawing which, lacking the means to procure pencils and crayons, he indulged with chalk, charcoal, or bits of burnt stick. His artistic bent, however, was but coldly regarded by his relatives, and at thirteen he was apprenticed to a barber in Dalkeith. Having served his time, he came to Edinburgh to follow the same trade, and in 1771 became a member of the Society of Surgeon-Barbers. All his leisure hours were devoted to miniature-painting and engraving; and there is little doubt that had he been properly trained, he might have become a good portrait-painter. But being wholly self-taught, there is in all his work a suggestion of the amateur. His unique and obvious gift lay in seizing a likeness and expressing it in terms of caricature. So popular and successful were his prints, which he was wont to exhibit in his shop, that by 1785 he decided to abandon his business, and instead of merely shaving the heads of his customers, to "take them off" completely. So he opened a small print-shop on the south side of the Parliament Close, the windows of which were always "embellished" by the latest examples of his art. The Max Beerbohm of his day, to be caricatured by Kay was a hall-mark of distinction, and for well-nigh half a century the most notable inhabitants of Auld Reikie "sat" for him, consciously or otherwise, to the joy of their contemporaries and the enrichment of their successors.

The social and historical value of his work is inestimable. But for it we should have known nothing of the personal appearance, say, of Deacon Brodie, and of a score of other eighteenth-century characters, whose "likeness" we could ill have spared. John Kay died in 1824 at the ripe age of eighty-three. His monument was in due season provided by a collection of his work, published in the two quarto volumes so well and widely known as *Kay's Portraits*. Of his achievement Chambers has justly observed:—"It may with safety be affirmed that no city in the Empire can boast of so curious a chronicle."

# I

There is a brief mention of our case in *Kay's Portraits*, accompanying the plate above referred to; also an adequate account in the *Scots Magazine* for July-August, 1814 (between which is surprisingly sandwiched a rather condescending review of the day's best seller: *Waverley: or, 'Tis Sixty Years Since*), as well as newspaper notices in the Edinburgh *Advertiser* and *Courant* of 15th and 16th July. Above all, we have an excellent report of the judicial proceedings: "The Trial of Thomas Whyte, Midshipman of H.M.S. *Unicorn*, before the High Court of Justiciary, on the 13th July, 1814, for the Murder of William Jones, late Seaman on board the *Unicorn*. Leith: Printed by Gilchrist & Heriot; sold by James Burnet, Bernard Street, and all the Booksellers. 1814."

The diet was called before the Lord Justice-Clerk (David Boyle of Shewalton), Lords Meadowbank, Hermand, and Pitmilly. Counsel for the Crown were the Lord Advocate (Archibald Colquhoun of Killermont), the Solicitor-General (Alexander Maconochie), and Mr. Home Drummond, Advocate-Depute; for the accused were John Clerk and Henry Cockburn, both of whom later ascended the judicial Bench. Clerk had won his spurs in 1788 at the famous trial of Deacon Brodie; Cockburn was to be remembered as the delightful author of the *Memorials* and of the *Circuit Journeys*.

The accused is described as "a good-looking young man, seemingly about twenty years of age; was dressed in naval uniform and behaved with great propriety." The indictment upon which he was brought to trial set forth, in the customary legal verbiage of the day, the crime with which he was charged. Stripped of its forensic garniture this was: that on 15th June, 1814, on the wooden part of the Pier of Leith, he did assault William Jones, seaman in His Majesty's navy, and then under his command, and did repeatedly strike him with a drawn dirk or hanger, and did stab and mortally wound him therewith in his belly, of which wound, so inflicted, he the said William Jones immediately died, and was thereby murdered by him the said Thomas Whyte. "No objection being made to the relevancy of the libel, a short paper was read for the pannel [accused] in which it was stated that the unfortunate occurrence for which he was now placed at the bar of the Court had occurred in the discharge of his duty; that the blow by which Jones was killed was merely accidental; and that not having any intention to hurt the deceased, he considered himself innocent of the crime laid to his charge."

The libel having been found relevant and a jury empanelled, the Lord Advocate called his first witness: James Allan, journeyman baker, Leith. Cockburn objected to this witness that he had a strong prejudice against the pannel, and had said that he ought to have been hanged when he committed the offence. The Court repelled the objection and admitted the witness.

Allan then stated that on the date in question he saw a King's boat lying below the bowsprit of a store-ship, which was moored off the wooden pier. There were in the boat five or six men and a midshipman. The accused came from the Britannia Inn to the west end of the pier. He asked whether Jones was come yet? and was answered, No. The boat's crew were singing, and Whyte said: "Sing on, you b——s!" and went back to the Shore. He returned in ten minutes, asked the same question, and was answered, Yes. "Where is he?" cried Whyte. Jones was seen lying on his side at the edge of the pier, "knocking his hat on the posts," and joking along with the rest of the crew in the boat below. Whyte ordered Jones into the boat; Jones said: "No; I am going to get up the basket to give the girl, and then I will go." (The basket had contained beer for the men, brought from a tavern by "a girl of colour," who was waiting for its return.) Jones then asked the crew to hand up the basket. Witness saw it and the empty bottles of ale lying in the bottom of the boat, "and the mulatto girl waiting for the basket about ten yards from Jones." The accused said to him: "Won't you go on board when I desire you, Sir?" Before Jones had time to answer, Whyte struck him twice on the head with his dirk, "and immediately he stabbed him near the navel." Drawing out the dirk, he struck him again on the belly. Witness was a yard from them at the time. On receiving the stab Jones sprang up and hung upon the side of the pier by his hands, with his feet resting on one of the posts below. The accused stamped upon his hands; he let go and fell down on to the stones below the pier, the tide being then out. The accused waved his weapon and bade the onlookers stand back or he would do the same to them: he said he had stabbed a man, but had only done his duty, as he, Jones, "was going to run away from His Majesty's service." Some gentlemen on the pier called out to seize him, "and the pannel ran after them with his dirk in his hand, towards the out-end of the pier, saying he would be about with them." He then boarded the store-ship and sat on the bowsprit with his drawn dirk, threatening to stab the first who should attempt to seize him. The boatswain came out of the boat and approached him, whereupon he leaped on to the pier and again pursued the crowd with his dirk. The boatswain, following, asked him to deliver up his sword, when, on his refusing to do so, the other closed with him and disarmed him, cutting his own hand in the process. He was then secured and carried to the Council Chamber. During the affray, the other midshipman, who was in the boat, cried up to the pannel: "You damned idiot! see what you have done; you have stabbed the man, when he would have come into the boat." The affair happened at exactly twenty minutes past seven by the witness's watch. The accused "did not altogether appear to be sober"; Jones also had been drinking. Cross-examined—The mulatto girl was standing on the east side of the pier; witness heard her ask for her basket. He had seen her before in Anderson's public-house on the Shore. Jones, when stabbed, was lying upon his side, resting on his elbow.

David Thomson, journeyman baker, Leith, stated that he was at Leith Pier that Wednesday night along with the preceding witness, whom he corroborated generally as to what occurred. When the accused ordered Jones to go aboard the boat, he answered, "very civilly," that he would not do so till he had handed back the basket to the girl. Whereupon the pannel drew his dirk and struck him twice on the head and stabbed him "under the navel." When Jones got up and tried to get over the pier, he lost his hold and fell below among the stones. Witness then described what further happened, up to the disarming and capture of the pannel by the boatswain of the *Unicorn*, assisted by one Ferguson, who secured his sword. In witness's opinion the accused "had got a glass"; Jones also appeared to be in liquor. Cross-examined—He and Allan were together the whole time. Jones seemed to speak civilly to the pannel.

Fowler Ferguson, publican, Leith, stated that when first he saw the accused, he was on the store-ship, brandishing his dirk. He came ashore and chased the people. The boatswain of the *Unicorn* asked him to sheath his weapon; he refused, and witness took it from him. There was blood upon it then. He identified the sword as now produced.

Robert Houghton Wright, midshipman of the *Unicorn*, stated that he was sent in a boat under Mr. Levit's command to the naval yard to ship some rigging. The accused was afterwards sent with another boat to bring the men back from the yard. Mr. Carroll, midshipman, was with him. The first party were six in number, of whom Jones was one. Witness went with the accused and Carroll to the Britannia Inn, where they had some ale. Whyte went out, and returning, told witness that two of his party and one of his own were missing, and desired him to search for them, which he did. He met Jones on the pier and asked him to go to his boat; Jones replied, "He would be damned if he would." He muttered and grumbled when the accused came up and ordered him into the boat, and said: "Damn his eyes if he would." Jones appeared to be in a bad humour and seemed to be drunk. On his refusing to obey, the accused drew his dirk and struck him twice with the flat of it on the breast, and again lower down. Jones then attempted to go over to the boat and got about a third down, when he fell under the pier among the stones. The accused pushed back the crowd, saying that no one should impede the King's service, as he was doing his duty in getting the man aboard. The injured man, having been lifted into the boat, was examined by Dr. Smith of Leith and Dr. M'Caroghir, surgeon of the *Unicorn*. The body was taken to the ship and afterwards brought ashore. Witness thought Whyte was drunk; after the accident he became quite frantic. All the drink witness had with Whyte was one bottle of ale, which Carroll shared.

Archibald Morrison, carpenter, Leith, gave much the same account of what happened. When the accused went on board the store-ship witness called out to him that he was a murderer and ought to be apprehended. The accused then came ashore, and brandishing his sword, cried: "Who calls me a murderer?" whereupon the witness prudently "retired about twenty yards." The pannel appeared to have been drinking, and Jones also seemed hearty.

John Duff, stocking-maker, Leith, stated that on the 15th of June, about half-past six o'clock at night, he saw the *Unicorn's* boat lying in the harbour, with ten or twelve men on board, who were "hearty and singing." The midshipman in charge gave liberty to have more drink, but the pannel came up and would not allow it. He asked for Jones, who was not there, and then went away. Meanwhile a girl of colour arrived with the beer, which was handed into the boat, and while the crew were drinking it Jones came up, "in high spirits and good-humour, running and jumping up and down the pier." Witness, who was 12 to 18 inches from Jones at the time, then described what he saw of the incident. "Pannel came up and seized Jones by the collar and damned him to go into the boat. Jones said: 'I will go, but don't collar me.' Pannel then drew his sword, and struck him across the neck and across the face with the flat side. Jones at this time was turning to get over the pier, when the pannel thrust the sword into his body. He gave him another stroke or push and damned him to get down to the boat. Jones instantly lost his hold and fell down. Witness saw Jones's face, and when he received the stab it directly lost colour."

Andrew Carroll, midshipman of the *Unicorn*, stated that he came ashore with the accused in a boat at four o'clock to take some rope to the naval yard. Witness was left in care of the boat. He then described several visits to the Britannia Inn, accompanied by the accused and Mr. Midshipman Wright, where they had divers bottles of ale, and subsequently dined together. Thereafter witness went back to the boat and remained there. He heard that Jones was missing; "but does not recollect when he saw Jones after that, as he has a very imperfect recollection, having drank too much." In view of this frank admission, the witness was not further examined.

John Bayne, apprentice baker in Leith, stated that he remembered the night the man was stabbed. Witness was sitting on one of the cross-bars under the pier when he heard the accused order Jones aboard. His account of what occurred thereafter is substantially the same as that of the other witnesses. "Witness was just getting upon the pier with his feet when the pannel stabbed Jones; he was quite close to him. After Jones received the stab he fell under the pier, from whence he was immediately lifted into the boat, and turned quite pale."

Dr. John Smith, Leith, stated that he was called to a man who had been stabbed on the pier, and found him lying on his back in a boat, apparently lifeless. A report was next day drawn up by order of the Magistrates of Leith, and was signed by Drs. Kellie, Sanders, and himself. Witness then read the report, which bore that in the opinion of the surgeons Jones died of the wound inflicted upon him, the sword having cut the aorta or largest artery, and been arrested by the backbone, thus occasioning instant death. The witness then explained the position in which seemingly the sword had been when the blow was struck. Even had the deceased been rising at the time, it must have required very considerable force to pierce the clothes and integuments. There was no other wound on the deceased but the fatal one.

Dr. George Kellie, Leith, concurred in the report and corroborated his confrère. The wound must have been inflicted by a sword-thrust, horizontally directed. It was the only wound.

Two declarations emitted by the accused, one on the night of his apprehension, the other on the following day, were then proposed to be read. Counsel for the defence objected to their admission, because "the Public Prosecutor had only libelled upon the last," and had not referred to the first. The Lord Advocate answered that the declaration emitted upon the 15th was merely a declinature by the pannel to be examined till next day, he having been in a state of intoxication at the time. His Lordship had not libelled on that declaration out of motives of humanity to the pannel. The Court (Lord Meadowbank dissenting) sustained the objection and refused to admit the declaration, holding that the Public Prosecutor is bound to produce all declarations emitted by a person charged with a crime.[1] The case for the Crown was then closed.

## II

The first witness called for the defence was Rear-Admiral William Johnstone Hope, who stated that orders had lately been received from the Admiralty regarding the reduction of sea service: those who had served longest were to be discharged first. There had been in consequence a number of desertions from the ships under his command on that station, and very strict orders had been given to prevent seamen getting away. The *Unicorn* had only been in the Firth ten days, and it was reported to him that already thirteen seamen had deserted from that ship.

Captain Smith, commanding the flag-ship of Admiral Hope, concurred with that witness as to the effect of the Order upon desertions. From his own ship, the *Latona*, five times more men had deserted than in the preceding two months. Strict orders were given to all officers that they should look watchfully after their men when on shore.

Lieutenant Kedger, of the *Unicorn*, stated that his ship came to Leith Roads on 14th June. The men had been paid at Sheerness ten days before. On 15th June the Master and

---

[1] The grounds of Lord Meadowbank's dissent from this ruling are fully set forth in Hume's *Commentaries on the Law of Scotland respecting Crimes*, Second Edition, 1819, Vol. II, p. 317.

Mr. Levit were sent with stores to the naval yard in a boat
with ten men. Mr. Whyte, the accused, was afterwards sent
in the cutter to bring the working-party back, as witness
feared some of them would desert, desertions having been
frequent since the Admiralty Order was issued for the reduction of the older men. Jones, the deceased, had been five
years on board the *Unicorn*. Of twenty-four men who were
ashore at Leith, thirteen deserted, two of them on the day
that Jones met his death. The latter was of a discontented
character, particularly when in liquor; witness thought he
would desert at Leith as, being a good seaman, he might get
a ship there. He had been punished for striking the Master-
at-Arms. Witness had known the accused for three years
as a zealous and attentive officer, remarkably sober, and much
esteemed by his messmates, captain, and ship's company for
his mild behaviour. Three days before the occurrence Mr.
Whyte had saved Jones from punishment by not reporting
him when drunk.

R. H. Wright, midshipman of the *Unicorn*, stated that he
landed with the party under the command of Mr. Levit.
Jones asked leave to go out of the yard, which witness refused to grant. Jones afterwards went out and returned
voluntarily, bringing some ale with him. He saw Jones on
the pier, who said, when ordered by Mr. Whyte to go into
the boat, he would be damned if he would do so for him.
Jones had served five years on the *Unicorn*, during which
he was very troublesome when drunk and was frequently
punished. The accused was sober and good-natured; he
was rather liked by the men.

John Levit, senior midshipman of the *Unicorn*, stated that
he took the working-party ashore, and that Whyte joined
him later with three men more to assist. Jones twice asked
leave to go out of the yard, which witness refused. He said:
"You know if I want to go out you cannot stop me." Jones
then offered him a two-pound note, which witness took from
him and kept, again refusing to give him leave. Jones then
cried: "Here goes!" and ran out of the yard, pursued by

witness, who overtook him and lodged him in the guard-house, but he escaped from the sentinel and joined the other men, who, the boat being aground, had come ashore and gone in a body to a public-house. There Jones gave witness 11s. 6d. more to keep for him, which he took "for more security." He then got the men out and down to the boat, except Jones and three others, leaving them in charge of Carroll; and having reported their absence to Whyte and Wright, went himself in search of them. While he was so doing the "accident" happened. Witness had served five years on the *Unicorn*, and gave Whyte an excellent character for efficiency and sobriety; he was well-esteemed both by officers and men. Jones, when drunk, was very quarrel-some and insolent to his superiors; he had knocked down the Master-at-Arms when ordered into the boat. The accused had three days before screened him from punishment, "but he would as soon abuse the pannel for his forbearance as anything else."

Sergeant Merrell of the West Norfolk Militia—whose name is pleasantly reminiscent of *The Yeomen of the Guard*—stated that he had orders not to let any of the sailors leave the yard unless passed by an officer. Witness described how Jones was committed to the guard-house and rushed out. He behaved very insolently to his officer.

Christian Christie, Leith, stated that she was on the pier when the man was killed. She heard the accused order Jones into the boat, who said he would see him damned first; he would go when he was ready, "and gave a good deal of imprudent language." He said "that the *Unicorn* was liker a prison ship than any other thing." Witness's husband was Captain's steward and coxswain of the *Apelles* sloop of war, a boat from which lay alongside the store-ship that night. While she was in that boat she saw the crowd use the pannel badly. One man struck him on the mouth, which bled much. Witness had been married to her present husband three years, and fifteen years to her first husband, who also was a seaman. She had been much aboard ship, but never saw a man behave worse to his officer than did Jones to the accused.

David Dick, publican in Leith, corroborated. He saw the pannel come down the pier and order three men into the boat; they obeyed. Jones was not then there, but when he came, he called to the boat's crew: "You b——s! you are all high and dry"—which, indeed, in a double sense, they were. On Mr. Whyte ordering him to embark, Jones went down upon the anchor-stock of the store-ship; he had a knife in his hand, and called out to two Portuguese sailors in the boat to come up to him and he would cut their throats —an invitation which the foreigners declined to accept. Witness then left the pier and saw nothing more of the affair.

Margaret Alexander, the dusky Hebe of the public-house, told how an officer ordered a dozen of ale, which she carried to a boat's crew in the harbour. After giving in the basket, witness went down below to get it, and had just done so when Jones fell. She had waited on the pier an hour, but said she knew nothing further of the matter.

John Boskin, captain of the main-top on board the *Unicorn*, said he had known Jones ever since the expedition to Flushing. He had a very indifferent character, was quarrelsome when in liquor, and refused to obey orders. Witness had served under the accused for three years. He was sober in his habits and well liked by the crew. Whyte had no ill-will at Jones, but rather the reverse; he had saved him from punishment for getting drunk after they had sailed for Leith from the Nore. George Tough, seaman on the *Unicorn*, gave similar testimony. This closed the case for the defence.

### III

The Lord Advocate then addressed the jury. Of the speech for the prosecution we are only informed that his Lordship was brief but stern, contending that the crime charged in the indictment was completely proved. However painful might be the duty which he was called upon to discharge, he felt bound to require from them a verdict of guilty. John Clerk, we read, addressed the jury at great length on behalf of his client. He argued, first, that the unfortunate event was the mere result of an accident, and that there was no intention on the part of the pannel to inflict even a serious injury on the deceased; and, second, that if the jury, contrary to his opinion, should think that the pannel had any such intention, he, counsel, was convinced they would have no doubt whatever he did not exceed the bounds of his duty, and that in that case they would return a verdict of justifiable homicide.

The Lord Justice-Clerk then charged the jury in "a most eloquent and perspicuous speech," in the course of which his Lordship laid down the law of Scotland as applicable to the crime of murder. He dwelt much upon the rash and unprovoked manner in which the crime had been committed; the unlawfulness of the weapon; the defenceless state in which the deceased was lying at the time; and "the impropriety of resorting to so desperate an alternative." He was decidedly of opinion that neither of the views of the case taken by the prisoner's counsel was well-founded on the evidence, according to the principles of the law of Scotland, and that the crime of murder had been clearly made out.

The jury were then enclosed, and directed to return their verdict next day at eleven o'clock.

# IV

On Thursday, 14th July, in the hour of cause, the jury returned their verdict, finding, "by a plurality of voices," or, as we should now say, by a majority, the pannel Guilty of culpable homicide (manslaughter). The Solicitor-General having moved for sentence, their Lordships severally delivered judgment.

Lord Meadowbank said that they were to administer the law of Scotland as handed down by their forefathers. By that law all species of culpable homicide was punished with severity; and the degree of punishment applicable to each particular case rested with the Court; but not so as to trench upon the verdict of the jury, which had reduced the crime from murder to culpable homicide. The Court was too versant in the law not to be aware that this case shewed the fatality so often attending human nature. The young gentleman at the bar, proved to be humane, to bear the best of characters, beloved and respected by his brother officers, commits a crime of a most violent nature upon a man under his protection who, while lying upon the ground, is stabbed with a sword, not sparingly inflicted, but which is proven to have penetrated even to the back-bone. Human nature, no doubt, must shudder at such a crime and account it murder; but as the jury had found that this is not murder, the responsibility rested with them. He, for one, would never depart from the law as handed down, which gives security to every man, whatever be his rank in society. He felt most severely for the young gentleman at the bar, as much as for one of his own children if placed in the same unfortunate predicament. But what could he do? It appeared to him impossible that the Court could do otherwise than to inflict such a degree of punishment as would mark its abhorrence of the crime which had been committed. Transportation was the very least degree of punishment that could be inflicted. Imprisonment would not answer the ends of public justice. He was sorry for it, but it seemed to him impossible that a less punishment could be inflicted than transportation for fourteen years. Transportation for life might be said to be necessary; yet he considered it would be pitiable to deprive so fine a young man of a chance of once more returning to his native country.

Lord Hermand concurred entirely in the opinion delivered. The present case was a striking example of the effects of unruly passion, and that in a man who bore so excellent a character. He was much struck with the evidence of several witnesses as to the pannel's humanity, sobriety, and even indulgence and forbearance towards the unfortunate individual who met his death at his hands. He was sensible that the pannel had not been himself at the time; still that was not excuse nor palliation, in the eye of the law, in the case of murder. Another defence set up was disobedience of orders on the part of the deceased; but unfortunately, in the situation in which the parties were at the time, there was no necessity for so violent an alternative as that resorted to. He believed that there had been no serious intention upon the part of the pannel to commit murder; but still the use of so deadly a weapon and the defenceless state of the deceased incurred a responsibility of murder. Transportation for life had been condemned by political writers as wrong, in respect that few instances had ever occurred of any person having been reclaimed who had been condemned to that punishment, all hopes of returning to their native land having been cut off. He would therefore agree with their Lordships that transportation for fourteen years was sufficient punishment in this case.

Lord Pitmilly said that throughout the long evidence that had been led in this most afflicting and distressing case, he could not quit the verdict of the jury without saying that he should not here, for himself, draw the line betwixt culpable homicide and murder. This young man had been proved to bear a most exemplary character, for these very qualities must have weighed with the jury—humanity, sobriety, indulgence and forbearance to the man who had met his death at his hands. These are the motives which strike professional men; and these in all probability were the views he presumed had weighed the minds of the jury after cool deliberation. This young man, flushed with liquor, and actuated by a false notion of duty, did that rash act for which the law holds him responsible; but the jury had by their verdict taken the responsibility wholly on themselves, and it only remained with the Court to measure out the punishment. Transportation for life was the highest degree of punishment; but considering the verdict of the jury and the character given the pannel, he would concur in a sentence of transportation for fourteen years.

The Lord Justice-Clerk said he was of the same opinion with the rest of their Lordships. Although he had laid down the case to the jury as one of murder, yet he must now, by their verdict, take it as a case of culpable homicide. Sure he was, however, that their Lordships would concur with him in what was the undoubted law of Scotland: that this was a most aggravated case of culpable homicide. The circumstances had made such an impression on his mind that in justice to the law, and for the security of the community at large, he was called upon to pronounce a most exemplary punishment, that it might not only have a salutary effect upon the mind of the pannel, but be attended with lasting good consequences to him hereafter. His Lordship then addressed the pannel as follows:—

"Thomas Whyte, you have heard from all the Judges who have spoken the painful duty I have to fulfil in announcing to you the punishment of the crime of which you have been convicted. It is distressing to me to address you on this occasion, who have been proved to have borne so good a character. Honourable mention has been made of you by your companions in arms, and it is most painful for me to pronounce the sentence of the law. The punishment which awaits you will remove you from the honourable profession to which you have been bred, from your happy country, and from your friends and acquaintances. You may probably in your mind conceive the sentence to be hard, but it is one absolutely necessary. The crime you have committed approaches next to murder, and shews the dreadful consequences of ungovernable passion. You was possessed with a most mistaken notion of duty; the arms given you were not to be used with unnecessary severity and buried in the bowels of a fellow-creature. This is the dreadful consequence of the improper use of liquor, especially with you, who bore so excellent a character for sobriety. Drunkenness is no excuse, in the eye of God or of the law, for that crime of which you have been convicted. I hope this will have a proper effect upon you, and teach every one of your profession that while the law will protect them in the lawful exercise of their duty, it will at the same time prevent the undue use of weapons in slaughtering their fellow-creatures.

"There are two circumstances which I beg leave seriously to impress upon your mind: First, I warn you, in the country you go to, not to indulge in passion or intoxicating liquors; it is a proof you cannot govern yourself, and therefore it becomes you in your temporal state to put a watch upon your conduct. For be convinced, if you are there concerned in murder, the law of that country will visit you with immediate and condign punishment. Therefore follow actions of a different description. Another and more important duty is this: endeavour to settle your account with Almighty God. It is said: 'Whosoever sheddeth man's blood, by man shall his blood be shed; and He who searches hearts knoweth the secrets of man.' If, therefore, you are really guilty of murder, it is known to the Searcher of hearts, and no verdict of a jury nor mitigated punishment at the hand of man can wipe away your guilt. [This was a rap at the jury for finding a verdict in the teeth of the judicial charge.] Humble yourself, therefore; make your peace, and pray for forgiveness, otherwise your punishment in the world to come will be ten thousand times ten thousand more severe than any you can receive from the hand of man."

A startling view, this, of the lad's chances of mercy in the hereafter. His Lordship then sentenced him to be transported beyond seas for the term of fourteen years, under the usual certification. The condemned man, we are told, bowed respectfully to his judges and jury, and the Court then rose.

## V

Hume, in his *Commentaries*, has a long footnote on the case, with reference to his account of the historic trial and conviction of the famous Captain John Porteous in 1736, for ordering his men to fire upon the mob at the execution of the smuggler Wilson.[1]

He cites two other relevant cases, both of which, curiously, concern murderous midshipmen. The first is that of Henry Lloyd (3rd December, 1810). He was an officer of the gun-brig *Gallant*, then acting as a guard-ship in the Firth of Forth, with orders to examine all vessels entering the Port of Leith. Lloyd was sent with a party in the ship's boat to overhaul a Danish galliot that was making for the harbour. He fired a shot ahead of the vessel; and no attention being paid and the master continuing his course, Lloyd, from a distance of half a mile, fired a second shot, which was intended to pass over her. Unfortunately it struck her in the stern and killed the man at the helm. The galliot, however, pursued her way, and was only brought to after a third shot. It appeared from the evidence led at the trial that Lloyd had acted according to the known rules of the service, and rather within than beyond his warrant, so the jury found him Not Guilty of the crime charged, "and do therefore honourably acquit him thereof."

The second case is that of James Henry (12th July, 1813), who was a midshipman of the armed tender *Maria*, employed on the west coast of Scotland on what is euphemistically termed "the impress service." Henry was ordered to go ashore at Campbeltown, in Kintyre, with a boat's crew, for the purpose of securing involuntary recruits for His Majesty's navy. Having captured six men, he proposed to rejoin his ship; but in this the party was opposed by a large crowd of the inhabitants, who resented the forcible abduction of their fellow-townsmen. Armed with sticks, stones, bricks, and

---

[1] *Op. cit.*, Vol. I, p. 205.

other impromptu weapons they beset Henry and his crew, urging one another "to murder the pressing vagabonds." Several of the party were beaten and knocked down, a marine was disarmed, pistols were fired from adjacent windows, and three of the captives were rescued. One of the landing-party returned the fire, but Henry was heard to call out: "For God's sake not to fire among the mob, but over their heads." Doubtless he had not only before his eyes the fear of God, but also the fate of Porteous. With great difficulty the landing-party forced their way back to the boat, pursued so long as within range by stones and curses from the shore, and safely rejoined their ship. One seaman was found to be missing, whom the mob had retained as a hostage. In the exasperated state of the townsfolk it might have gone hard with him, for his life was violently threatened; but the magistrates intervened, and took the man to the pier-head, whence they hailed the tender, asking that a boat be sent ashore to take him off.

Now the officers of the *Maria* had their doubts as to whether this was not a treacherous device to bring a party ashore and renew the attack; so two marines accompanied the boat's crew, armed with muskets, pistols, and some rounds of ball cartridge. Two of the captured men, not being found up to His Majesty's standard, were to be returned, without thanks, to their friends. On approaching in his boat the stairs at the middle of the pier, Mr. Midshipman Henry was confirmed in the impression that the hailing had been a mere decoy; for no sooner did the party near the shore than the crowd greeted them with shoutings and threatenings and a fusillade of stones. Keeping his boat off, Henry ordered the marines to fire over the heads of the multitude, and as this had no effect, he announced that if they did not desist he must and would give orders to fire upon them. But the mob increased in numbers and violence, so, finding that the seaman could not be brought off without danger to the landing-party, Henry took a musket from a marine and fired three times upon the mob. They speedily dispersed, but unfortunately a girl of fifteen, who had been in the crowd, was mortally wounded. The boat then rowed to the pier, landed the discarded captives, and recovered their own man. "It is quite obvious," remarks Hume, "that in the whole circumstances of this case, the charge of *murder* was out of the question; and the prosecutor accordingly gave it up. The Court were, however, of opinion that it was a case of culpable homicide [manslaughter], and it does indeed rather appear that there was a precipitancy and an excess. . . . The jury, however, considered the violence and obstinacy of the assault, the great patience of the seamen in the first stages of it, the personal injuries recently sustained, and the many warnings given the mob without effect. . . . They found accordingly that he had committed an act of *justifiable homicide*. With that phrase in the verdict, of which this is said to be the first instance in our practice, the Court was not entirely satisfied. What the jury had to consider was: *Guilty or Not Guilty of culpable homicide*, to which extent only, and no farther, the Lord Advocate had insisted in his charge."

With regard to the case of Thomas Whyte, Hume observes: "Taking this case as between officer and private seaman (for nothing can be made of it as between man and man), it does not appear that Jones's behaviour, according even to the worst account of it, was such as to require or excuse the use of inferior, much less of mortal violence. Whatever suspicions might have been previously entertained, the man had now plainly no purpose of deserting. He was there upon the spot, ready to answer at a call, and talking in good humour with his comrades; and he could have come hither with no purpose but that of ultimately going on board along with them. Taken in its worst construction, the man's refusal to get into the boat (if he ever did absolutely refuse) was not an act of mutiny, but a piece of drunken and humoursome absurdity, or peevishness at the moment, for which, if it were thought worth notice, he was answerable to the service. His instant compliance was a matter of no moment, for the boat was but beginning to float at the time; and if the man had been mad enough to think of flying or resisting, there was ample force at hand to compel him. In these circumstances the pannel ought to have considered that, as under his command, this seaman was also under his protection. Before resorting to force he was bound to give him time, and to admonish and warn him; and if force was at last to be used, it ought to have been of that sort—certainly quite within the pannel's power at the time—which was calculated to compel his obedience and to save, instead of losing a man to the service.

"If, again, the result of the evidence be (and I rather think it is so) that the man never did absolutely refuse to get on board, but delayed only and for a reasonable cause, then the homicide admits of no excuse but that very bad one in any man's case, and least of all to be allowed to an officer upon duty—the excuse of intoxication. It was there and there only that the source of the misfortune really lay. For Mr. Whyte received a high character as a good-tempered and humane officer, and so far from ill-disposed towards this man Jones that he had recently screened him from punishment for drunkenness by failing to report his offence.

"These circumstances were, however, for His Majesty's consideration rather than for the jury, farther than as they might suggest to the jury to recommend him to mercy, while they did their own duty by convicting according to law, and thus holding out a salutary example to the public and the service of the Navy."

I cannot find that any attempt was made to move in the convict's behalf the Royal bowels of mercy, and doubtless he was carried beyond seas in terms of his sentence. Whether or not their Lordships' optimistic forecast of his future was justified in the event, and Mr. Whyte survived to return to "his happy country," is not recorded. One hopes that he did, and being then but thirty-four, had a better time before him.

It is not necessary to be a member of the Band of Hope Union in order to extract a moral from this so lamentable finish to a promising career. All such as are called upon to discharge responsible and onerous duties, whether it be to drive a car or command a boat's crew, ought sedulously to eschew other than the softer drinks. Here it would seem that the ale of the Port was curiously potent, and the pannel was, moreover, unaccustomed to take liquor.

# THE WEAVER'S HAND:
## A TALE OF TWO GRAVES

# THE WEAVER'S HAND:
## A TALE OF TWO GRAVES

Death will close the eyes and ears against the sights and sounds of earth; but even the tomb secures no secrecy. The dead themselves declare their dreadful secrets, open-mouthed, to the winds.

J. SHERIDAN LE FANU: *Wylder's Hand.*

THERE are degrees in murder, artificially and naturally considered. Some are good, others bad, many merely indifferent. That of which I here propose to give a brief account must, I fear, be placed in the third category. Not because of its intrinsic demerits, for duly and deservedly handled it should prove a capital yarn, but by reason of the inadequate report of the case which, so far as my research extends, is the sole separate authority.

The man accused and convicted of this particular murder was tried in 1830. At that date the official series of Justiciary Reports, so invaluable to students of Scottish crime, was not yet begun. The newspapers of the day, if they chanced to chronicle the event, or the enterprise of such private publishers as might put forth a shilling pamphlet on the subject, are all that the legal historian can hope to find. Here we have an account of the affair, extending to twenty-seven pages of small type, illustrated with a repellent portrait of the criminal, and a delightful view of the scene of his crime. Indeed, so charming is this woodcut that, for pure pleasure of reproducing it in this essay to furnish a coherent story, I am content to suffer gladly the manifold shortcomings of the reporters.

These persons design themselves on their title-page as "Teachers." What, as such, they were doing in that criminous galley at all is not apparent; but what is painfully so is that however competent they may have been to teach others, they had much themselves to learn about reporting. As one who

has conscientiously and carefully edited many criminal cases
—like that fair litigant Miss Rugg, I can truthfully say I have
had my trials—I stand aghast at the light-hearted and casual
manner in which these "editors" have discharged their duties.
Their method of presenting the evidence of the witnesses can
only be described as telegraphic, with results provokingly
scrappy; and they are much more concerned for the moral
to be drawn from the facts of the case, than to supply a full
and satisfactory text. Yet despite the sins of commission and
omission of which they are self-convicted, but for their slip-
shod labours we should have known nothing about the trial,
and so must make the best of what undoubtedly is a bad job.
I have, however, been able to glean some further factual
grains from such notices of the case as are contained in the
contemporary Press, to wit, the *Scotsman* and *Edinburgh
Courant*, of 11th September, 1830.

The title of the work, as so often provokingly happens,
promises much more than is therein performed: "A Full
Report of the Trial of John Henderson, for the Murder of
Mr. Millie, before the Circuit Court of Justiciary, Perth,
September, 1830. Together with a Memoir of Henderson,
collected from the most Authentic Sources. The whole accompanied with a Portrait of Henderson, View of Whinny Park,
Plan of the Grounds, Interior of the House, Workshop, &c.
By James Ewan and John White, Teachers, Edinburgh."
The book bears the imprint of no less than eight publishers,
and so must have enjoyed a wide circulation at the time,
although I have never come across another copy than that
now before me, which is in the Signet Library at Edinburgh.

"The propriety of publishing the Lives of Criminals,"
observe the learned editors in introducing their hero, "has
been often a subject of keen discussion; and, indeed, it is a
subject which ought to be seriously inquired into. For our
own part, we cannot but think that the manner in which
some of these memoirs have been drawn up cannot be
censured too severely. The object of most of these publica-
tions has been to please, to amuse, to gratify the curiosity of

74

the public; hence the blackest actions in the catalogue of crime have sometimes, nay, frequently, been surrounded with such a fascinating kind of elegance as to captivate the hearts of youthful readers, and thus render such works highly dangerous to the improvement, and destructive to the morals of the rising generation.

"Such Works, on the contrary, when intended to be laid before the Public, ought to be drawn up in a style totally different. They ought to shew the Individual as he really is, in his own native colours, and in all his inherent ugliness. Criminals ought to be held forth to the world in general, and to the rising generation in particular, as beacons to warn them from the shoals and quicksands, the rocks and shallows, on which these poor wretched, miserable individuals have made shipwreck of a good name, and of a fair and honourable reputation. Such is the Object of the following Memoir."

"Heavens and earth!" as Trollope so often makes his characters exclaim. And here have I, in my ignorance, been writing these many years on matters criminal with the single aim "to please, to amuse, to gratify" my small public! If only I had received earlier a lesson from these wise men, how different would have been the form and content of my productions. I ought to have bored the reader stiff with lay sermons on the heinousness of homicide, the disadvantages of adultery, and the gross impropriety of theft. Instead of surrounding the blackest actions with elegance, I should have frightened him into fits by depicting VICE, personified by capitals, in all its inherent ugliness, whereas this long time, with the best possible intentions, I have striven to camouflage the frightful, to disinfect the decadent, and generally, by a discreet employment of whitewash, to make my sepulchres as presentable as possible. Well, I hope I am not too old to learn, and I shall see to it that my sketch of Mr. John Henderson is as ugly as his picture in the frontispiece. I cannot put it higher than that. Further, I shall make it abundantly plain that to assassinate one's benefactor with a hammer, and (adding insult to injury) to bury him in his own back garden, are acts not only in themselves highly reprehensible, but calculated to conduct the perpetrator to the scaffold.

With respect to the baneful effect of my system upon the morals of the young, I can assure the Teachers, however, that they may rest in peace: the rising generation are in this regard perfectly secure from contamination, and that for the best of reasons, namely, that they do not read my work, and even if they did, would fail to appreciate its purport. So let it be known that from henceforth I am definitely on the side of the angels.

## I

John Henderson, as his biographers inform us, was when a boy "as highly esteemed as anyone." But after this fair beginning his character and reputation gradually declined; his conduct became ever more flagitious, he fell from crime to crime, "until he was now arrived at such a depth in guilt and misery as places him on a level with the most atrocious monsters that ere disgraced a civilized country." His downfall is attributable to drink and bad company. "Let old age, let manhood, let youth in particular, take warning by the fate of John Henderson."

He was born, it appears, in 1806 of the usual respectable parents, in the good town of Dunfermline in Fife, so long famous for its linens, where his father was a damask weaver and owned some property. He received a suitable education, and was thereafter bred to his father's trade. At school he was popular with his playmates, who often chose him as leader in their juvenile sports and ploys, "although he was considered by the Teacher as rather thoughtless." While working with his father, his leisure hours were spent with dissipated companions; "John also, we are sorry to say, resorted too frequently to the public-house." Nay, more; his biographers blush to record that "he frequented the haunts of women of doubtful character." *Enfin*, John was an idle apprentice in the approved Hogarthian tradition.

Having left his father's employment, whether of his own motion or by request of his indignant progenitor we are not informed, he got work with a weaver in the suburbs of Dunfermline, where he continued for two years. One morning, however, John was absent without leave and certain webs of cloth were simultaneously found to be missing. It was supposed, not without reason, that he had taken them with him. No trace of either could be discovered, and as the weaver was determined to bring his nefarious hand to justice, he went to the expense of advertising "a very considerable reward" for his apprehension and for recovery of the stolen goods. The search, stimulated by such inducement, was renewed, and presently John was captured near his native town. He denied all knowledge of the webs, and as none of these could be found he was discharged for lack of proof.

John, having by this time "taken a disgust at the weaving trade," began business on his own account as a hawker or travelling merchant throughout the country. He does not seem to have been over-scrupulous as to how he procured his stock in trade, for we read that one day in Kirkcaldy he contrived to carry off from a local bookseller a quantity of books, some of which the owner afterwards recovered. He must have had a taste for letters, as the proprietor found the name of "John Henderson" inscribed in one of the ravished volumes. For some reason or other no proceedings were taken against him; but it was predicted by many, who, as we shall see, were justified in the event, "that sooner or later his actions would bring him to an untimely end." This episode put a period to his hawking activities; he reverted to his original trade as a handloom weaver, being engaged as such by one Mr. Millie at Whinny Park.

James Millie is quaintly designed as "a damask customer weaver," which, being interpreted, means that he did not manufacture for the trade, but sold direct to private buyers. In his employment John continued until the "horrible transaction" that resulted in the death of both. Millie, we are told, was a stout, good-looking man of some 45 years, and was possessed of great abilities. "His habits, however, were repulsive and retired"—*i.e.* not that they were objectionable, but that he did not encourage company—"and he thus afforded a favourable opportunity of becoming a prey to a cold-blooded, heartless miscreant." He pursued his "repulsive" social attitude and conducted his business pursuits at Whinny Park, a three-roomed cottage and workshop, standing in a considerable garden, situated at a bend of the road between Monimail and Collessie, half a mile east of the latter place. On the west the property was bounded by a wall 12 feet high, which joined the wall separating it from Melville Park, the seat of the Earl of Leven and Melville, by which it was bounded on the south. On the north and east it was bounded by a high thick hedge, "with laburnum trees at short intervals, which ornament and shelter it." Thus no one could see into the garden unless they climbed the wall. The only entrance to this secluded pleasance was by a narrow iron gate at the south-east corner.

And now, just when their narrative had reached the point where even Teachers might have had something interesting to tell us, the biographers unblushingly shirk their job. "It would be useless for us to say anything regarding the murder, the facts brought out in evidence speak more decidedly than we can possibly do." No doubt of that, if only they had been properly reported; but as the editors have left out the speeches of counsel, the charge of the presiding judge, the declarations of the accused, the Inventory of Productions (exhibits), and the medical report, together with many other things which they ought to have included, and worst of all, have dispensed the evidence of the witnesses in such homeopathic doses, we must take the case as it is stated or leave it alone, which, because of the illustration aforesaid, I am loth to do.

## II

The scene was a Circuit Court, held at Perth on Wednesday, 8th September, 1830, by my Lords Meadowbank and

Mackenzie. Mr. George Smythe, Advocate-Depute, appeared for the Crown; Mr. George Deas, advocate, for the defence. Meadowbank was the friend of Sir Walter; Mackenzie was a son of the famous author of *The Man of Feeling*; Smythe was a kinsman of David Smythe, Lord Methven; and Deas was in the fulness of time to become the Draconic judge before whom criminals quailed. It is of interest to find him here as *advocatus diaboli*, defending a murderer. I never miss occasion to refer to an old Edinburgh directory, and as a result of my research I can gratify the local reader with the information that Lords Meadowbank and Mackenzie then respectively "resided" at 13 and 9 Royal Circus, the Advocate-Depute at 12 Gloucester Place, and Mr. Deas at 33 Scotland Street.

From the summary of the indictment as printed in the report we learn that the accused was charged with the crimes of murder, theft, and forgery. Now forgery is not in itself by Scots law a crime; that is constituted by the *uttering* as genuine the forged document, and this must have been the crime that Henderson was charged with having committed. As regards the first charge, he was said to have murdered, on 26th June, 1830, James Millie, damask weaver, Whinny Park, at his house in Whinny Park, with a hammer or other lethal weapon. As regards the second, that between 26th June and 24th July (the date of his arrest) he stole and carried away "a number of articles which formerly belonged to the deceased James Millie." It otherwise appears that these articles were described in two Inventories of Productions (exhibits), which the reporters, with criminal negligence, omit. But from the evidence we gather that these included a quantity of unbleached linen: tablecloths, towels, etc; the title deeds of the property and divers other documents, including a deposit receipt; sundry silver spoons; a watch, a gold brooch or pin, a tortoiseshell snuff-box, and a "spy-glass"; also a number of books, one of which was, curiously enough in the circumstances, a Bible, another a legal work. The accused, says the *Courant*, "assumed an appearance of great composure, but it was evident he was not at ease," which in the circumstances is not surprising. "He was dressed in a black coat and vest, and white trowsers"—his customary "Jane" or "Cassamere" nether-garments were among the productions for the Crown.

I do not propose to take the witnesses in the order in which they were called. The evidence, as led, begins with the discovery of the crime, but it is more interesting, and makes a better yarn, to start with the disappearance of the victim.

Elizabeth Blyth, ten years of age, servant to Alexander Simpson, farmer, Hallhill, who in view of her youth was not put on oath, stated she had been taught to read her Bible and knew that her duty was to tell the truth. Mr. Millie got his milk from the farm and she was in use to deliver it daily. On the morning of Saturday, 26th June, she took the accustomed quantity to Whinny Park. Henderson received the milk and told her that his master was then at St. Andrews, but he expected him home that night. As she left the garden gate she met Mr. Millie himself, who asked her to bring his account in the afternoon as he wished to pay it. She returned with the account about 3 o'clock, passing Henderson "above Monimail," a little distance from Whinny Park. Arrived there, she found the doors were all locked and there was no response to her knocking. Going back again at 8 o'clock she found the garden gate shut and fastened with a "muckle" (large) nail. She was sure of the date, because it was the last time she had taken milk to the house.

Mrs. Blyth, her mother, stated that she was in the habit of supplying milk to Mr. Millie. Saturday, the 26th, was the last day it was sent. On Sunday, the 27th, Henderson came personally for the milk about 10 o'clock. He told her to send no more in the meantime, as Mr. Millie was going away to Edinburgh on Monday morning and he himself was going to Dunfermline.[1] The accused was then wearing dark grey "Jane" trousers. Cross-examined by Mr. Deas—she saw

[1] The declinature of the milk was also an important feature of the famous Sandyford Mystery. Cf. *The Trial of Mrs. Jessie M'Lachlan* in 1863, edited by the present writer.

VIEW OF WHINNY PARK
(*Showing the grave in the path beside the well*)

nothing strange in Henderson's demeanour that Sunday. A fortnight later she met him on the road and asked him whether Mr. Millie had come home yet. He answered, "No." Witness then made the arresting observation that she thought James Millie must have been murdered; whereupon the accused hung his head and muttered some "laigh" (low) word which she did not catch. Witness denied that he laughed at her remark.

Elizabeth Balfour, wife of the blacksmith at Monimail, stated that she saw the accused at her own door about 3 o'clock on the 26th. He mentioned that Mr. Millie had gone to Cupar and was going to Edinburgh on Monday. He (Henderson) appeared to be in a great hurry. On Saturday, 24th *July*, witness said she received from a little girl a message from the accused. Bell Dalgleish, aged 10, stated that at 9 o'clock that morning Henderson gave her a message for Mrs. Balfour. He told her to say "that James Millie came home last night." We shall see later in what fashion he returned.

William Wallace, vintner, Letham, stated that his house was situated a mile from Whinny Park. Henderson, whom he knew, came there at 3.30 on Saturday afternoon, 26th June, and called for a dram. Witness noticed that his hand shook and that he seemed much agitated. He asked the cause of these symptoms; Henderson replied it was "the horrors." He said he had been at Auchtermuchty—that word of fear for the Sassenach—and that his master was going to Edinburgh on Monday about a lawsuit against Lord Leven and Melville.

Thomas Greig, head gardener at Melville House, stated that he and Mr. Millie were joint subscribers for the *Fife Herald*. On Sunday, 27th June, Henderson brought the paper, saying that Mr. Millie was too busy to bring it himself, as he had to go to Edinburgh next morning. Henderson had on "Jane" trousers. Witness next saw him on 4th July; asked for the *Herald*, and inquired as to Mr. Millie's continued absence. Accused said he would be home next week. He was then wearing black clothes.

David Ford, weaver, Auchtermuchty, stated that at 7 p.m. on Friday, 25th June, accused came to his shop. He bought cloth for a new suit, and paid £4. A tailor was summoned and instructed to have the clothes ready by Monday morning. Ford, who knew his customer's pecuniary resources, asked him where he got the cash. He said he had been paid £5 for working a web and £1 more for doing it so quickly. He produced five keys, which he said were those of Mr. Millie's house; explaining that his master had gone to Cupar to consult a lawyer about a law process with Lord Leven, and that he himself was going "to set on two men to work plain work at 5 o'clock next morning, *as he was not like Judas, who betrayed* HIS *master*." Henderson mentioned that Mr. Millie was going to Edinburgh on Monday and he himself to Dunfermline. He invited witness to accompany him there, which Ford agreed to do. After divers drams, for which Henderson paid, between 3 and 4 in the morning he set out for Whinny Park; witness, in the Scots fashion, convoying him a mile on his way. On Monday he returned as arranged. On this occasion he was furnished with a watch, which he said he had bought from Mr. Millie for 35s., that gentleman having, as appeared, no further use for it. Henderson then assumed the new suit and hired a gig, in which the two friends proceeded to Dunfermline. He took with him, and exhibited to his companion, a Bible, which he said he had bought cheap at Cupar, and a gold brooch or pin, which he said he had acquired from a packman for 7s. 6d. This—the brooch, not the Bible—he presented to a damsel of his acquaintance in that town, both being afterwards identified as the property of his master. Witness next saw Henderson on 7th July, taking his "morning" at the Trafalgar Inn, Auchtermuchty. He promised witness and his brother a pair of trousers; but these not materializing, they went in quest of them to Whinny Park, where they found the door locked, but saw Henderson washing his face in the burn. "He had the trousers with him," which then, presumably, changed hands, or rather legs. He saw him again on 16th July; "he was away with a woman in a gig." A week later the accused called and shewed witness a keyed trumpet; he said he had got a letter from Mr. Millie to begin work, and proposed to do so. Jean Barrowman, the damsel in question, corroborated and said that in addition to the brooch Henderson gave her the tortoiseshell snuff-box produced. She could not read; but it bore the late owner's name inscribed upon the lid: "James Millie."

Isabel Brebner, washerwoman, Monimail, stated that a week after he had been at Dunfermline, the accused brought her two unbleached cotton shirts to wash, one of which had upon the shoulder a great "splerge" (splash) of blood, and further blood-stains on the breast. She was certain it was blood, and knew from professional experience that it was due neither to currant nor blackberry stains. He came back for them on Friday, 16th July. She asked how the shirts were so stained; the accused said "it was a glass of shrub," *i.e.* cordial made of fruit juice and spirit. Witness knew Mr. Millie well and bought some yarn from him in his shop about ten days before his disappearance. The accused was then working on the big loom. She did not do Mr. Millie's washing.

Christian Rollo, wife of the change-keeper at Lindores, stated that early in July the accused called and offered some unbleached tablecloths for sale. One Lyall, who was present, remarked that nobody but Mr. Millie made that kind of linen. Asked whether he was not Millie's "young man," the accused said he came from Dunfermline. He then hastily put up his goods and departed. After he had left, her girl found a parcel of silver spoons wrapped in paper. Henderson later returned, complaining of having lost these. Witness referred him to the girl. Mary Melville, the maid in question, stated that she found the parcel at her mistress's door. The accused gave her 2s. for finding it.

Andrew Wilson, grocer, Newburgh, stated that in the beginning of July the accused was selling tablecloths. Witness bought one, which he now identified as produced. He noticed that it was spotted with blood and asked the accused how it came to be so. He replied that he had laid it down on something bloody in Speedy, the flesher's, shop. He said he came from Dunfermline. Matthew Speedy, butcher, Newburgh, stated that he bought a tablecloth from the accused in July. He never saw him before. Accused got no blood on his tablecloths while in the shop. George Anderson, manufacturer, Newburgh, stated that the accused sold him some yarn in a bag on 6th July. He said he got it at Perth in exchange for some tablecloths. Later, witness found Mr. Millie's name marked upon the bag. Several other witnesses spoke to buying from the accused in July tablecloths and towelling.

Robert Taylor, writer in Cupar and factor to the Earl of Leven, stated that on Thursday, 15th July, the accused called at his office with a deposit receipt for £18, 4s. 7d. by the Commercial Bank in favour of Lord Leven, indorsed in blank by that nobleman. Witness had seen his Lordship personally hand that receipt to Mr. Millie. Asked how he (the accused) obtained it, he said he had been working for Mr. Millie, who, being then in Edinburgh, had instructed him to uplift the money. Witness told him that Mr. Millie must indorse it and then the Bank would cash it. A teller and clerk in the Commercial Bank, Cupar, stated that on 16th July accused presented the deposit receipt, indorsed "James Millie," and received payment of the amount.

James Watt, servant to the Auchtermuchty innkeeper, stated that on Friday, 16th July, he drove the accused and a young lady, named Bell Chalmers, to Dunfermline, whence he and Henderson proceeded in the gig to North Queensferry, where they put up that vehicle, and crossing the Forth, took the mail coach to Edinburgh. There the accused went to the shop of Mr. Robertson, music seller, and bought a keyed bugle and a trumpet, for which he paid £4. They then adjourned to a public-house, where Henderson wrote a letter and put it in the post office. They next went down to Trinity, and at the Chain Pier boarded a steamboat for Queensferry, where they resumed possession of the gig, and drove back to Dunfermline, joining Miss Chalmers at the Old Inn. There the party stayed all Saturday night. The accused's demeanour throughout this singular expedition was very restless: "When he went into a public-house he was anxious to get out again, and when he was out he was anxious to get in"—behaviour not necessarily betokening blood-guiltiness.

George Mackenzie, innkeeper, Auchtermuchty, stated that he met the accused on Monday, 19th July. He said he was going to Whinny Park, as he expected a letter from his master. He then went into Lawson's shop and came out with a letter, which he said was from Mr. Millie, part of which he read to witness. It contained instructions as to his work, and ordered him to send the title deeds of Mr. Millie's property to Mr. Robertson, music seller, 27 Princes Street, Edinburgh. Henderson then went to Whinny Park, and called again that night at witness's house with a parcel, which he said contained the writs referred to. Witness asked to see the letter, but Henderson said he had destroyed it, adding that "everything was all right and he had good news from Mr. Millie." Henderson came back on Thursday, 22nd July. He was still idle and thirsty, and witness told him he ought to return to his work: "he had been long enough on the ball [spree]." The accused replied, with a laugh, that there was no hurry: "*Millie might be* BURKED *in Edinburgh!*" (The revelations of the Burke and Hare murders were then but two years old.) So far as witness knew he continued "on the ball" until the discovery of the crime.

Mrs. Lawson, Collessie, stated that on Monday, 19th July, the postman delivered at her house a letter, addressed: "John Henderson, care of Robert Lawson, merchant, Collessie." The accused came in as she was paying the postage; he read to her the letter, which he said was from his master in Edinburgh. It was in these terms: "John, You will begin your work with a rose and sprig pattern. You will send the papers that are lying in the East Room; you will direct to me at Mr. Robertson's, No. 27 Princes Street, and by doing so you will oblige, JAMES MILLIE." (This was, of course, the letter written and posted in Edinburgh the day before by Henderson himself.) He returned in the afternoon with certain documents, and having called for pen, ink, paper, and cord, wrapped them up and addressed the parcel to "Mr. James Millie," care of Mr. Robertson, as above. Witness identified the parcel, as produced. Cross-examined—Henderson sometimes said he thought he should inform Mr. Millie's friends as to his staying so long away, which witness strongly advised him to do. A clerk in Croal's coach office in Edinburgh having identified the parcel as delivered there and forwarded to Robertson, that music seller himself stated that it arrived at his shop on 20th July. He knew nothing of the person to whom it was addressed; no one called for it; and after it had lain for some time in his shop, he opened it, found the documents and a letter addressed: "James Millie, Whinny Park, near Cupar," and handed the whole, as now identified by him, to a Sheriff Officer. Witness had sold to the accused for £4 a keyed bugle and a trumpet; he seemed to be in a great hurry. The Sheriff Officer in question stated that, acting on instructions, he went from Cupar to Edinburgh and obtained from Mr. Robertson the parcel of documents referred to.

Robert Heggie, Newburgh, stated that on 6th July the accused called at his house, hawking unbleached tablecloths. Witness bought one, which later he delivered to the Sheriff, and now identified as produced. On the 23rd Henderson returned with a carter, whom he had engaged to carry certain goods belonging to him, as he alleged, at Monimail. These included some books which he emptied out of a bag and took away with him, leaving the bag behind.

John Brough, carter, Newburgh, stated that on Thursday, 22nd July, the accused employed him to go to Monimail for goods. They reached Whinny Park at midnight. The accused said "that the people knew he was coming, and the key would be lying beneath the door." As it was not there, he said the maid must be out; "and he put up his hand and opened the door." The arrangement of the interior, as we know from the plan of the house, was (1) the principal living room, (2) the kitchen, (3) Mr. Millie's bedroom, and (4) the workshop and "loomstead." There was above a loft, where Henderson slept. They entered the room, where was a fire nearly exhausted, which had been "happed up" with ashes. Henderson took up a "spunk" and lighted the lamp, remarking that the maid was out, probably "with the lads." He said "he did not wish to disturb the folk of the house"— even had he blown his keyed bugle he could not have done that: it would have required the Last Trump to rouse his master—and as the goods were in the loft, they would go quietly upstairs and secure them, which they did. Witness, at his request, held a bag and the accused filled it with un-bleached linen. Going downstairs, Henderson left witness in the kitchen, and taking the lamp with him, remarked that he would go "ben," *i.e.* into the inner room, "and see what they [the inmates] were about." Coming back, he said "it was all right, and that was all he was to take that night." Thereafter they returned with divers bags to Newburgh, witness buying from the accused a coat as a souvenir of the expedition. One of the bags was left at Heggie's house.

A merchant and a cooper of Newburgh stated that on 24th July Henderson offered to them for sale some books, which he described as "Law Statutes." Naturally enough, they declined to buy them. The accused had better luck with the next witness, Gavin Stewart, writer, there, who purchased the legal treatises. Henderson consulted him as to selling a property, the titles of which he said would be in his hands the following week. Witness advised him to employ a lawyer in Dunfermline.

Catherine Millie, sister of James Millie, stated that until some 15 months before she had kept house for her brother for upwards of 30 years. The cause of the severance of this old habit is not reported. She was thoroughly familiar with his belongings, and identified as his property the several table-cloths sold by the accused, the silver teaspoons, the snuff-box, the gold brooch, the watch, the "spy-glass," the law books, and three shirts of her own making. The books were also sworn to by an Auchtermuchty bookseller, who had sold the very volumes to Mr. Millie himself. A tailor in Letham identified as his work for that gentleman the coat which Henderson had sold to the carter.

Jean Millie, another sister, who lived at Strathmiglo, stated that having heard nothing of her brother for some time, on Saturday, 24th July, she went to Whinny Park to "look after him." Arriving about breakfast time, she found Henderson working in the garden and inquired for her brother. The accused said he had been away but had come home, and had gone off to Cupar on business that morning. Henderson said he had orders not to let anyone into the house during his master's absence.

## III

Now, whether at the suggestion of Jean Millie, or of some other person dissatisfied with the statements of the accused, or suspicious on account of Mr. Millie's unusual and protracted absence, later in the day Henry Heggie, coachman to Lord Leven at Melville House, went over to Whinny Park to see what he could see. Henderson was absent, presumably engaged either in realizing the remainder of his ill-gotten stock, or being still "on the ball"; but Heggie somehow obtained access to the house and examined the premises. The first thing he noticed was that a portion of the workshop floor—an earthen one—bore marks of having been recently disturbed. Just then John Rushforth, a plasterer who was working at Melville House, happened to pass by, and Heggie called to him to come in. They got a spade and began to dig at the spot, which presented the appearance of a rude grave. The earth was loose and readily excavated, but though they dug down till they reached rock bottom, they found nothing: the grave was untenanted. Stimulated to fresh endeavour they examined the garden, and in a pathway at the back of the house, near a well which supplied the inmates with water, they noticed that the ground was in one place soft. So they started to dig again, and at a depth of 8 inches were horrified to find, protruding from the soil, the left hand of a dead man. "It was about half-past seven o'clock in the evening," says Heggie, "when we found the hand." They forthwith informed the Procurator-Fiscal of the discovery. John Rushforth corroborated.

Drs. Grace and Malcolm were speedily on the scene; so soon as the Sheriff of the County arrived at 10 p.m. the digging was resumed, and presently the body of James Millie was uncovered. It was raised and carried into the house, the clothes were taken off, and an examination was made by the two surgeons, who subsequently prepared a joint report—which our authorities, with culpable and characteristic carelessness, fail to print. Dr. Malcolm, who was Mr. Millie's medical attendant, at once recognized the body as that of his former patient. The doctors considered that death had taken place about five weeks earlier. There were two severe wounds, some 3 inches in length, upon the scalp, and corresponding fractures of the skull ; both doctors were clearly of opinion that these injuries caused death and that they had been inflicted by blows with a heavy instrument. The hammer produced was, in their judgment, a likely weapon, and on subsequent examination was found to be stained with human blood. From the nature of the injuries, the man must have died "almost immediately": he could have made no resistance whatever. Cross-examined—witness was aware that a person might die suddenly from natural disease. By the Court—He was also aware that a person could not die of a fractured skull without external violence.

The Sheriff, whose name was Andrew Jameson—a fact which pleasantly calls to mind the genial memory of a later Sheriff of the same name, afterwards the well-known judge, Lord Ardwall—stated that he was present at the exhumation and superintended the ensuing search of the premises. In the workshop, "underneath the place where the weaver sits" at the loom, he saw a large quantity of blood upon the treadles and a portion of tablecloth in the loom was spotted with blood. All these stains were obvious. An iron hammer found on the floor near the treadles bore marks of blood upon the claw and handle. This was all that was observed that night: it was dark, and the search was made by candlelight. The doors were then sealed up and the inquiry was resumed next morning in daylight. One of the party was placed as if working the loom. There was blood on the right side of the seat and on the tenter; the largest blood-stain was directly opposite where the weaver sat. There were marks of lime on the floor and on the treadles; it appeared to have been sprinkled over the blood-stains for the purpose of obliterating them. A pair of "Jane" pantaloons, belonging to the accused and found in the house, were seen to be spotted with blood. All these matters were also sworn to by the doctors and by Rushforth, the plasterer, who were present at the time. A pick and two spades were found in the workshop.

Rushforth further stated that on the night of Saturday, 26th June—the day of the murder—he met Henderson about half-a-mile from Whinny Park, "on the brae" above Collessie; he was "wanting" his coat and had on a hair cap. Witness was aware that his wardrobe included a pair of "Cassamere" trousers, but could not swear he was wearing them that night. The accused was much agitated and could not stand still; he kept constantly moving backwards and forwards. We are not told what, if anything, he said.

David Heggie, weaver, Collessie, stated that he was present when the body was "lifted." He knew James Millie very well and recognized it as his. Shewn the accused's "Jane" trousers, witness said he saw him wearing them on Thursday, 24th June, two days before Mr. Millie's disappearance. When he next saw him, two days before the body was found, the accused was appropriately dressed in black. On that occasion witness asked him how he had got so much money, to which the accused replied that before his master went to Edin-

burgh he gave him £6, in respect of his having "wrought"
since February without fee or reward. Accused also said that
his own father had contributed an additional £3. Witness
remarked he had heard that Henderson had lately spent some
£9, independent of £4 for "gig-hires," which the accused
repudiated as a lie. Heggie, who seems to have been a
collector of local scandal, next made the unfriendly remark
that it was reported of the accused that he had murdered
Mr. Millie and buried him under a tree in his garden! Henderson replied that they, the gossips, "would soon see about
that"; his master would shortly be home again. Witness
observed that he had a mind to get some men to search the
place, and Henderson obligingly offered to be of the party.
Heggie then counselled him that if he had stolen anything, it
were well for him "to cut his stick"; but if he had done no
wrong, he should go back and resume his work. The accused
said he was about to do so; he could not work before for want
of a pattern, but he had now received a letter from his master,
telling what pattern he was to work. Witness advised him to
inform Mr. Millie's sisters why his master was so long absent.
And so they parted company.

## IV

The Crown case closed with the reading of the accused's
declarations, of which our reporters, instead of printing them
in full as they ought to have done, afford a bare synopsis.
He told how he entered James Millie's employment "last
spring," and wrought for him on the loom in the workshop.
The last time he saw Mr. Millie was "about 5 weeks ago"—
this declaration would be emitted soon after his arrest on
25th July—when his master left for Edinburgh. He knew
that Mr. Millie arrived there, for he received from him a
letter of instructions after he went away. In this letter he was
asked to forward certain papers which were lying in the east
room of the house; this he accordingly did. He was in the

workshop when Jean Millie came; his master had told him that if any of his (Millie's) friends called while he was away, the declarant was not to admit them. He never struck James Millie with a hammer and did not bury him in a hole in the garden; nor did he know that his master was dead, until informed of the fact by the officers by whom he was apprehended.

Mr. Deas called only one witness for the defence. This was John Kennedy, Sheriff Officer, who, on 25th July, took the accused into custody in Dunfermline. Henderson, he stated, made no attempt to escape and said he was as innocent of the crime as witness. Since his incarceration in Cupar Jail he had behaved himself "with great propriety."

The Advocate-Depute then addressed the jury for the Crown. His task cannot have presented any serious difficulty, for the guilt of the accused was manifest. From a sketch of his speech in the *Courant* account of the trial, it appears that it followed the usual lines. As regards the second charge: theft: the articles produced had been fully identified by Catherine Millie and other witnesses as having belonged to the deceased, and the possession and sale of these had been fixed upon the prisoner. As regards charges three and four: forgery and uttering: there was upon the deposit receipt, when shewn by the accused to Mr. Taylor, no indorsation by James Millie; yet next day, when presented to the Bank for payment, it was so indorsed, Mr. Millie being then dead and buried, and even, according to the accused's own statement, in Edinburgh. His lies and misrepresentations throughout; his false assertions of Mr. Millie's return, etc., not only warranted the jury in convicting him, but rendered it a duty imperative on them to do so. One would like to have heard how the learned Advocate-Depute dealt with the more interesting and important first charge: murder; but as to this matter we are told nothing!

Only little less unsatisfactory is the report of Mr. Deas's speech for the defence. He admitted that it was with some degree of anxiety that he rose to address the jury. We are not surprised to hear it. He cautioned them not to be misled by the false representations which had appeared in the local Press. They must not rest satisfied with mere circumstantial evidence, whatever colour of probability it might carry along with it. "He could multiply instances where the innocent had been sacrificed by a jury setting too much weight upon circumstances, but he would just bring one under their notice." (The case of Mrs. M'Lachlan, above cited, at which counsel was himself to preside as judge thirty-two years later, would have afforded a palmary example of the evil of which Mr. Deas complained.) "It was," he continued, "but little more than 6 years ago that a jury, sitting in that very box, had convicted a poor woman from Montrose. Her sentence was carried into execution; and it had been publicly recorded within these few months that another person in England had confessed to that murder for which she suffered." [1] Mr. Deas concluded a long and earnest appeal for his client by urging that the murder, at least, was not proven.

Lord Meadowbank, we read, in charging the jury, addressed them in very impressive terms as to the caution and consideration with which they should approach a decision in this case. "His Lordship adverted with indignation to the report which had been most falsely circulated as to the confession of a murder for which another was condemned by that Court, and entered at much length upon the nature, efficacy, and safety of circumstantial evidence. His Lordship then recapitulated the leading points of the evidence with much minuteness and perspicuity, and expressed an opinion"—in which I humbly concur—"that the pannel [prisoner] must be held guilty of the whole charges libelled in the indictment." The jury then retired to consider their verdict, but returned "almost immediately" with a unanimous finding of Guilty on all the charges.

"The trial did not terminate," says the *Courant*, "until

[1] The case to which counsel referred was that of Margaret Tindal or Shuttleworth, tried and convicted at Perth, on undeniable evidence, on 19th September, 1821. The alleged "confession" turned out on inquiry to be a bogus one. The woman was clearly guilty and justly condemned. Of her crime and trial I have elsewhere given a full account. See "The Vintner's Wife," in a book of essays entitled: *In Queer Street* (Edinburgh: 1932).

between 12 and 1 o'clock on Thursday morning, having occupied more than 13 hours. The Court was extremely crowded during the whole time"—the local interest in the case being widespread and intense, due to the very remarkable features with which (even in the truncated account that has survived) it bristles.

Lord Mackenzie having, according to the quaint practice of the day, "proposed" the inevitable sentence, Lord Meadowbank addressed the pannel upon the aggravated nature of the dreadful crime of which he had been found guilty. This unfortunate man was cruelly murdered by an assassin while sitting at his honest trade, and that by his companion—his only companion, who was bound rather to defend him even at the risk of his own life, had that been required. It was a crime committed for the sake of base lucre, and with a coolness and perseverance unexampled. "The murderer returned to the house, at the door of which the mangled body of his master had been buried. He continued living in it day by day and sleeping in it night by night; and all the while availing himself of the crime he had thus committed, to perpetrate a series of new crimes and carry on a continued system of plunder. Considering the circumstances, he must suffer death with all the aggravations directed by the Statute in such cases. "The judgment of the Court is, Lords Meadowbank and Mackenzie decern and adjudge you, John Henderson, to be hanged till dead, by the hands of the common executioner, at the county town of Cupar, in the shire of Fife, on Thursday, 30th September, betwixt the hours of 2 and 4 afternoon, and your body to be afterwards delivered to Dr. Alexander Monro, Professor of Anatomy in the University of Edinburgh, to be by him publicly dissected." On hearing this grim forecast of his fate the prisoner, who throughout the proceedings had displayed an amazing degree of firmness, "appeared to be considerably agitated." This form of post-mortem punishment was reserved for criminals of peculiarly atrocious wickedness. Two years before, Science in general, and the Professor of Anatomy in particular, had similarly benefited by the judicial bequest of the body of the notorious William Burke, the West Port multiple-murderer. It is doubtful whether Henderson appreciated the distinction.

## V

The *Scotsman* and *Courant* of Saturday, 2nd October, chronicle at somewhat gruesome length the circumstances of Henderson's final exit. "The execution of this great criminal," records the latter journal, "took place on Thursday about 3 o'clock, at the back of Cupar Jail. A platform was constructed for the purpose in the courtyard behind the jail, fronting a large park, in which is a hillock, known by the name of the Skevie Brae, and other rising ground, so that the immense crowd, amounting to not fewer than 12,000 or 15,000 persons, brought together from every part of the large and populous county of Fife, had a full view of the criminal. . . . To preserve order the staff of the Fife Militia was on duty, as also several of the respectable citizens in the character of special constables." I do not propose farther to follow the grisly report of the ensuing ceremonial; but it is satisfactory to learn that this natural grandstand was so largely patronized. "An execution in Cupar," says the *Scotsman*, "is a novelty of no common description, there not having been one since 1743, when a man of the name of James Hay suffered the last punishment of the law for horse-stealing." Probably he did not prove such a popular "draw" as the Whinny Park murderer.

As to the personal appearance of the chief actor, the reporters of the trial observe: "John Henderson is of rather diminutive stature, not perhaps above 5 feet 5 inches. His face is not at all peculiar and can lay little claim either to intelligence or spirit, and would never induce us to suppose that he was capable of perpetrating such a horrid and diabolical deed. He has all along firmly and uniformly denied his guilt, and maintained a composure truly astonishing."

This, of course, was written prior to the last act; but on

30th September the *Courant* was able to publish in its columns a full confession by the condemned man, made to the magistrates before the end. "According to his account, he perpetrated the foul deed on the afternoon of Friday, 24th [? 25th] June.[1] He says that on that day he had a quarrel with Mr. Millie about his work, in consequence of having broken some part of the machinery of the loom. Mr. Millie went to put it right, and was sitting on the loom, repairing the machinery and using two hammers. He began to chide Henderson for his carelessness, and an altercation took place, when Henderson came behind Mr. Millie, lifted one of the hammers, and struck the fatal blows." After securing his victim's ready money, he went to Auchtermuchty, where he met Ford at 7 o'clock, ordered his new suit, and remained drinking there till 3 o'clock in the morning, when he returned to Whinny Park. "He did not sleep that night in his own bed, which was upstairs, *but in Mr. Millie's bed*, which was on the ground floor. Next morning he entered the workshop, dug a grave, and buried Mr. Millie." He then locked up the premises and spent the rest of the day at the Crown Inn, Letham. On the Sunday he remained at Whinny Park; but on the Monday he again visited Auchtermuchty, taking with him divers articles which he had discovered during the week-end, to wit, the watch, snuff-box, pin-brooch, etc., together with "a considerable sum of money." Having donned his new clothes and bought some shoes and stockings, he set out with Ford in the gig upon the expedition described at the trial. On his return from this Dunfermline excursion on 3rd July, he at once perceived that the presence of his victim's body was powerfully indicated to the sense of smell. Next morning, being Sunday, the 4th, he dug a fresh grave in the garden—as an airier situation—a little distance from the well, and having disinterred the body from the workshop floor, he dragged it to the garden path and there re-buried it. For

---

[1] The reader may remember that the little girl Blyth said she saw and spoke to Mr. Millie on the morning of Saturday, the 26th. Yet Henderson truly says he went to Auchtermuchty and met Ford upon the *Friday* night. The child may have mistaken the day, although as to the date she is corroborated by her mother.

the rest of his doings up to the time of his arrest, his account coincides with the evidence given at the trial. Apparently his spirits were lightened by thus making a clean breast, for the narrative concludes: "His conduct after condemnation evinced somewhat of levity."

This confession must have proved for Mr. Deas but painful reading. At least it filled the bill and fitted the proved facts, which that false one wherein he trusted indisputably failed to do.

## VI

I promised to point a moral, although owing to the insufficiency of my material, I have been unable to adorn a tale. So I shall conclude with a quotation from one who is an acknowledged master of the subject and a high authority for such as profess to be, in his own happy phrase, "curious in homicide": that connoisseur of the macabre, De Quincey. In the Supplementary Paper to his immortal essay *On Murder* you will find these wise and weighty words, which I commend to the prayerful consideration of my less gentle readers, who may be contemplating manslaughter: "If once a man indulges himself in murder, very soon he comes to think little of robbing, and from robbing he comes next to drinking and Sabbath-breaking, and from that to incivility and procrastination. Once begin upon this downward path, you never know where you are to stop. Many a man has dated his ruin from some murder or other that perhaps he thought little of at the time." The truth of this admirable passage is strikingly exemplified by what we are permitted to know of the late Mr. John Henderson's career.

Despite the meagre and fragmentary form in which the chronicle of his crime has come down to us, I venture to hold that in some respects it would have satisfied our author's rather exalted standard. It is bloody and violent enough, in all conscience; and as an artist, he appreciated blood and violence: witness his award of the palm to Mr. John

Williams, the slayer of the Marr and Williamson families in Ratcliffe Highway, for the supreme technical excellence of that achievement. The rudeness of the weapon would have had his warm approval, and above all, the novel and picturesque introduction of the second grave. There are, too, such minor beauties as the expedition to Edinburgh in the gig, recalling as it does the memory of that historic vehicle in which Mr. William Weare took his last drive; the egregious purchase of the keyed bugle and trumpet; the ingenious letter of instructions respecting the rose and sprig pattern for the new web; and the attaching declaration of the murderer that he would not prove a Judas to *his* master. The man who, in such circumstances, could say that, was a murderer nor unworthy of De Quincey's regard.

## BIBLIOGRAPHICAL POSTSCRIPT

Since the foregoing narrative was completed, I have acquired another account of the case, bearing to be a second edition of that upon which I worked. For the benefit of brother collectors I give here for comparison the title-pages of the respective editions:—

(1) A Full Report of the Trial of John Henderson for the Murder of Mr. Millie, before the Circuit Court of Justiciary, Perth, September 1830. Together with a Memoir of Henderson, collected from the most Authentic Sources. The whole accompanied with a Portrait of Henderson, View of Whinny-Park, Plan of the Grounds, Interior of the House, Workshop, &c. By James Ewan and John White, Teachers, Edinburgh. Published by D. Morison, Junr. & Co. and J. Dewar, Perth; Stillie Brothers, 140 High Street, Edinburgh; R. Griffin & Co., Glasgow; J. Paul, Cupar; E. Donaldson and J. Adam, Dundee; Wilson, St. Andrews; G. Bernard, Kirkcaldy; and J. Miller, Dunfermline. 1830.

8vo. pp. 27.

(2) Whinny Park Murder. Report of the Trial of John Henderson; with his Confession in Jail; a Notice of his former Life; and a short Memoir of Mr. Millie, &c. With a View of Whinny Park, and a Ground Plan of the Premises. Second Edition. Cupar: Printed and Published at *The Fife Herald* Office; and sold by the Booksellers in Fife, Perth, Dundee, & Edinburgh. 1830.

12mo. pp. 72.

The revised version is unquestionably the better one. The chief improvements are these. For the original Introduction by the egregious educationalists, with its moral reflections and pedantic comments, no less irritating than irrelevant, is substituted a plain, straightforward statement of the facts, and an adequate account of Henderson and his hapless victim. These would have saved me a lot of trouble had they come timeously to hand; but such things seldom do. The omissions of the Teacher-Editors are in some manner supplied. The Indictment, and the Inventories of Productions thereto annexed, are printed verbatim, as also are the pannel's Declarations, emitted by him on 25th July, the day of his arrest, together with the Medical Reports by Drs. Grace and Malcolm, dated 27th July; and ampler reports are furnished of the addresses of counsel and the Charge of the learned Judge. Lastly, the Confession of the convict is printed at length. Thus the most material of my many grievances against the earlier editors have been by their anonymous and more competent supplanter removed.

On the other hand, the text of the evidence is substantially the same; no worse, but certainly no better. There were not at that date any official shorthand-writers' notes, and both accounts doubtless derive from those published in the contemporary local Press. The portrait of Henderson, which served for frontispiece, is silently dropped, whereby Art has sustained no serious loss. But I regret that the admirable woodcut of the cottage has been re-drawn, possibly with greater accuracy, but to my mind at least, at some sacrifice of its original charm.

As I have done the former editors the unmerited favour of quotation, I shall in justice to their successor give two examples of his superiority as a narrator: the one being a dramatic description of the discovery of the murder; the other a just appreciation of the nature and quality of the crime:—

"The popular suspicions had now become uncontrollable. The whole of this day (24th July) one or other, without any concert, was continually approaching to examine the state of the premises, and towards eight o'clock in the evening two or three of the nearest neighbours met in the garden. These were quickly joined by others, who happened to be passing, and who, though they came only by accident, all entertained the same suspicions. It was agreed immediately to enter the house and examine it. The first suspicious circumstance was a part of the floor of the workshop, which exhibited the appearance of having been freshly broken; the earth was soft, and it was conjectured that here was the grave of poor Millie. On turning up the mould, it was found to have been dug almost sufficiently deep for such a purpose, but the corpse was not there. The ideas it excited confirmed all the previous alarm, and one party went immediately to search the dwelling-house, while another examined the appearance of the garden.

"Among the latter, Henry Heggie (one of Lord Leven's servants), jumping down from a high bank on the footpath which led to the well, perceived something suspicious in the yielding of the ground under him; the earth also seemed here to be more fresh than in the rest of the path; and on a spade being procured, one minute's work brought to light the appearance of a man's hand. The heavy corpse-like smell from the uncovered earth sufficiently told what remained. The appearance of the hand, already discoloured and blackened by the progress of putrefaction, and protruding in the dusk from the broken clods, was sufficiently fearful;[1] and prepared as they were for the result, this confirmation of their suspicions produced emotions of horror among the country people hardly to be described. One of the spectators describes his feelings as so overpowering that his knees smote one another with the violence of an ague. A number of those present were females, who from their natural aversion to the vagrant character of the man (Henderson), had been most active in alarming suspicion against him. The feelings of these, on seeing this horrible confirmation of what they had

---

[1] Cf. Chapter LXXII of *Wylder's Hand*, by that master of the macabre, J. Sheridan Le Fanu.

dreaded, were intense and overwhelming. It was judged proper not farther to disturb the body till the arrival of some person in authority. No time, however, was lost; and one of the Earl of Leven's servants (he who had observed the spot) was sent off directly to Cupar.

"It was now near ten o'clock at night; but the rumour of what had been discovered spread immediately to the neighbouring farms and the villages of Letham and Collessie, so that numbers of the country people arrived from all directions and crowded round the premises. Some respectable persons had, however, been placed as sentries, that no one might be admitted to disturb the place or disarrange any appearances on which evidence might depend.

"The distance from Cupar to Whinny Park is about seven miles, yet in less than two hours Mr. Jameson (Sheriff-Substitute) was on the spot, with two medical gentlemen, Dr. Grace of Cupar and Dr. Malcolm of Letham, and Kennedy, the Sheriff Officer. The country people, though it was now past eleven o'clock at night, had assembled in great numbers from the whole neighbourhood; and the scene presented in disinterring the body, which was done by torchlight under the direction of the Sheriff, was truly appalling. The evening was perfectly calm, so that the flame of the torches glared quietly on the discoloured features of the corpse, as they were gradually disincumbered of the earth; and the strange, lurid reflection from the overhanging trees and the faces of the surrounding people, gave an interest to the scene almost too painful for recollection. From the length of time it had been in the ground there was some hazard of the body falling to pieces in the disinterment; and had it not been for the dress, and certain marks known to one of the medical gentlemen, the features were so fearfully changed that no evidence could have identified it.

" On being brought into the house and washed, the marks of violence were dreadfully visible. One heavy stroke had been given on the back of the head, which had seemingly stunned the victim; and two blows near the temples (apparently with a common wright's hammer) had perforated the skull and driven fragments of it down to the very centre of the brain."

.    .    .    .    .    .

"The crime is in its whole circumstances one of the most atrocious that has been known.  In the coolness with which it seems to have been projected and carried into execution, it comes nearest to the murder of Weare by the miscreant Thurtell.  But there the criminal and his victim had both equally forfeited the respect of honourable men; in the present case Millie was a person who, if somewhat remarkable for his secluded habits, was valued both for his ingenuity [? ingenuousness] and integrity.  He had afforded the person upon whom suspicion has fallen an asylum and decent means of subsistence, when he was wandering the country in rags, without even shoes or stockings; and had become security for him when he wanted credit for purchasing the most ordinary necessaries of life.  The coolness with which the wretch had continued for a whole month to carry on his depredations after the murder is not the least striking indication of his hardihood, and will scarcely find its parallel in any of the former records of crime."

# THE PLIGHT OF PLEASANT RAWLINS;
## OR, THE PRETENDED BROTHER

# THE PLIGHT OF PLEASANT RAWLINS;
## OR, THE PRETENDED BROTHER

"The World, my Dear, hath not such a Contempt for Roguery as you imagine."
MR. PEACHUM: *The Beggar's Opera.*

VALUABLE, nay indispensable, as are the serried volumes known as the *State Trials* compiled by the industrious Howell, I prefer when possible to read these old cases in the fine form in which they were first presented to contemporary connoisseurs. The spacious folio pages, the ample margins, the quaint type with its lavish employment of capitals, all have for me a flavour not to be found in the packed double-columns and modern orthography of the revised version. The old-fashioned format, the erratic spelling, better become these eighteenth-century figures than the more correct uniform of a later age.

For example, that particular one with which we are here concerned is thus entitled by Howell: "The Trial of Haagen Swendsen, at the Queen's Bench, for forcibly taking away and marrying Mrs. Pleasant Rawlins: I Anne, A.D. 1702"; and "The Trial of Sarah Baynton, John Hartwell, and John Spurr, at the Queen's Bench, for forcibly taking away Mrs. Pleasant Rawlins, and procuring her to be married to Haagen Swendsen: I Anne, A.D. 1702." Compare with this bald and unattractive announcement the inviting programme— I wish I could reproduce the picturesque stateliness of the original page:—"The TRYALS of *Haagen Swendsen, Sarah Baynton, John Hartwell,* and *John Spurr,* for Feloniously Stealing MRS. PLEASANT RAWLINS, a Virgin and Heiress of a Considerable Fortune: with an Intent to Cause and Procure the said *Pleasant Rawlins* against her Will, to Marry the said *Haagen Swendsen.* At the *Queens Bench Bar*

at *Westminster*, *Nov.* 25. 1702.   Before The Right Honourable the Lord Chief Justice *Holt*, and the rest of the Judges
of the said Court, of which Fact the said *Haagen Swendsen*
and *Sarah Baynton* were found Guilty, and the said *Swendsen*
was executed for the same, *Decemb.* 9th following.   The said
*Baynton* being with Child was Reprieved after sentence.
LONDON, Printed for *Isaac Cleave* next *Serjeants* Inn in
*Chancery-Lane.*   1703."

That, in my submission, is something like a title-page,
although perhaps it errs in giving away at the start rather
too much of the story.   But the facts are in themselves so
curious that the interest resides in their adequate present-
ment.   For the comfort of the common reader I shall take
my quotations from the current text.

By an old Act of 3 Henry VII. c. 2, the abduction of an
heiress was felony and punishable by death.   Yet the crime
was ever a popular one among impoverished spendthrifts,
from the ruined rakes and bloods of the past to the needy
fortune-hunters of a later age.   There was Captain Clifford,
who in 1663 carried off a rich widow to Calais and married
her by force; and Count Königsmark's attempt in 1682 to
marry the heiress of the Percys, whom he had widowed by
slaying her lord.   There was Sir John Johnston, a Fifeshire
baronet, executed in 1690 for his part in the subreption of
Miss Wharton; the conspiracy of which our Mrs. Pleasant
Rawlins was in 1702 the unhappy victim—the style of
"Mistress" being applied to her, though unmarried, according to the custom of that day as designating a lady of position
and property; and the forcible caption of Mrs. Lee by the
brothers Gordon in 1804.   The last, so far as I can find, of
these predatory husbands was the celebrated Edward Gibbon
Wakefield, who kidnapped his child-wife from school in
1827, and after a series of remarkable adventures was sentenced to three years in Newgate, a private bill being brought
into the House of Lords to annul the marriage.   I have told
this amazing tale as that of "The Stolen Heiress," in *Malice
Domestic* (Edinburgh: 1928).   Fortunately for the future

Empire-builder, the penalty of his crime had, by the Act, 9 Geo. iv. c. 31, been reduced to transportation or imprisonment.

I

On 25th November, 1702, the four prisoners were placed at the bar of the Court of Queen's Bench, the judges presiding being the Lord Chief Justice (Sir John Holt) and three puisne judges, Sir John Powell, Sir Littleton Powis, and Sir Henry Gould. The Solicitor-General (Sir Simon Harcourt, afterwards Lord Chancellor and Baron Harcourt), with Mr. Serjeant Darnell and Mr. Montague, conducted the prosecution. The prisoners, according to the practice of the time, were not represented by counsel, and had to conduct their own defence as best they might.

The indictment charged Swendsen with the forcible taking away and marrying one Pleasant Rawlins, gentlewoman, and a virgin, and unmarried, grand-daughter and heir of William Rawlins, senior, deceased, and daughter and heir of William Rawlins, junior, also deceased, she being above the age of 16 and under the age of 18, she having substance and estate in moveables and in lands and tenements, to wit, in money, goods, and chattels to the value of £2000, and in land and tenements to the value of £20 per annum. The text of the indictment is so delightful that I quote it verbatim:—

And that the several persons, Swendsen, Baynton, Hartwell, Spurr, and Tho. Holt, the said 6th day of November, with force and arms, the said Pleasant Rawlins, as aforesaid, being unmarried, and heir, and having substance and estate in the parish of St. Giles-in-the-fields in this county, for the lucre of such estate and substance of the said Pleasant Rawlins, did unlawfully, feloniously, violently, and against the will of the said Pleasant Rawlins, take, carry, and lead away, with intent to cause and procure the said Pleasant Rawlins, against her will, in matrimony to the said Haagen Swendsen to be joined, and to him to be wedded and married; and that the said Haagen Swendsen, being a man of a dishonest conversation, and of none or very little estate or substance, then and there, by the help and procurement of the other defendants, did feloniously marry the said Pleasant Rawlins, and was joined to her in matrimony, and then and there did carnally know; to the great displeasure of God, against the laws of the Queen, to the disgrace and disparagement of the said Pleasant Rawlins, and to the great grief and disconsolation of all her friends, to the evil example of all others, against the form of the statute, and against the Queen's peace, her crown and dignity. And that the said Tho. Holt, after the said Pleasant Rawlins had been so unlawfully, violently, and feloniously taken, carried, and led away, and to the said Haagen Swendsen married and wedded as aforesaid; well knowing the said Pleasant Rawlins to have been so taken and led away against her will, and to the said Haagen Swendsen to be wedded and married, afterwards, viz. the said 6th day of November, in the said first year of the reign of this Queen, at the parish aforesaid, the same Pleasant Rawlins, and also the said Haagen Swendsen, did wilfully, knowingly, and feloniously receive, abet, comfort, conceal, and assist the said Haagen Swendsen, with the said Pleasant Rawlins to lie, and her carnally to know, then and there did feloniously incite, abet, help, cause, and procure, against the form of the said statute, and against the Queen's peace, her crown and dignity.

Our old Scots indictments used to be long-winded and involved enough, but compared with this rambling rigmarole they are models of brevity and clearness. To this indictment the defendants pleaded Not Guilty. Swendsen asked for pen and ink, so that he might take notes of the evidence; also that his case should be tried separately. The Court granted both requests. The other prisoners were then "put aside" to await their trial; but the Solicitor-General moved that as "the facts were so twisted together," the jury for the second trial should attend this one also, in order that they might hear the evidence in both. So the case proceeded before the two juries.

The Solicitor-General, in addressing the first jury, said that Pleasant Rawlins was the daughter of the late Mr. William Rawlins, who had left her a considerable estate, and appointed George Bright and William Busby to be her guardians. Mr. Bright being dead, the other guardian, Mr. Busby, for the better education of Mrs. Rawlins, placed her under the care of his sister Sabina. Mrs. Busby and Mrs. Rawlins had for about three years lodged at the house of the widow Nightingale. Haagen Swendsen and Mrs. Baynton lodged at Mrs. Blake's, in Holborn, and there they first projected and contrived how they might make a prey of this young gentle-woman. The first step they took towards executing this design was to get lodgings at Mrs. Nightingale's house for Mrs. Baynton; for which purpose she was to pass for a country gentlewoman of a plentiful fortune. One Mrs. St. John was sent to Mrs. Nightingale to take lodgings for Mrs. Baynton, commending her to be a very good woman; and that having the misfortune of a lawsuit, and being for that reason obliged to attend in town, it was her greatest care to lodge in so reputable a house as Mrs. Nightingale's. Under this pretence lodgings were taken for her. At her first coming she was forced to put on a disguise; she seemed to live a virtuous life that she might ingratiate herself into the favour of the family, as often as she had an opportunity of conversing with them. She pretended she had a brother of good estate, one of the best men in the world; and she hoped he would shortly come to town that she might see him. In a little time after came this Swendsen (being nothing related to her), and appeared as her brother, and frequently visited her under pretence of that relation. But Mrs. Baynton was too well known in town to continue long undiscovered; notice was soon given to Mrs. Busby of the vicious life Mrs. Baynton had led, and that she was not fit to be in the same house with her. Mrs. Baynton having discovered this, and finding she had no time to bring about her design by frauds and wiles, and that no other ways were left but open force, the prisoner at the bar and she took measures accordingly; and in order thereto it was agreed that a writ should be taken out against Mrs. Rawlins. Mrs. Baynton contrived to get Mrs. Rawlins and Mrs. Busby into a coach, and at a place appointed a signal was given and the writ executed. Mrs. Busby, Mrs. Rawlins, and Mrs. Baynton were all carried in the coach to the Star and Garter tavern in Drury Lane, where particular care was taken to separate Mrs. Busby and Mrs. Rawlins, because unless they did that, they could not hope to accomplish their designs. Mrs. Busby was by force kept at the tavern, without any process against her, till the marriage was over; but Mrs. Rawlins was forcibly carried to Hartwell the bailiff's house. At the Star and Garter Mrs. Baynton pretended to be much concerned for Mrs. Rawlins, and went in all haste to call some of her friends to be bail for her. Some time after Mrs. Rawlins was got to Hartwell's, in comes Mrs. Baynton, pretending that by mere accident she had discovered her being there, hearing her name as she was passing by the door; that she had been in search, but could find no help; and that her last hope was her brother Swendsen, and she doubted not but he would bail her. He by agreement had been placed near the bailiff's and so was soon found and brought thither, and was very ready to assist her. In order to her discharge, the prisoner, the bailiff, and Mrs. Baynton carried Mrs. Rawlins to another tavern, where they had a parson ready for the purpose; and there this young gentlewoman, through divers artifices, was constrained to marry. These were the principal circumstances, which would be plainly proved.

Then Serjeant Darnell "thought it necessary to open a little the manner of getting this young lady away," which he proceeded to do at greater length than the Solicitor-General! But as we shall hear all about that from the witnesses themselves, I have not "thought it necessary" to trouble you with the learned Serjeant's version.

The first to be called was Mr. William Busby, who bore out the Solicitor's opening statement as to his ward's parentage and estate, and told how he committed her to his sister's care. Sabina Busby and Mrs. Nightingale, the landlady, were next called together.

"My Lord," said the prisoner, "I beg the favour that only one witness be heard at a time." This reasonable proposition being granted, Mrs. Sabina was meantime put aside, and Mrs. Nightingale told her tale.

*L.C.J.* Did Mrs. Busby lodge with you?

*Nightingale.* Yes, my Lord, we were very intimate before; and since it pleased God to take away my husband, I was pleased with her, and very willing to take her into my house.

Sabina and Pleasant Rawlins had, she stated, occupied her lodgings for the last three years. She became acquainted with the prisoner Baynton in this wise: a lady, naming herself Mrs. St. John, called and asked whether witness took boarders, explaining that she had a friend, a widow lady, that was come out of Wiltshire about a lawsuit, "*and would be in a sober family, near a church.*" The widow's character, she said, would speak for itself. Upon this fair shewing witness agreed to take her, and presently Mrs. Baynton arrived, accompanied by her maid—"a modest girl and a neighbour"—which gave witness the more security. The new lodger commended her being "very curious in taking boarders," and said she liked her the better for it. Like her maid, she was at the outset very modest in her behaviour and garb. "She carried herself very well until Michaelmas-day at night, when we heard of her new brother; she seemed elevated at the news, and fell into convulsion fits"—due, as appears, to the unexpected joy of seeing him so soon. She described him as "a dear brother, a good Christian, and he would come on the morrow." This was the first witness had heard of this paragon of brothers. Next day the gentleman called, accompanied by two ladies, "very modest, whom I never saw before nor since," and of whom we, likewise, hear nothing further. Mrs. Baynton sent for a bottle of wine, and spoke most highly of the lodgings, expressing a wish that her brother could share them, "for she knew he had but a puny stomach, and believed he would like the victuals." She instanced, as an additional attraction, a near-by bowling-green, where he might divert himself. But the brother said it would not be convenient for him to lodge there, as his business called him every day to 'Change. Mrs. Baynton then suggested that he might drop in occasionally for a meal. Witness said that if her boarders' friends did so, she "had twelve-pence a meal of them," which, if the lady kept a good table, seems a moderate tariff. "On the Friday before the Sacrament," Mrs. Baynton's new-found brother, availing himself of this privilege, came to dinner. "I went to church," says Mrs. Nightingale, "and left them together at cribbage, as I found them on my return." Yet the lodger had chosen the apartments as being near a place of worship!

> Mrs. Baynton said to Mr. Swendsen before Mrs. Busby: "You have an extraordinary hand at making punch"; so they agreed to make a bowl the Monday following. But Mrs. Rawlins hardly drank any, she not liking any strong liquors. . . . Mrs. Baynton said she had an interest in a Norway ship and invited us all aboard. We concluded to go on Saturday. . . . We went, and had much discourse. After having a glass of wine, the cloth was laid, and the master offered a bowl of punch. Says Mr. Swendsen: "Ladies, I would please you all, and leave you all to your liberties to drink what you please."

The hospitable master-mariner reminds one of the immortal Bunsby's inquiry, which so shocked Captain Cuttle, when Florence Dombey and Susan visited the *Cautious Clara*: "Shipmet, what 'll the ladies drink?"

Witness identified the prisoner as the supposititious brother. It was not long, she said, before she began to have suspicions as to the relations subsisting between Mrs. Baynton and her fraternal kinsman. "There seemed to be an extraordinary love between them, more than is usual between brother and sister." "Madam," said she, ironically, "I wonder you do not marry your brother." She said she thought that it was not lawful. "I said there was such a thing done at Westminster, of a man's marrying two sisters"—Swendsen being, as Baynton alleged, the husband of her deceased sister. Witness was now anxious to be rid of her questionable lodger: "but being all women and fearful of her, thought not fit to give her warning till her month was up." Before that period, however, Mrs. Baynton, perceiving that her landlady's suspicions were aroused, announced that she had heard from the country "that the trustees will agree"; there was an end to the lawsuit, and when her month was up she designed to resume a rural life, "for this town is very chargeable."

Mrs. Nightingale announced the welcome news to the other members of the household, "and expressed her joy to them"; their relations with the widow had become unfriendly. Her maid had said to her: "Madam, do you not see a strangeness in the family?" "Yes," she replied, "I can see and bear a great deal; but when I am roused, I'll be like a lion!" Fortunately for "the family" the occasion did not arise. Mrs. Nightingale continues:—

> She told me on Wednesday that her time was out; but said: "There is a fellow in town that I fear will cheat me, and I am taking out a statute of bankruptcy against him, which will cause me to stay in town a week longer." She also told me she had taken a place in the coach to go on Thursday, but must lose her earnest, for this business would detain her a week longer. . . . We never had any suspicion of Mr. Swendsen, but of the woman, for she could put on all manner of disguises.

Mrs. Sabina Busby stated that four years ago her brother placed his ward, Pleasant Rawlins, in her care. They then lived in Stretton Grounds, Westminster; but on the death of her husband she "left housekeeping," and three years before the trial took lodgings with Mrs. Nightingale, in her house "near Tuttlefields," i.e. Tothilfields. Witness then described the coming of the gentlewoman from the country, the arrival of her brother, and the arrangement that, when so disposed, he should dine there "at 12d. per meal." He did so on nine or ten occasions, sometimes when "the family" was not at home. Asked what impression she formed of Mrs. Baynton, Sabina said:—

> We thought very well of her, till at last we discerned too much freedom between Mr. Swendsen and herself. We suspected her, and thought she would drink, and were informed she would swear. She said she must stay in town about a month or six weeks about a suit of law. Her maid told her of the strangeness of the family; she said they had best be civil or else she would stay and plague them. She told Mrs. Nightingale at length the town was chargeable and her business done, and that she would return into the country.

It was the ladies' pious custom to go every Friday morning to Oxendon Chapel. One day Mrs. Baynton offered them a lift: she was going in a coach to Golden Square and would drop them near their place of worship.

> When we came to Dartmouth Street somebody bid the coachman stop. I expected she would set us down as she promised. All of a

sudden I saw a man in the coach, which was Hartwell, the bailiff. Mrs. Rawlins and I were in a very great fright, knowing nothing. I said: "For God's sake let's come out; we are not concerned." Hartwell said we were the persons that he came for.

Despite the protests of the terrified girls, the party proceeded to the Star and Garter in Drury Lane. Mrs. Baynton told them to put on their masks—apparently these were carried by ladies at that time for use when they wished to avoid publicity. Sabina refused, saying she had done nothing amiss, and she would not. They were taken to a room in the tavern, Mrs. Baynton hastening away, as she averred, to summon their friends. The two girls were, naturally, "in a great consternation," wondering what their captors meant to do with them. "I took hold of her arm," says Sabina, "and told her I would live and die with her. The bailiffs came in and said she was their prisoner, and took her by violence from me," saying that Pleasant was arrested by a writ out of one Court and witness by another. Sabina put her head out of the window and cried: "Murder! murder!" several times. Spurr, one of the bailiffs, said: "What have you got by your bawling? We are better known here than you." The landlady then came up and rebuked Sabina, saying she "had done a diskindness to her house by crying out murder." The man produced a writ, bearing to be against Sabina Busby at the suit of one Jones. He offered to go to her friends, "as cheap as a porter and as soon"; but as he did not return that night she doubted his good faith. The man who had carried off Mrs. Pleasant came back with the cheering news that "the young woman was well, and he had left her eating fowl and bacon." Some neighbours came in, but no one would interfere, "as it was an arrest." So Sabina remained in custody till nightfall.

I did not know what I was arrested for: it might be murder or treason for aught I knew. There was a little boy by, said: "Madam, I know Mr. Unkle, your friend in Newmarket, and I will go for him." He went, but when he returned again he said he was not at home; which I thought was a lie. There was a poor man, a labourer, working in the chimney; he gave me a wink and said: "Madam, I will go for him"; but I said: "Pray do not leave me." I began to be afraid, for I did not know how my life might be concerned.

But Sabina had misjudged the juvenile messenger. "Said the little boy: 'I will go anywhere for you'"; so she dispatched him to fetch two gentlemen, her friends, who presently came and offered bail. The bailiffs were "very impudent and shuffled about awhile"; but in the end abandoned their captive, who departed with her rescuers.

> *Prisoner.* Have you done?
> *Witness.* I think so.
> *Prisoner.* If you have, I will ask you a question: Did you know of any love between Mrs. Rawlins and me?
> *L.C.J.* Did you know any thing of love between Mrs. Rawlins and the prisoner or no?
> *Witness.* No, my lord.

Mrs. Baynton's maid told how she was engaged by that lady to go to Mrs. Nightingale's, where she remained a month. The family had a mistrust of her mistress long before she went away; they thought her a loose sort of woman. Witness had never seen the prisoner until he turned up at the house. "They went for brother and sister." She gave up her place the day after Mrs. Rawlins' abduction.

Mrs. Berkeley, a neighbour, who frequently saw Baynton and Swendsen together, said she was present when the prisoner was apprehended.

> I went to Mr. Swendsen and said: "Is this wicked woman your sister?" Says he: "I cannot say she is; but I have made her my tool and she has done my business, and I would get rid of her tomorrow, but that being Sunday I will not; but on Monday I will give her a reward for what she has done, and then I will discharge her and never see her more."

Mr. and Mrs. Blake stated that the prisoner and Baynton lodged in their house in Red Lion Street. They had known the lady for twelve years. Asked whether she was a country widow with a good jointure, they said they knew nothing about her, "but that she works for her living." The nature of her employment is not specified, but, like the Sirens' song, is not beyond all conjecture. Swendsen had lodged with them some seven months. Mrs. Baynton occupied "the opposite room against the gentleman." She left about five weeks before the affair of Mrs. Rawlins.

Wakeman, a bailiff, stated that he was instructed by Hartwell to arrest Mrs. Busby and Mrs. Rawlins upon a Marshal's Court writ. He described how Hartwell, Spurr, and himself lay in wait to intercept the coach. "I was ashamed to stand in the street," says this sensitive officer, "so I went into an alehouse and drank a single pot of drink." Spurr stopped the horses; Hartwell gave the word of arrest, "and into the coach he went; but I did not go in, because there was no room, but rid behind it." Having lodged the captives in a back room at the Star and Garter, one Holt, landlord of the Mitre in King Street, led witness to the Five Bells in Wych Street, where was a gentleman whom he now identified as the prisoner, to whom he reported the successful issue of the adventure. "At that Mr. Holt filled me a full glass, which I drank off." Witness then went to Hartwell's house " to inquire for the gentlewoman" (Pleasant Rawlins), and was informed that Hartwell had taken her to Holborn "to make an end of the matter." Witness followed to the Vine tavern, where he found Hartwell and a tallow-chandler, "going to eat steaks." They invited him to eat some with them, and told him he was now discharged of his prisoner. As he went away he saw the gentlewoman looking out of a window of the Vine.

Pleasant Rawlins was then called. She told how she was arrested by three bailiffs and carried from tavern to tavern, as before described.

I was in a very great fright, but Mrs. Busby saying: "We will die together," they took me by force from her. Hartwell swore a great oath, and thrust me down the stairs and forced me out of a back door into an alley. When he went to put me into a coach I cried out: "Murder!" Then he threatened to put me into Newgate. He carried me to his own house and nobody came to help me for a great while; but Mrs. Baynton said that as she was going by the door, she heard my name and came in in a mighty fright. She said to me:

"Madam, I pity you. Will nobody bail you?" She told me: "I will send to my brother, who shall be bail for you." She sent for him; he came into the room and he said: "What is the matter with you?" I said: "Enough is the matter when I am arrested for £200, and owe no man a penny!" Said he in a jocose way: "What makes you affrighted at that? I have a good mind to arrest you myself!" They took me then to the Vine tavern in Holborn, where I was an hour or two before I heard any thing of marrying.

The first suggestion that she should change her maiden state came from Mrs. Baynton, who said that the only remedy for her sad situation was to marry her brother. Pleasant refused the proposal, and demanded to see and consult with her own friends. Mrs. Baynton said that if she did not marry her brother she would be ruined for ever. She forcibly possessed herself of Pleasant's ring; with this she went out and returned with a wedding-ring of similar size, which she said she had bought.

There was a minister in the house; they brought him with the clerk upstairs, the parson saying: "I hear there is a couple to be married." He asked no questions, but told me if I did not marry this gentleman I should be sent to Newgate. . . . So with many threats and persuasions they at last prevailed with me to marry. I was forced to marry him out of fear, *not of going to Newgate, but of being murdered.*

It is not surprising that a girl of seventeen, helpless in these sinister circumstances, should have feared the worst and consented to anything.

The examination is resumed by the Lord Chief Justice:—

Where did they carry you? To Blake's house in Red Lion Street, Holborn.

What time of day was it? I cannot give an exact account, but I think it was candlelight.

*Prisoner.* It was about 12 o'clock at noon.

*L.C.J.* What time was it that you were married? It was about 3 o'clock.

When you went to Blake's, who was with you there? None but Mr. Swendsen, Mrs. Baynton, and I.

Was there any force or threats used when you were at Blake's house? Yes, there was, my Lord.

Give an account of it. They thrust me upstairs, and ordered to have a bed sheeted. Mrs. Baynton said to me: "Undress, and go to bed." I said I would not. She said she would pluck my clothes off my back. I said she should not. She said she would pluck off my clothes and make me go to bed.

What did she do with you? She put me to bed.

Did she use any violence with you? Such violence that made me go to bed.

How came you to be released? It was Saturday morning before I was released; there was some of my friends came to the place where I was.

Then you were with him all night? Yes, my Lord.

The Solicitor-General having stated that this closed the Crown case, his Lordship asked the prisoner whether he had any questions. Swendsen then began a rambling account of the affair, which he broke off to desire that his "wife" might stand by herself, "and none of them [her friends and supporters] near her." "There is none near her that will hurt her," observed the Chief Justice. "Must I grant it only for your humour?" "It is not a humour, my Lord," retorted the prisoner, "but of a great consequence to me." "There is nobody near her that concerns you at all," said his Lordship." "There are those by her that will do me no kindness" was the reply. "My Lord," protested the Solicitor-General, "he does it on purpose to fright her"; but Pleasant Rawlins was ordered to be removed.

The accused then described divers punch-brewings held by him at Mrs. Nightingale's, in the produce of which the ladies duly shared. After their visit to the ship, where they were "very merry," the parties became well-acquainted. He was invited to the house for the following week, "to partake of a treat"; he did so, and prepared the inevitable bowl. One of the guests, Mr. Pugh, was then courting Mrs. Rawlins, but the accused perceived that "she had a kindness for him [Swendsen], and complained that he could not be easy while she suffered Mr. Pugh to kiss her." "She desired me to be easy, and it should be remedied." In reply to the Court, Pleasant indignantly denied that such words ever came out of her mouth.

*Prisoner.* Did you not say this, Mrs. Rawlins—Mrs. Swendsen, I should say—did you not say if I would not sit by you, you would not eat a bit or a crumb? When I sat by you and proferred my place to another, can you say you were not offended? No, I was not.

Are you not upon your oath? Did not you give me some encouragement? I do not know how I could shew it you; I know not of any such thing.

*L.C.J.* You ought to speak the truth, because his life depends upon it. Did you, in the first place, admit of his courtship in order to marry you? No, my Lord, I do not remember any such thing.

Did you ever shew any kindness to him upon any such account? No, I do not know I shewed him any more kindness than all the rest of the family shewed him.

Was you ever in his company alone? No, my Lord.

"To give me more ease and satisfaction," continued the prisoner, "after dinner we had our bowl and walnuts. Mrs. Swendsen peeled the kernels and gave them to me; she gave them faster than I could eat; she heaped my plate with them. Everyone at the table took notice of it, and she jogged me with her knee that I should take them, and gave some to Mrs. Baynton and bid her take them and give to me."

*L.C.J.* Mrs. Busby, were you there? Yes, my Lord.

Did you see anything of this kind? No, my Lord.

*Prisoner.* Will your Lordship be pleased to ask her yourself?

*L.C.J.* Mrs. Rawlins, did you ever give peeled walnuts or send them to him in particular?

*Rawlins.* No, my Lord. I do not know that I was more kind to him than the rest of the company.

*Prisoner.* Everybody took notice of it, and Mr. Pugh in particular. If he were here he would say the same as I do. He was afraid I should get away his lady.

*L.C.J.* Where is he?

*Court.* He is in Court.

*L.C.J.* You may have him for a witness if you will.

Even had Mr. Pugh corroborated, the walnuts seem but a frail foundation for the prisoner's defence, namely, that Pleasant made love to him from the first and went to him as a willing bride. But he did not call that gentleman, preferring to adduce the evidence of an artist, irreverently designed "picture drawer," whose name was, appropriately, Scoreman. It appeared that Mr. Scoreman had been engaged in painting a portrait of Mrs. Baynton at his lodgings. On one occasion when Mrs. Busby and Mrs. Rawlins attended the sitting, "they fell into discourse relating to a matter of love between Mr. Swendsen and the young lady [Pleasant]. She [Mrs. Baynton] said the young lady had a love for Mr. Swendsen more than the other [? Pugh]. She [Pleasant] should have said so. I did not hear her myself; but upon a discourse, she afterwards said, What she had said she would stand to." The prisoner interposed: the witness could not speak English "right"; might he speak for him? witness was a Dane. So a member of the jury, who knew the language,[1] was sworn as interpreter, and having conferred awhile with the witness, reported to the Court: "He is none of my country, he is a Dutchman. I do not understand him." Whereupon his Lordship justly remarked: "You must have a better witness, or you are in a dangerous condition."

> *Prisoner.* My Lord, Mr. Pugh complained to Madam Busby that she slighted him very much.
> *L.C.J.* What, for love of you? Yes, my Lord. I could tell you of divers things that pass between lovers that would be impertinent for me to relate to wise men.

His Lordship, however, desired to be informed.

> *Prisoner.* When we were by ourselves she kissed me, and squeezed me by the hand when we walked privately in the garden.
> *L.C.J.* Did you think her very coming? Yes, I did; and when we talked of marriage she seemed to be very well pleased. Mrs. Rawlins, you hear what he says. Did you squeeze him by the hand and kiss him? Is that true? No, my Lord, I did no such trick, not I; and as for walking in the garden, I did not walk in the garden alone with him.
> *Prisoner.* I could mention a great many of these little things; but if she denies them I cannot help it. My Lord, the last time I was at the house we had a barrel of oysters. I stood with my hands behind me, and as she passed by at anytime she gave me squeezes by the hand.
> *L.C.J.* What do you say to this, Mrs. Rawlins? My Lord, I did not do so, upon my oath.

And even if she did, it seems very little to the purpose. With regard to the marriage, the prisoner maintained that Pleasant was wedded to him "with as much freedom as could

---

[1] According to the practice of the time, when a foreigner was on trial the jury was one of mixed nationalities.

be in a woman." Whereupon the bride was called upon by the Judge to repeat all she had said as to the events leading up to and culminating in that irregular ceremony.

The prisoner then called the officiating clergyman, who was none other than the notorious Chaplain of the Fleet. "Come, Doctor," said his Lordship to the witness, "you are not upon your oath"—presumably because of his sacred calling; "How came you to be concerned in this match?" The parson explained that he and his clerk were fetched from the Fleet by a gentleman, who conducted them to the Vine tavern. "When we came there, the clerk and I went up one pair of stairs and drank a pint of wine." They were then led into another room, where they found the prisoner and two ladies. "I asked him what I was to do. He told me, for to marry him to that young gentlewoman." He produced a licence, which was in order.

> *L.C.J.* Do you think that they should grant licences to marry in a tavern and out of canonical hours? I never did it in all my life before, and never will do it again.

The parson stated that he asked the damsel whether she were willing to be married. She said that she was; and the other gentlewoman that was with her (Mrs. Baynton) said she was her sister. He said to her: "Madam, if you consent, and your sister is willing, here is the licence for I believe there is no danger to marry you." It was not "the gentleman at the bar" that came for him to the Fleet. The licence, which was dated 14th October, 1702, bore the names of Haagen Swendsen, in the parish of St. Paul's, Shadwell, and Mrs. Pleasant Rawlins, in the parish of St. Mary, Whitechapel. There was a blank left for the place of the marriage. After the ceremony "the gentleman bespoke a fowl," of which, doubtless, the parson partook.

Mrs. Cotchett, the landlady of the Vine, stated that on the occasion of the wedding she heard no noise nor saw any violence offered to the bride. "They came in and asked for a room," said witness, "and I shewed them a lower room, but

they would not have that, but went up. Soon after, Mr. Holt,
the vintner, came down and went out, and Mr. Hartwell called
for a pint of wine for the coachman; but the drawer grumbled
at it, and said he did not know who would pay for it. Then
Mr. Hartwell told me it was an arrest, and that the person
was to be bail for the lady, and at that I very much wondered.
Afterwards they told me there was a wedding above, which
we admired at: that there should be a wedding and bailiffs.
After all was over, the gentleman and the lady went out at
the back door and took a coach." "Did you see Mrs.
Swendsen discontented when she went out?" asked the
accused. "She seemed not discontented," replied the witness,
adding with sound judgment: "What I know I will speak,
and no more." It were well did all witnesses follow her
example.

Sarah Walker, cook at the Vine, said she was in the bar
"when that young gentlewoman was carried prisoner there."
Witness heard there was a wedding. She was sent upstairs
to the gentlefolks, to receive directions for the supper. The
bride sat at one end of the room and seemed to be very
melancholy. "When orders were given about the supper,
I asked her what sauce she would have? She said she would
eat nothing at all." Sarah's evidence cannot have done much
for the defence.

Mrs. Blake's daughter, called and examined by the accused,
said that when the bride was brought to their lodgings, "she
carried it very well."

> The lady was pleased to say that I should wait upon her. I offered
> to pull off her shoes and stockings when she went to bed. She held
> out her legs, and I pulled off her shoes and stockings.
> *The Solicitor-General.* Were you present before she began un-
> dressing? Yes. . . .
> Do you know Mrs. Baynton? Yes, Sir.
> Pray did she ever lie in at your house? Yes, Sir.
> Hath she a husband? I cannot tell.

In reply to the Judge witness said that the newly married
pair went to bed about four o'clock, arose at seven, and after
having had supper, left the house between eight and nine that

night. Mr. Blake, father of the preceding witness, stated that he had known Mrs. Baynton for twelve years. He could not say whether or not she had a husband. "It was reported that she had one," but witness had never seen him. Mrs. Baynton lay in at his house four months ago.

*The Solicitor-General.* When she was such a woman as this, and brought a gentlewoman to your house and ordered a bed to be made, how could you admit her into your house again? I did not know that it was any clandestine thing.

*L.C.J.* Have you any more witnesses, Mr. Swendsen?

*Prisoner.* Let the constable be called for.

Pleasant Rawlins' friends having procured a warrant, they accompanied this officer to Blake's house in Red Lion Street, for the purpose of effecting her liberation and apprehending "such men as took the young gentlewoman away." The constable stated that one of the lady's friends asked her: "Are you married?" to which she answered: "Yes; there is my husband." She seemed to witness very well satisfied with her condition. He said to her: "Madam, I wish you much joy."

*Prisoner.* My Lord, I desire she may be asked what she said to the constable.

*Mrs. Rawlins.* My Lord, I do not know whether I said such a thing. If I did, I was not in my senses. I did not know what I said.

*Prisoner.* My Lord, I hope you will give me leave to speak. She said to the constable: "I am very well content with the marriage, and this is the ring that married us."

*L.C.J.* What say you to that, Mrs. Rawlins? I do not know but I might; but I did not know what I said.

Had you been in bed then? Yes, we were in bed about an hour.

Were there any threats used by Mrs. Baynton? Yes, my Lord; *she said that I must own him for my husband, or else we were all ruined.*

Mr. Baber, a Justice of the Peace, stated that on the night of Friday, the 6th, the prisoner, with Mrs. Rawlins and another gentlewoman (Baynton), came to his house in York Buildings, and desired him to administer to the young lady a "voluntary oath" that she was married to the prisoner. This witness declined to do, on the ground that it was not his business to confirm marriages. "What sort of frame was the young woman in?" asked counsel. To which witness made answer: "In very great disorder; not like a gentlewoman, but in a very confused condition."

One Bulkley, a barber, was next called. He stated that on 7th November, the day after the marriage, in the forenoon, the prisoner "stopped at the porch of his door and gave him orders to wait upon him upon the business of his calling," *i.e.* wished to be shaved. "He told me," said the barber, with the usual loquacity of his class, "that he was married. I asked him: 'What! are you married?' 'Yes,' said he, 'I am; and here is my wife,' and the gentlewoman said so too. At that I wished them much joy and happiness. The young woman said she did not question it, since what she had done was with her own voluntary consent." Hudson, an upholsterer in the employment of Mr. Blake, stated that on Saturday morning, the 7th, the prisoner brought Pleasant to his master's house, and bid her shake hands with Mr. Blake and ask him how he did. "Mr. Swendsen said: 'This is my dear wife'; and she said: 'This is my dear husband,' and took him about the neck and kissed him."

> *The Solicitor-General.* If they lay there overnight what necessity was there for Swendsen to tell Mr. Blake that was his dear wife? He did not say so to him, but to his wife; and she kissed him.
>
> What need to tell Mr. Blake that was his wife, when he knew it before? Why may not I, if I had a wife, come to her and say: "My dear wife"?

Blake, recalled, said he had never seen the lady before.

Mr. Green, who designed himself as "belonging to the General Post-Office," was called to prove that before the Recorder, whither she had been taken by the prisoner, she declared that she was married to that gentleman "by her own consent without any force or compulsion." Cross-examined, witness believed she did not continue in that tone all the time she was at the Recorder's; that when she so declared, the prisoner had hold of her hand; that the Recorder said he was afraid she had "been drawn in by this man, who he feared was a spark and bully of the town"; that the prisoner was then "withdrawn"; but witness did not hear what the gentlewoman thereafter said, "as he was thrust out."

This imputation on his fair fame was highly resented by the prisoner, who desired he might have his friends heard "as to his walk and conversation." So three witnesses were adduced who had divers business dealings with him, "and found him to be a very honest and ingenuous man."

The prisoner here closed his case; but the Solicitor-General was allowed to lead further evidence as to what occurred before the Recorder. Another witness was called, who stated that on Saturday, 7th November, he was present when Mrs. Rawlins made her declaration. "While Mr. Swendsen held her by the hand," said he, "she owned the marriage; but when he was withdrawn, she threw herself upon me and desired me to stand by her, or she was undone! She spoke much to the same purpose as she has done here: that what she had done was all by force and out of fear."

Mr. Taylor, who issued the licence, stated that it was dated *three weeks before the time of the marriage*, and that the prisoner swore that the lady's age was 25.

## II

The Lord Chief Justice began his summing up by stating to the jury the law of the case. Anyone carrying off an heiress by force and marrying her, was guilty of felony by the statute. It was proved that this young woman had personal estate to the value of £2000 and land to the value of £20 per annum. It was proved that she was placed by her guardian under the tuition of Mrs. Busby, with whom for the past three years she had lodged at Mrs. Nightingale's. That lady was prevailed upon to take the woman Baynton into her house as a boarder. Mrs. Baynton pretended she had a brother, the prisoner at the bar, and introduced him as such into the family, with whom he became friendly. It was noticed that the pair were too familiar as brother and sister, and that Baynton was "inclinable to drink"—a charming phrase. Perceiving the "strangeness" of the family, she gave notice that she would leave at the month's end. His Lordship then reviewed the evidence of the *enlèvement*: Baynton's offer of a lift in her coach, and the arrest of the young ladies by Hartwell, the bailiff, who told the passers-by who asked what was amiss, that they were "cheats and trading-women that owed people money." Upon this pretended arrest they were carried to the Star and Garter in Drury Lane and put into a back room, where they were "in a great consternation," their captors telling them that one was to be taken to Newgate and the other to the Marshalsea. Mrs. Rawlins was then carried off to Hartwell's house, where Baynton proposed her "brother" to be bail. Under that pretence she was taken to the Vine tavern in Holborn. Bail being refused, "Mrs. Baynton proposes a marriage between the prisoner and Mrs. Rawlins, as the best way to make an end of this troublesome business." As the young lady declined this artful proposition, she was threatened that if she did not marry, she would be committed to Newgate. They had a parson and clerk ready; and Mrs. Rawlins being under terror, the office of matrimony was performed. She was then conveyed to Blake's house, "and by constraint there was put to bed in the day-time." Violence was used to force off her clothes; she lay in bed about an hour, "and thereby the marriage was supposed to be consummated." (The prisoner, as we shall see, denied this supreme act of villainy.) "After all this evidence," continued his Lordship, "the prisoner doth insist upon his innocence, because he was not present at the arrest; and hath produced several witnesses to prove that this young woman was very well satisfied with the marriage; and that reverend divine, the parson, asked her whether she was willing to be married to the gentleman, and she said she was willing." His Lordship then dealt with the visit that same night to the Justice of the Peace and the call next day upon the barber; the return to Blake's house, and the coming of the constable with the warrant for her release.

He pointed out the significance of what happened at the Recorder's: how, while the prisoner held her hand, the young lady declared her consent to, and satisfaction with, the marriage; but on her "husband" being withdrawn, she declared it was effected by force and violence, and that she consented only out of fear. There was also the remarkable fact that the licence was taken out by the prisoner three weeks before the marriage was accomplished. Having referred to the high character given to Mr. Swendsen by his business friends, the Chief Justice gave the jury the following directions on the law, as applicable to the facts established by the evidence:—

"1. You are to know that if she be taken away by force and afterwards married, though by her consent, yet he is guilty of felony. For it is the taking away by force that makes the crime, if there be a marriage, though by her consent.

"2. In the next place it is to be observed that she was taken away by force and a stratagem was used to give an opportunity thereunto, and the arrest was but a colour.

"3. You may consider upon the evidence how far the prisoner was concerned in the first force. It is true he was not at the arrest, and did not appear until she was brought to Hartwell's house; and that under pretence of bailing her, she was carried to the Vine tavern, where there was a parson ready, and the marriage was had in such a manner as you have heard. Now, considering these matters, it is left to you to determine whether the marriage was not the end of the arrest; and if so, how it would be possible for such a force to be committed to effect the prisoner's design, and he not be privy to it.

"4. If it can be imagined that he was not privy to the colourable arrest, yet she was under a force when he came to her at Hartwell's house; and from thence she was carried by force to the Vine tavern, where she was married. That is a forcible taking by him at Hartwell's house; and though when she was at the Vine tavern she did express her consent to be married, yet it appears even then she was under force and had no power to help herself. Her marriage was by force when she was taken to Blake's and put to bed: all this was force; nay, when she was carried to the Justice of the Peace, even then she was under a force; and all she said was not freely, but out of fear. Such a force would avoid any bond, for she was under imprisonment. But, however, if the first taking was by force and she had consented to the marriage, the offence is the same: it is felony."

Regarding the prisoner's reputation as spoken to by his friends, it was possible he might once have been an honest man. "A man is not born a knave," observed his Lordship; "there must be time to make him so, nor is he presently [at once] discovered after he becomes one. His former reputation will signify nothing to him upon this occasion." Finally, if they were satisfied on the evidence of the prisoner's guilt, they must find accordingly; if not, they ought to acquit him.

> *Swendsen.* I desire, my Lord, that my wife may be asked whether she did not upon her knees swear she went away from me as good a maid as she came to me?
> *L.C.J.* That is a question need not be asked, since the marriage is so plainly proved, which is sufficient to bring you within the statute.

The jury then retired to consider their verdict, and three hours later—in the middle of the second trial—returned a finding of Guilty. Sentence was postponed until the conclusion of the other prisoners' trial.

### III

Counsel for the Crown moved that the trial of Sarah Baynton, John Hartwell, and John Spurr be put off till Friday, 27th November; but the Lord Chief Justice refused, "and ordered it to begin presently [forthwith]." Accordingly, on the afternoon of Wednesday, the 25th, the second trial started with a fresh jury. Judge and counsel can hardly have been so fresh, seeing that they had been engaged upon the Swendsen case from an unknown hour of that Wednesday morning. But it appears from the report that the 25th was "the last day they could be tried to have sentence given against convicted persons in that term."

The indictment upon which the prisoners were arraigned was the same as in the former trial, except that the charge against Thomas Holt was now dropped. The Solicitor-General again described the conspiracy of which Pleasant Rawlins had been the victim. "In this contrivance," said he, "you will find every one of the prisoners at the bar had their several parts to act." Hartwell got the writ; Mrs. Baynton brought the two victims to the place of "execution"; Hartwell and Spurr arrested them and carried them in the coach to the Star and Garter, where Mrs. Busby was detained by Spurr, and whence Mrs. Rawlins was carried by Hartwell to his own house. Then came the business of the pretended bail and her removal by Hartwell, Baynton, and Swendsen to the Vine, where, under threats of undergoing the miseries of a jail, she was married.

The evidence for the Crown being practically that given by the same witnesses adduced at Swendsen's trial, it were tedious to discuss it at length. I shall, therefore, only mention such supplementary points as call for notice. Further light was thrown by Mrs. Nightingale upon the perfidious Mrs. St. John, whose false representations induced her to admit the infamous Mrs. Baynton beneath her blameless roof. "She told me," said the landlady, "that she [Baynton] was akin to the Lady Ann Baynton; that she was an extraordinary good woman, and that her husband was well-acquainted with the family, and gave her an extraordinary character. She said she would not have parted with her herself, but that she [St. John] did not take boarders." Mrs. St. John commended to her as maid a neighbour's child, "which was a pretty civil girl; she hired her, which made me still like her the better." The lodger spoke much of a dear brother who had come to town: "an extraordinary Christian, that had married her sister." This lady, on her deathbed,

had counselled Mrs. Baynton to be both wife and sister to
the widower. Witness then told how "the abundance of
love" displayed by the lodger for her brother when he came
to the house aroused suspicion in the family, which, coupled
with her swearing "above stairs," and the fact that she sometimes came home "elevated with drink," led to a hint being
given her to vacate the rooms.

The prisoner Baynton here interposed to remind the witness that the first time Swendsen came to her house, "you
said you loved punch entirely, and I said: 'If you please,
Madam, Mr. Swendsen shall make a bowl'"—this, apparently,
to shew that Mrs. Nightingale herself, like Mrs. Diana Trapes
in *The Beggar's Opera*, was "very curious in her liquors."

Mrs. Busby re-told the tale of the arrest and her subsequent sequestration at the Star and Garter. Mrs. Baynton
pretended to take her part, and offered to go to her friends
for help, which Hartwell would not permit. "She argued
with the bailiff, and said: 'May I not go where I will?' and
seemed to be very angry with him. Mr. Hartwell also
seemed to be very angry with her, and called her 'Mrs. Pert,'
saying if she were civil she should have the more respect."
It is plain that the tragi-comedy had been thoroughly re-
hearsed. Witness asked Spurr whether the charge upon
which she was arrested was treason or felony. He replied
that he did not know: "he was only hired for a crown to
keep her." She was taken at ten o'clock forenoon, and it
was "not till near night" that her friends effected her rescue.

Pleasant Rawlins again recounted her sufferings at the
hands of the prisoners, whom she severally identified as the
persons responsible. "Mrs. Baynton said if I did not marry
her brother I must go to Newgate. I replied that I would
not marry without my friends' advice; but I was not so much
afraid of going to Newgate as I was of being murdered, or
sent away somewhere into the country, where I might never
see or hear of my friends." She then described the marriage,
and how she was forced by Baynton to undress and go to bed
at Blake's house.

When Pleasant had finished her sad story, his Lordship said: "Mrs. Baynton, it is now time for you to make your defence." "My Lord, I will," said the accused; adding with a laudable desire to preserve the purity of the witness's testimony: "Pray, my Lord, let her stand by herself a little, that nobody may speak to her." The cross-examination was directed to shew that from the first appearance of Swendsen, Pleasant set her cap at him, talked much of him to Mrs. Baynton, and was disappointed if he did not come to take his twelve-penny dinner at Mrs. Nightingale's—all which the witness steadfastly denied.

> *Baynton.* My Lord, Mr. Swendsen had a cold, and she told me she would not be easy till he was cured of it.
>
> *Witness.* I never said such a thing. How can you say so, Mrs. Baynton?
>
> *Baynton.* My life upon it; and I will not for my life say any thing but the truth.

Pleasant admitted that she had wished Mr. Swendsen a good wife, but not with reference to her own qualifications for the post. "Mrs. Baynton told me he was a very good-tempered gentleman and never out of humour"; wherefore she wished him, matrimonially, well. She swore that never once was she alone with Swendsen, and particularly that she did not often walk with him in the garden.

> *Baynton.* Pray, Mrs. Rawlins, did you not once come up to me and say you wished that you could see Mr. Swendsen, and that you could not be easy without his company?
>
> *Witness.* As I am upon my oath, I never said such a thing.
>
> *Baynton.* Mrs. Rawlins, did not you say a hundred times that you loved Mr. Swendsen above any man in the world?
>
> *Witness.* I never said any such thing in my life.

Pleasant swore that there was no truth in the alleged peeling of the walnuts; and that although she did in fact return to Mr. Pugh his letters, "it was upon things that we heard of Mr. Pugh that was not very handsome," and she had never mentioned the matter to Mrs. Baynton. As that lady became more violent in her manner and exceeded even the licence allowed to counsel in browbeating a witness, his Lordship intervened. "I pray, Mrs. Baynton," said he, "do not put yourself into a passion. I speak in favour to you; you will not deliver yourself so well in passion as without." But Mrs. Baynton had the last word: "She lay baiting of me night and day, and always speaking to me of her love to Mr. Swendsen. And to hear her speak the quite contrary, really it moves me, my Lord." Mrs. Baynton called, as her only witness, her maid Betty, who had been a witness for the prosecution in the previous trial. But as this damsel flatly denied everything put to her by her late mistress, that lady's defence was scantly benefited.

At this point the first jury, who had been considering their verdict in Swendsen's case for three hours—from which we may estimate the time occupied by these trials—returned to court, the Foreman intimating that they were agreed. Whereupon one of their number, Erasmus Johnson, described as a Dane (it was probably he who had acted as interpreter), said that he differed in one respect from his brethren:—

*Johnson.* If it shall please you, my Lord, I am not satisfied. I do not find from any of the evidence that hath been given that he [Swendsen] was privy to the arrest. My conscience will not let me comply with the rest that he is guilty.

*L.C.J.* What kind of a conscience have you? Do you not believe what the witnesses have said? Have you any evidence that Mrs. Rawlins went away with her own consent?

*Johnson.* I do not find, my Lord, that it was done by him.

*L.C.J.* Did he not go to Hartwell's house, and from thence, while she was under force, went with her to the Vine tavern, where he married her? which was a forcibly taking by him.

*Johnson.* But, my Lord, it was with her consent; else how could he marry her?

*L.C.J.* Though she did consent to the marriage, yet if she was taken by force it is the same offence.

The Foreman said it was agreed to be a point of law, which should be left to his Lordship; who thereupon advised the dissident juryman to "govern himself by reason"—in his case, a counsel of perfection. But Johnson, explaining that his objection was "merely out of a tender conscience," continues to argue the point with the Judge throughout two closely printed columns of the report, until he finally re-marked: "I can say no more. I must agree with the rest." So Swendsen was found guilty, unanimously. One is familiar with this type of juryman—which is not confined to Denmark—who, whether from vanity or pig-headedness, loves to differ from his fellows, and causes to all concerned much unnecessary trouble. Here his Lordship's capacity to suffer fools gladly must have been sorely tried.

After this episode our indefatigable friend Mrs. Baynton returned to the charge and subjected the unhappy Pleasant to further badgering, but without appreciable result. Hartwell and Spurr had more regard for propriety and the time of the Court; they presented their respective cases in briefest compass. Hartwell maintained that he was instructed to take out the writs by Holt, who, it seems, had fled from justice; Spurr alleged that he only acted as assistant in the matter on Hartwell's instructions.

The Lord Chief Justice then proceeded to charge the jury, his summing up of the evidence being on much the same lines as in the previous case. He directed them to acquit Spurr for lack of proof. "But as to Mrs. Baynton and Hart-well," observed his Lordship in conclusion, "if they are privy to the design of a forcibly taking away of Mrs. Rawlins with an intent to marry her to Swendsen, as it is plain that he was an actor and she abettor in the force, then, gentlemen, you are to find them both guilty. If you are not satisfied, you are to acquit them." The jury, after an absence of half an hour, returned the following verdicts: Baynton, Guilty; Hartwell, Not Guilty; Spurr, Not Guilty. "You have had a very merciful jury," said his Lordship, in discharging Hartwell. "Let it be a warning to you for the future." But the last word was, as usual, with the fair defendant:—

*Baynton.* My Lord, I am with child.
*L.C.J.* That will be considered on Saturday.

The Court then rose. One recalls a similar plea in arrest of judgment made in behalf of Katharine Nairn or Ogilvy, convicted in 1765 at the High Court, Edinburgh, of the murder of her husband. See also the case of Black Moll, cited by Mr. Peachum in *The Beggar's Opera*, of whom that specialist remarks: "Why, she may plead her Belly at worst; to my Knowledge she hath taken care of that Security." It is always well to be prepared for the worst.

## IV

On Saturday, 28th November, the prisoners were brought up for sentence. "My Lord," said Swendsen, "my trial has already made a great noise in the world, and I do not know but that by this time it may be come to the Queen's ear. Therefore I desire that your Lordship would be pleased to make a favourable construction of it to her." "Well," replied the Lord Chief Justice, "I do not question but Her Majesty hath heard of it.—Crier, make an O Yes while judgment is given." Mr. Justice Powell then pronounced sentence of death upon both prisoners.

> *Swendsen.* My Lord, now I am bound to do this woman justice. She hath not been the contriver of it. It was all done by my direction; and for her sake I desire the Queen may know of it.
> *L.C.J.* Well, that will clear up the doubt to some of your countrymen, who did think you were not the contriver of it.

One wonders whether Johnson, the Dane with the tender conscience, felt the force of his Lordship's observation.

It is recorded of Mrs. Baynton that "upon the hearing of her sentence she fell into fits." In view of her plea, a Jury of Matrons was summoned forthwith, and being duly sworn "to view and diligently inquire and a true verdict give according to your evidence, whether Sarah Baynton be with child, quick with child, or not," after concluding their scientific investigation in private, they returned to court within half an hour, and by the mouth of their Forewoman found and declared the prisoner to be quick with child. Addressing the prisoner, his Lordship said: "Hark ye, Mrs. Baynton.

These women by their verdict give you longer time to prepare you for death, and therefore I hope you will improve your time. For the judgment remains the same, and will be executed soon after your delivery." Notwithstanding this dread pronouncement, Sarah Baynton's sentence, respited in consequence of her being *enceinte*, was afterwards reprieved. It is hoped that she took to heart her lesson and amended in future her manner of life.

On 9th December, Haagen Swendsen paid at Tyburn Tree the extreme penalty of his offence. Thus was vindicated the ruthless justice of those bad old days. Contrary to the custom of the time he made no dying speech at the gallows; but he left in the hands of the two divines by whom he was attended a paper, in which he admitted that he had conspired to make Pleasant Rawlins his wife, but still maintained that she was a consenting party to the marriage. It is interesting to note that in this posthumous protestation the condemned man takes occasion indignantly to assert the falseness of divers current aspersions upon his moral character, to wit, that Mrs. Baynton was his mistress and that he already had two children by her, as well as being responsible for that to which she owed her life. The only load on his conscience was, he averred, her death, of which he acknowledged himself to be the unhappy instrument. But that burden had, as we have seen, been lightened by the Queen's clemency.

A further source of his expressed vexation was this: "I expected," he writes, "my trial should be published, that the world might see my treatment: what I have done and what I have left undone in my case; but I am informed it may not be printed." Here also he was grieved without just cause; for, as I have said, an excellent report of the proceedings in which he played his part was issued in due course, and in the fulness of time was incorporated in the fourteenth volume of the *State Trials*, becoming thereby assured of permanent fame. Nay more; the late Peter Burke, of the Inner Temple, Barrister-at-Law, that admirable author of studies in old crime, has, under the title of "The Abduction of Mrs. Pleasant

Rawlins," treated of the case in his *Celebrated Trials connected with the Upper Classes of Society, in the Relations of Private Life* (London: 1851). And I, even I also, have here done my modest bit to help keep green the memory of Mr. Swendsen's achievement.

As for poor Pleasant Rawlins, her plight was indeed peculiar. Not only was she what is picturesquely known as a hempen widow, but the circumstances attending her bereavement were exceptionally painful. Let us hope that her old flame Mr. Pugh did, after all, do the handsome thing despite his former failure, and gave her a further and less perturbing experience of matrimony.

# THE ORDEAL OF PHILIP STANFIELD

# THE ORDEAL OF PHILIP STANFIELD

In a secret Murther, if the dead carkasse be at any time thereafter handled by the Murtherer, it will gush out of blood; as if the blood were crying to Heaven for revenge of the Murtherer.

KING JAMES THE SIXTH: *Daemonologie*.

AS one of the few parricides recorded in Scottish criminal annals, and the last person convicted in that country upon the ancient ordeal of *Bahr-recht* or Law of the Bier—the bleeding of the slain corpse at the murderer's touch—Philip Stanfield has attained some eminence of infamy. He has pointed a moral for Wodrow and furnished footnotes for Sir Walter Scott, who doubted the evidence of his guilt. He has his part in Howell's dismal repertory. More recently he has adorned a tale by Mr. S. R. Crockett, in which he plays the villain for the circulating libraries at some sacrifice of truth, and, despite an undeniable gibbet and dismemberment, continues by the author's favour his criminous career. The contemporary report of his trial at Edinburgh in 1688 is appreciated by the bibliophile, but to the general reader the facts of his strange story are unknown. It is a tragedy of old years of blood and superstition; grim, indeed, but with here and there quaint glimpses of the ghostly marvellous, wherein we perceive malice domestic incite to midnight murder, and in the end the guilty designated by the manifest finger of God.

Philip Stanfield—the name is variously given as Stansfield, Standsfield, and Stamfield—was the eldest son of Sir James Stanfield of New Mills, in East Lothian. A Yorkshireman by birth, the elder Stanfield is said to have held the rank of colonel on the Parliamentary side in the Civil War. He settled in Scotland after Cromwell's victory at Dunbar, having purchased certain lands lying on the south bank of the river Tyne, a mile east of Haddington, formerly belonging to the local abbey. There he established a cloth manufactory upon the site, some thirty years earlier, of a similar undertaking. Colonel Stanfield's enterprise enjoyed the patronage of the Protector, and after the Restoration he was further encouraged by divers privileges granted to him by the Scots Parliament. Later he received from Charles II a knighthood, presumably in recognition of his mercantile rather than his military achievements. In 1681, with the approval of James, Duke of York, then resident in Scotland, proposals were made for establishing a cloth manufacturing company on a large scale, to compete with the English industry. Among the promoters of this patriotic scheme was Sir James Stanfield, and from him the new company acquired upon liberal terms a lease of "that great manufactory stone house on the south side of the village of Newmylnes," with the offices thereof, "which are many, great, and spacious."

At this time Sir James was a wealthy man. The cloth manufactory had prospered, and we learn from the decisions of the Lords of Session that in addition to his estate of New Mills he owned other lands at Hailes and Morham in the same county. But he was more blessed in his business than in his home. Lady Stanfield was no ideal helpmate, while Philip, his son and heir, was a prince of prodigals. Sir James complained to his friends that "he had no comfort in his wife and family," whom he described as "very wicked," observing that it was "sad that a man should be destroyed by his own bowels." His chief cause of anxiety was the conduct of his elder son, of whose misdeeds a lurid account is given in the indictment upon which Philip was convicted of the murder of his long-suffering sire. Apart from that catalogue of iniquities we know little of Philip's youth, but an anecdote preserved by Wodrow shows him to have been a student of St. Andrews University. While at that seat of learning, he one day attended the preaching of John Welsh, the great-grandson of Knox, and, disliking his doctrine, "threw somewhat or other at the minister, which hit him." Mr. Welsh promptly prophesied that "there would be more present at his [Philip's] death than were hearing him preach that day." This retort seems to have been a favourite one with outraged prophets. Similar predictions are recorded of Captain Porteous and others, the seers being justified by the event.

It is stated in the indictment that, notwithstanding the advantages of an excellent education, Philip, "being a profligate and debauched person, did commit and was accessory to several notorious villainies both at home and abroad." He had, it is said, "entered a souldier in the Scots Regiment," but most of his time was spent in retirement in the Marshalsea and the public prisons of Brussels, Antwerp, Orleans, and other places on the Continent. At Treves he was condemned to death, but managed to escape. From these retreats he was time and again released by his father's liberality; but so far from exhibiting either gratitude or sign of amendment, it was his habit "most wickedly and bitterly to rail upon, abuse, and curse his natural and kindly parent," and on two occasions he actually attempted his father's life. On the first of these he "did chase and pursue his father upon the King's highway at Lothian-burn, and did fire pistols upon him"; on the second he "did attempt to assassinate his father for his life at Culterallors," by similar methods.

Some years before the murder, Philip, married, was living with his wife at the house of New Mills, as appears from a case reported by Lord Fountainhall, a contemporary judge. In 1682 an action was raised in the Court of Session by an Edinburgh merchant against Philip, for payment of £1100 Scots for clothes "taken off" by himself and his wife in two years' time. Sir James was also called as defender on the ground that although his son was major and married at the time of the furnishing, yet the young couple were then living *in familia* with him, and had no separate estate, so that he was bound to clothe and aliment them. The Lords decerned against Philip, but assoilzied (discharged) the father, "because he made it appear that he had paid 5000 merks of debts contracted by Philip during that very space, and that his son was a prodigal waster."

Sir James, finding his pecuniary affairs embarrassed by the unnatural encroachments of his family, proposed, in 1686, to sell "the houses and lands of Newmilns" to the cloth company. The negotiations were interrupted by his death in the following year, but were shortly thereafter completed. Meanwhile he had decided to disinherit the peccant Philip in favour of John, his second son. But Jacob, of whom "he had some comfortable hopes," was little less unsatisfactory than Esau, and "several times came in drunk as the other."

In this unhappy situation it is not surprising that Sir James at times exhibited a certain lowness of spirits, which the wicked Philip artfully attributed to mental derangement. So far, however, from being driven mad by his troubles, it appears that Sir James bore his afflictions with fortitude, and though he suffered in mind, body, and estate, his reason was unimpaired.

Matters reached a crisis in November, 1687. On Saturday the 27th of that month Sir James Stanfield rode into Edinburgh for the last time, and having transacted his business there, returned in the evening to his house of New Mills, accompanied by a friend, one John Bell, "minister of the Gospel, aged 40 years," who was to occupy the pulpit of the neighbouring church at Morham next day. This divine was probably Mr. John Bell, parish minister of Gladsmuir, the learned contemporary author of certain treatises on witchcraft. They supped together after their long ride, and, according to Mr. Bell, Sir James's discourse was rational and pertinent, both before and after supper. At ten o'clock Sir James, having conducted his guest to his chamber, went to bed. The minister's experiences of the night must be described in his own words: "I declare that having slept but little, I was awakened in fear by a cry (as I supposed), and being waking, I heard for a time a great dinn and confused noise of several voices, and persons sometimes walking, which affrighted me (supposing them to be evil wicked spirits); and I apprehended the voices to be near the chamber-door sometimes, or in the transe [passage] or stairs, and sometimes below, which put me to arise in the night and bolt the chamber-door further,

and to recommend myself by prayer, for protection and pre-
servation, to the majestie of God; And having gone again to
bed I heard these voices continue, but more laigh [low], till
within a little time they came about to the chamber-window;
and then I heard the voice as high as before, which increased
my fear, and made me rise again to look over the window,
to see whether they were men or women; but the window
would not come up for me, which window looked to the
garden and water, whither the voices went on till I heard
them no more; only towards the morning I heard walking
on the stairs, and in the transe above that chamber where I
was lying. I told the woman who put on my fire in my
chamber that Sabbath morning that I had rested little that
night, through dinn I heard; and that I was sure there were
evil spirits about that house that night."

Next morning Sir James Stanfield was missing. The maid-
servant found his bed "better spread up than it used to be,
and the curtains more drawn about it."

Some distance behind the house of New Mills the river
Tyne flowed beneath a steep bank upon the south. Early
that Sunday morning a stranger named John Topping, going
from Monkrig to the village by the waterside, saw Philip
standing "at the brink of the brae," his eyes fixed upon the
body of a man floating in the pool below. Topping asked
whose body was in the water, but received no reply; when
he came to New Mills he learned the answer to his question.
About an hour after daybreak Philip entered the minister's
chamber and inquired if he had seen his father that morning,
adding that he himself had been seeking him by the banks of
the water. Mr. Bell "having gone without the gate and up
the cawsey that leads to the manufactory, one came running
and said they had found Sir James in the water." The minister then left to perform his Sabbath duties at Morham,
remarking, "If the majestie of God did ever permit the Devil
and his instruments to do an honest man wrong, then Sir
James Stanfield has received wrong this last night, which the
Lord will discover in His good time."

Umphray Spurway, the manager of the cloth mills, was a fellow-countryman of Sir James. Their relationship was intimate and friendly, and Umphray was often consulted by Stanfield in his unhappy domestic troubles. Apprised of his master's disappearance, he was leaving the mills to go up to the great house when he encountered Philip. The latter expressed wonder at the cause of his father's "discontent, that he should thus leave his lodgings"; whereupon Umphray plainly told him that in his view his (Stanfield's) family were responsible for what had happened. The search was then begun, and presently Sir James's body was discovered floating, face downwards, among the ice in a pool of still water some five feet deep, "a little by-west the town [village]." It was observed at the time that the ground at the water's edge nearest the body was "all beaten to mash with feet and the ground very open and mellow, although a very hard, frosty morning." When the dead man was carried by his servants to his own house, Philip met the bearers in the doorway, and "swore that the body should not enter there, for he had not died like a man but like a beast." It was accordingly deposited in an outhouse.

"The presumptions here were very pregnant against Philip," says Fountainhall, "for though other children in such dubious cases do ever ascribe their father's death to murder, yet he, being asked his opinion, asserted he thought he was not murdered, but rather took pains to persuade all that he was *felo de se* and his own executioner."

Philip's expressed opinion that Sir James had taken his own life was at first generally shared. Within an hour of the recovery of the body, the son ransacked his father's repositories, secured his valuables, and, appropriately enough in the circumstances, removed the silver buckles from the dead man's shoes and put them on his own.

When Mr. Bell returned to New Mills on the Sunday evening, he was informed by Philip that he had advertised several friends in Edinburgh of what had happened, and was expecting their arrival that night. The minister commended his prudence, deeming it highly desirable that the body should be "sighted" by the physician and friends of the deceased, for, from his midnight experiences, he was inclined to think it not a case of suicide, but "a violent murder committed by wicked spirits." In the morning he found to his astonishment that by Philip's orders the body had been secretly buried in the night. "They had very hastily buried him," says Fountainhall, "pretending that they would not have his body to be gazed upon and viewed by all comers."

Meanwhile "the fame of the country did run" that Sir James had been strangled by his son or servants, and Umphray Spurway, suspecting that all was not right, had, through a friend in Edinburgh, communicated with the Lord Advocate, Sir John Dalrymple (afterwards the first Earl of Stair). His lordship replied by letter, recommending that the body be viewed by Spurway, "along with two or three discreet persons," and if they saw no reason to suppose Sir James had met with foul play, that it should then be buried "privately and with as little noise as could be." When the messenger returned on the Sunday night, however, he was intercepted by Philip, who suppressed the letter.

At three o'clock on the Monday morning Umphray Spurway was awakened, and looking out from his own house at the mills saw horses and "great lights" about Sir James's gate. He arose, and going down to ascertain the cause met one of his men, who told him that Philip, "having received orders from my Lord Advocate for that purpose," was taking the body for interment to Morham churchyard. Umphray did not offer to join the funeral convoy to the lonely burial-place on the Lammermuirs some three miles off, where, in the black winter night, lit only by the torches of the murderer and his satellites, a grave was hastily dug in the frost-bound earth. He prudently went back to bed; but next day "the Englishmen in the manufactory, who were acquainted with the Crowner Laws, made a mutiny anent the burial."

On the following night Spurway was again aroused from sleep, and found at his door two Edinburgh surgeons, named

Crawford and Muirhead, and three other gentlemen from the city (one being Mr. James Row, a relative of the deceased), who exhibited an order from the Lord Advocate for the exhumation of Sir James Stanfield's corpse. He accompanied them to the churchyard forthwith. Mr. Andrew Melvil, minister of the parish, with whose services Philip on the former occasion had dispensed, attended in his official capacity. Sir James's brief rest was broken, and the body was carried into the church, where the surgeons conducted their examination by torchlight. Philip himself was present, how unwillingly and with what feelings may be imagined.

The autopsy concluded, the surgeons requested the relatives to assist in replacing the body in the coffin. It afterwards appeared from Sir George Mackenzie's address to the jury that this was done deliberately, with a view of subjecting Philip to the ordeal by touch. In accordance with the Scots custom the son lifted his father's head, but no sooner had he done so than the horrified onlookers "did see it darting out blood through the linen from the left side of the neck which the pannel [prisoner] touched." Philip, astounded, let the head fall with a loud crash upon the "furm" [bench], staggered back, wiping his bloody hands upon his clothes, and crying lamentably upon his Maker for mercy, fell fainting across a seat. The watchers, "amazed at the sight," looked at one another in awe. They had witnessed the immediate interference of the Deity—"God's revenge against murder."

In due course Philip Stanfield was arrested and brought to justice. His trial took place before the High Court of Justiciary at Edinburgh upon 6th, 7th, and 8th February 1688. George, Earl of Linlithgow, Lord Justice-General, presided, the other judges being Sir John Lockhart, Lord Castlehill; Sir David Balfour, Lord Forret; Sir Roger Hogg, Lord Harcarse; and John Murray, Lord Drumcairne. The prosecution was conducted by Lord Advocate Dalrymple and Sir George Mackenzie, the "Bloody Mackenzie" of Presbyterian tradition. Dalrymple had succeeded Mackenzie in the office of Lord Advocate a year before; within a month the political whirligig was again to bring about a similar exchange of parts. Sir David Thoirs, Sir Patrick Hume, William Moniepenny, and William Dundas appeared for the defence. The usual debate upon the relevancy of the libel, the formidable and unwieldy indictment of former times, setting forth at portentous length all (and sometimes more than) the Crown expected to prove, occupied the first day. Stripped of the cumbrous verbiage of their "qualifications," the crimes charged were three in number—(1) high treason, as having drunk confusion to the King; (2) cursing of parents; and (3) murder under trust, each of which was at that date equally punishable by death. The copious arguments of counsel were, according to the old practice, reduced to writing and are printed in the trial. We cannot here enter these learned labyrinths, abounding in quaint subtleties and citations from Carpzovius, Mattheus, and other ancient jurists. Fountainhall, who gives a curious abridgment of the pleadings, observes, "It was alleged, against the parricide, that the presumptions libelled were not relevant, such as his [Philip's] preceding threats, his hasty burying of him, the corps bleeding when he touched them, . . . and that his [Sir James's] murder might be ascribed to other causes, seeing it is notour [publicly known] that he was once mad, and that it can be proven that he was once melancholy and hypochondriac thereafter, and that he used to tell himself that in one of these fits he rode towards England with a design never to have returned, but his horse stopped and would not go forward, which he looked upon as the finger of God, and returned home again; that once he was throwing himself out at a window at the Nether Bow if Thomas Lendall had not pulled him in by the feet; and that the very week before his death he desired George Stirling to let blood of him because his head was light." The Lords, however, found the libel relevant, and repelled all the defences.

Next day a jury was empanelled, and the prosecutor adduced his proof. The charge of treason need not detain us. It was proved that Philip, in the kitchen of New Mills, had proposed to five persons the comprehensive toast of confusion to the

Pope, Antichrist, the Devil, and the King, "and did menace the witnesses with a great Kane that he would beat and brain them if they told it." The cursing of his father upon many occasions was fully established. For instance, Sir James's own servant deponed that, when asked to come to dinner with his father, Philip's ordinary answer was, "The Devil damn him and you both, and the Devil rive him, for I will not go to him, and if he [Philip] had a sixpence a day he would not go near him, for his father girned upon him like a sheep's head in a tongs." On another occasion, Philip having obtained some tobacco from a shop in the village without paying for it, the vendor hinted that Sir James might do so; whereupon Philip rudely retorted, "The Devil take him and his father both, for there never came an honest man out of Yorkshire" —a graceful allusion to his parent's original domicile.

With regard to the cause of Sir James's death, Mr. James Muirhead, one of the surgeons who made the post-mortem, was examined, but, curiously enough, only as to the miraculous bleeding of the corpse. The joint medical report stated that there was upon the neck "a large and conspicuous swelling, about three inches broad, of a dark red or blae colour, from one side of the larynx round backwards to the other side thereof," which, on incision, was found to be full of bruised blood. The neck was dislocated. Otherwise the body presented a healthy appearance, and was entirely free from water. Mr. Muirhead deponed that when he and the other surgeon were "putting on the clean linens and stirring and moving the head and craig [neck], he saw no blood at all." There were also produced for the Crown separate reports of the Chirurgeons of Edinburgh and the College of Physicians, based on the post-mortem appearances as reported, to the effect that strangulation, not drowning, was the cause of death.

It was proved that father and son were upon the worst of terms; that Philip had repeatedly threatened to take his father's life if he were disinherited in favour of his brother, "though he should die in the Grass Mercat for it," *i.e.* on the gallows; and that Sir James went in great fear of him, having twice narrowly escaped assassination at his hands. Mr. Roderick Mackenzie, an Edinburgh advocate and the old gentleman's friend, deponed that he met him in the Parliament Close eight days before his death, when "the defunct invited him to take his morning draught." While enjoying their "meridian" in an adjacent tavern, they discussed the unhappy situation of Sir James's domestic affairs. Mr. Mackenzie hinted that he had heard this was partly due to the disinheriting of the heir. "The defunct answered, 'Ye do not know my son, for he is the greatest debauch in the earth; and that which troubles me most is that he twice attempted my own person.'"

It further appeared that within a month of his father's death Philip had several times boasted that he would be "laird of all before Christmas," and would then "ride in their skirts that had been ill to him"; also that during this same period Lady Stanfield, being sick, said to him: "You will shortly want your mother, which will be a gentle visitation to Sir James," when Philip rejoined, "By my soul, mother, my father shall be dead before you!"

Lady Stanfield herself was not free from the dreadful suspicion of having been accessory to her husband's murder. That the relations between husband and wife were most unhappy, and that in the family quarrels she espoused the cause of her prodigal son, was clearly proved. Fountainhall records that "the mother had the dead-clothes all ready," that is, before the occasion for their use arose. "Some alleged that she was concerned in the murder"; and he adds an even more shocking accusation. In the opinion of Sir Walter Scott some countenance is afforded to these horrible rumours by the evidence given at the trial.

The manner of the murder, according to the prosecution, was in this wise. Philip, though young in years, was "old in—everything else." A married man, as we have seen, he carried on an intrigue with one "Janet Johnstoun, spouse to John Nicols," who lived in the village of New Mills. With the aid of this woman and of two other profligate companions,

George Thomson, significantly named "The Devil's Taylour," and Helen Dickson his wife, Philip was alleged to have compassed his father's death, producing incidentally those manifestations which caused the minister's "affrightment in the night." These three accomplices, we learn from Fountainhall, had been examined before the Privy Council on 8th December, "and tortured with the thumbikins but confessed nothing; which criminal lawyers say does purge and elide, at least debilitates and extenuates, all the former *indicia* and presumptions against themselves, if not those also which militated against others." For this reason they were not produced upon the trial, either in the witness-box or, more suitably, at the bar. The servants at New Mills had also been "questioned" regarding their knowledge of the facts in the practical manner of the Crown authorities of that day, for we find that on 13th December "Sir James Stanfield's servants are tortured," apparently with negative results, so far at least as their testimony was concerned.

It appeared from the proof that Janet Johnstoun and the Thomsons had been closeted with Philip in his chamber the night before the murder; that Janet, though a woman of infamous repute, "who was his own concubine and his father's known enemy," was alone entrusted by him with the duty of "woonding" (laying out) the old man's corpse; that she and Lady Stanfield quarrelled next day "about some remains of the holland of the woonding-sheet" (winding-sheet), when Philip bade his mistress hold her peace, "for he would reward her well for the kindness she had done to him at that time"; and that Thomson the tailor, bringing "the mournings" to the great house and learning that the body was to be raised, said it was the blackest news that ever he heard in his life, and "he would sew no more in the house of New Mylns for the world."

As these adminicles of evidence hardly went the length of sustaining a charge of murder, the Lord Advocate proposed to examine two children, James Thomson, son of "The Devil's Taylour," and Anna Mark, daughter of Janet Johnstoun, aged respectively thirteen and ten. In view of their tender years the Court refused to receive them as witnesses, but allowed their declarations to be taken "for clearing of the assize," which came to much the same thing. Their depositions are very interesting and full of curiously vivid touches, which a brief summary necessarily pretermits.

The boy Thomson deponed to the following effect: Philip and Janet came to his parents' house on the night of the murder between nine and ten. Drink was sent for, but as Philip had no small change "the ale was taken on upon trust." The boy, who had been beaten and sent to bed, heard Janet's daughter Anna call with a request for her mother to go home to nurse her child. He heard Philip say, "God damn his own soul if he should not make an end of his father, and then all would be his, and he would be kind to them." Philip and Janet went out about eleven, and shortly afterwards the boy's father and mother followed. In about two hours his mother returned alone and "came softly to bed." His father came in some time later, and called to him to know if he were awake, but he feigned to be asleep. The wife asked the husband, "What had stayed him?" and he replied, "That the deed was done; and that Philip Stanfield guarded the chamber door with a drawn sword and a bendet pistol, and that he never thought a man would have died so soon; and that they carried him out towards the waterside and tyed a stone about his neck." After some discussion, however, the murderers had thought it better to throw the body into the river without the stone, to produce the appearance of suicide. The boy added that, when his father received from Philip the coat and waistcoat found upon the body, his mother "was affrighted, for she thought that some evil spirit was in it"; and from that time she was afraid to be alone after nightfall.

The girl, Anna Mark, deponed that on the night in question Philip was at her mother's house, and sent her to see if Sir James had returned from Edinburgh. On learning that he had done so, Philip and her mother went out about eleven. Her "good-father" sent her to bring her mother back to nurse her child, and she found her with Philip at the Thomsons' house. Her mother, however, did not come home till about two in the morning, when Anna heard her "good-father" say, "Bitch and whore, where have ye been so long?" Her mother answered, "Wherever I have been, the deed is done!" and after that she heard them speak softly together, "but could not know what they said." Since that night Janet, like Mrs. Thomson, "was feared, and would not bide alone," a peculiarity also exhibited by Philip after his father's death.

The testimony of these two children concluded the evidence for the Crown; but Fountainhall states that the prosecution had certain affidavits from London, not mentioned in the report of the trial, "being the oaths of the keepers of the prisons where Philip, the pannel [prisoner], had lain, who deponed that he often cursed his father for not relieving him and boasted that if he were out he should dispatch him; and that one Betty Dolbry, being with child to him [Philip], had followed him to Scotland and might possibly be on the plot; but this was not produced to the assize."

No witnesses were adduced for the defence. Indeed, as appears from Sir George Mackenzie's address to the jury, the prisoner's counsel took the unprofessional course of throwing up their brief before half of the evidence for the prosecution had been led. The case for the defence, as disclosed upon the pleadings, was that Sir James had committed suicide "in a frainzie or melancholy fit," to which he was alleged to be subject. But even if he were in fact suffering from depression, it is, as Sir George pointed out, hard to believe that "after he had strangled himself and broke his own neck, he drown'd himself." No proof was offered in support of the allegations of his previous insanity and attempted suicide.

It is very rarely that one finds the addresses of counsel to the jury reported in a Scottish criminal trial even of a hundred years later, but here we have a full and excellent report of Sir George Mackenzie's speech for the Crown, probably a unique example of his forensic oratory, at which we can now only glance. "You will discern," said he, "the finger of God in all the steps of this probation as evidently as Philip's guilt; and this extraordinary discovery has been made as well to convince this wicked age that the world is governed by Divine Providence, as that he is guilty of this murder." The motive alleged was Philip's desire to prevent delivery of the disposition or conveyance of his property made by Sir James in favour of his younger son, "after which settlement Philip could gain nothing but the gallows by killing his father." Sir George noted in passing the affinity between the two crimes first libelled: "for to pray confusion to the King, who is *pater patriae*, is a cursing of our great parent"; and, dealing with Philip's former attempts upon his father's life, he described that "innocent and obliging Gentleman" as flying from his unnatural offspring like "a trembling Partridge pursued by a Haulk." The charge of treason was not pressed, but the learned counsel made the most of his trump card, the miraculous bleeding of the body, whereby "the Divine Majesty, who loves to see just things done in a legal way, furnished a full probation in an extraordinary manner." Therein, said he, "God Almighty himself was pleased to bear a share of the testimonies which we produce: that Divine Power which makes the blood circulate during life, has oftimes in all nations opened a passage to it after death upon such occasions." And this was specially remarkable in the present case, where the incision had been carefully bound up, and the body "designedly shaken up and down," having been some time buried, "which naturally occasions the blood to congeal"; yet at the murderer's touch the blood "darted and sprung out, to the great astonishment of the chirurgeons themselves, *who were desired to watch the event.*" Then, with regard to the hardly less marvellous discovery "by the mouths of babes and sucklings," Sir George observed, "If you had seen this little boy upon his knees begging his father to confess with so much affection, so much judgment, so much piety, you had needed no other probation." This refers to the confronting of the wicked parents with their accusing children before the Privy Council. The peroration is as follows: "If, then, such amongst you as are Fathers would not wish to be murdered by your own children, or such of you as are Sons would not wish the World to believe that you are weary of your Fathers, you will all concur to find this miscreant guilty of a crime that God has taken so much pains to detect and all mankind has reason to wish to be punished. May the Almighty God, who formed your hearts, convince them; and may this poor Nation cite you as the remarkable curbers of vice to all succeeding ages."

At the conclusion of Sir George's address, the Lord Advocate, to "mak sicker," protested for "an Assize of Error against the Inquest in case they should assoilzie the Pannel"; which, being interpreted, meant that if the jury so far forgot themselves as to acquit the prisoner they would be fined and imprisoned for the wilful error of absolving him against clear evidence! The jury, however, on 8th February, unanimously returned a verdict of guilty of the first and second, and art and part of the third charges libelled, and the Court pronounced sentence of death in the horrible form applicable to his crimes.

As to the ultimate fate of Janet Johnstoun and of "The Devil's Taylour" and his wicked wife, history is silent; but in Mr. Crockett's robustious pages a brilliant future awaited Janet as the wife of the Spanish governor of the Isle of San Juan de Puerto Rico.

"The 15th being come and the gallows and scaffold ready," says Fountainhall, Philip Stanfield "was reprieved for eight days longer by the Chancellor at the priest's desire. He craved by a bill that those already tortured for his father's murder might be re-examined. This he thought would clear him on their reiterated denial; but the Counsel refused it, lest it should harden him." The Lord Chancellor was James Drummond, Earl of Perth, who had adopted the faith of his sovereign, James the Seventh. Fountainhall adds that Philip "had tampered with the Popish priests and professed himself to be of their religion, hoping thereby to get his life"; but finding this move unsuccessful, he returned to the Presbyterian fold.

On the 24th the sentence was duly carried out. At the Cross of Edinburgh Philip Stanfield was hanged upon a gibbet. The tongue wherewith he had cursed his "natural and kindly parent" was cut out and burned upon the scaffold; the right hand raised by him against his father's life was cut off and affixed to the East Port of Haddington, "as nearest to the place of the murder"; his dead body was hung in chains at the Gallow Lee, between Edinburgh and Leith; his name, fame, memory, and honours were ordained to be extinct; his arms were riven furth and delete out of the book of arms, and all his goods and gear were forfeited "to our Sovereign Lord, to remain perpetuallie with his Highness in property."

He maintained to the last his complete innocence of the old man's blood, and "imprecated a judgment against himself if he was in the least guilty or in the foreknowledge of his father's death." Two incidents in connection with his execution and the fate of his remains were noted by the superstitious of the day. At his hanging the knot of the rope slipped, "whereby his feet and knees were on the scaffold (this I, Robert Mylne, Writer, saw with my own eyes) which necessitate the hangman to strangle him, bearing therein a near resemblance with his father's death." Application being made to the Privy Council, probably by Lady Stanfield, for permission to bury the body, "Duke Hamilton was for it, but the Chancellor would not consent, because he had mocked his religion." The recently converted Lord Chancellor evidently found Philip's taste in toasts offensive.

The body, as we have seen, was hung up in chains at the Gallow Lee, among those of other malefactors,

"Waving with the weather while their neck will hold."

It was, however, secretly taken down a few days afterwards and thrown into a neighbouring ditch, "among some water, as his father's corpse was." Once more the body was hung up by order of the authorities, but it was again mysteriously removed, "and no more heard thereof."

"This," concludes Fountainhall, whose account we have hitherto followed, "is a dark case of divination to be remitted to the great day, whether he was guilty or innocent. Only it is certain he was a bad youth, and may serve as a beacon to all profligate persons." But without seeking to anticipate that final finding, we may rest assured that Sir James Stanfield died by some hand other than his own, and that Philip, who clearly was *capable de tout*, was, in Braxfield's classic phrase, "nane the waur o' a hangin'."

The case of Philip Stanfield attracted the notice of Sir Walter Scott, who makes reference to it on several occasions. The earliest of these is in his private note-book, extracts from which are given by Lockhart, where, under date 15th March, 1797, he writes:—"Read Stanfield's trial, and the conviction appears very doubtful indeed. Surely no one could seriously believe, in 1688, that the body of the murdered bleeds at the touch of the murderer, and I see little else that directly touches Philip Stanfield. It was believed at the time that Lady Stanfield had a hand in the assassination or was at least privy to her son's plans; but I see nothing inconsistent with the old gentleman's having committed suicide." In later years, when Adolphus, who discovered the identity of the author of *Waverley* from his works, was visiting him at Abbotsford, Scott recommended his guest to read the trial, and lent him his own copy of the original folio for the purpose.

In his notes to "Earl Richard" in the *Minstrelsy*, Scott discusses the superstitious belief in the bleeding of the murdered corpse, and instances Stanfield's case as the last and leading example in Scotland. He also refers to the trial of Muir of Auchindrane, which took place in 1611, where a conviction was obtained by similar miraculous means, and of which he himself made a ballad, "Auchindrane, or the Ayrshire Tragedy," in 1830.

The last case of the kind in England reported in the *State Trials*, and one of the most remarkable instances of touching as a test for murder, is that arising out of the death of Joan Norkott in 1628, sixty years before the Stanfield affair. This woman was found dead in her bed with her throat cut, the knife with which the wound had been inflicted sticking in the floor, in a room within that occupied by her husband's mother, sister, and brother-in-law. At the inquest these persons declared that they had slept in the outer room that night, but heard and saw nothing amiss, and that no one could have entered the inner room without their knowledge. The coroner's jury accordingly returned a verdict of *felo de se.* In consequence of certain rumours, however, they afterwards desired that the body should be exhumed, which was done *thirty days after the death*, in presence of a curious crowd, including the three relatives above mentioned and the husband of the deceased, who had been absent on the night in question. All four were required to touch the corpse, "whereupon," in the words of Sergeant Maynard, who reports the case, "the brow of the dead, which before was of a livid and carrion colour, begun to have a dew or gentle sweat arise on it, which increased by degrees till the sweat ran down in drops on the face. The brow turned to a lively and fresh colour, and the deceased opened one of her eyes and shut it again; and this opening the eye was done three several times. She likewise thrust out the ring or marriage finger three times and pulled it in again, and the finger dropped blood from it on the grass."

These phenomena were attested by the minister of the parish and by his brother, who also was in holy orders. The former had dipped his finger in the supernatural fluid, and swore that it was blood.

The coroner's jury withdrew their former verdict. The four accused were duly tried at Hertford Assizes for the murder, and, against the expressed opinion of Judge Harvey, who tried the case, were acquitted. The miraculous wink was no better than an ordinary nod to so blind a jury. On appeal, the case was re-tried at the Bar of the King's Bench before Sir Nicholas Hyde, the Lord Chief Justice, when a less sceptical jury found the husband and his mother and sister guilty, but acquitted the brother-in-law. The two former were executed, but made no confession; the sister, owing to her condition, was reprieved.

The fact that the victim's neck was broken, as also was that of Sir James Stanfield, disposed of the suggestion of suicide; while apart from the bleeding of the corpse, "according to God's usual method of discovering murder," to quote Philip's indictment, the circumstantial evidence, as in his case, pointed plainly to the prisoners' guilt.

Echoes of the Stanfield case reverberated in the Parliament House for some years after the murder. On 22nd December, 1693, the children of one James Scott of Bristo "pursued" Sir James's creditors, who were in possession of his estates, upon an assignation of his share of the cloth manufactory granted to Scott by him on the day of his death. The deed, duly executed, was found lying on the table in Sir James's room, and directed to Scott, who called for it on the following day. Presumably it had escaped Philip's notice. The question being, Was there delivery of the document in a legal sense? the Lords thought this "a too nice and metaphysical tradition," and held that the deed was undelivered.

On 9th November, 1697, Sir James's creditors presented a petition to the Court, stating "that John Stanfield, his son and apparent heir, was *in lecto* dying and had the whole writs of the lands whereof they had raised a summons of sale, and there was hazard of his wife's putting them out of the way." The Lords, "this extraordinary case requiring haste," ordered the title deeds to be sealed up in the hands of the clerk of Court.

What became of John we are not told, but from the little we know of his habits it is probable that the illness was his last.

In 1713, on the winding up of the cloth company, its property was offered for public sale in various lots, and the lands of New Mills were purchased by the notorious Colonel Francis Charteris of evil memory, who changed the name to Amisfield, after his family seat in Nithsdale, which they still retain. Through him the estate passed in succession to the present owner, the Earl of Wemyss.

The stately mansion of the wicked Colonel has superseded Sir James Stanfield's old unhappy home, and the "great manufactory stone house, together with the walkmylne and dying house," even the busy village itself, are among the things that have been. Only the river is unchanged, and still the eddies circle in the quiet pool where Philip looked long upon his murdered father, that frosty winter morning two centuries ago.

## POSTSCRIPT

"World's End Close is the appropriate title of the last alley before we reach the site of the Nether Bow Port, which terminated of old the boundaries of the walled capital, and separated it from its courtly rival, the burgh of Canongate. In the earliest title deed we have seen connected with it, it is called Sir James Stanfield's Close. The name perpetuates that of an old resident once associated with a stranger mystery than that of the murdered Begbie. Sir James Stanfield of Newmills, whose death took place in 1687 under circumstances which excited great interest at the time, occupied the house at the head of the close looking into the main street."— Wilson's *Memorials of Edinburgh*.

The murder of Begbie, the bank-porter—one of Edinburgh's standard mysteries—took place in 1806 in the adjoining close, Tweeddale Court. I have dealt with the case in a chapter, "Mackcoull and The Begbie Mystery," of *The Riddle of the Ruthvens* (1919; new edition, revised, 1936).

For an admirable romance, based upon the facts of the Stanfield case, the interested reader should consult *Little Anna Mark*, by S. R. Crockett (1900).

# THE SHADOW ON SHANDY HALL;
## OR, "WHAT LOVE COSTS AN OLD MAN"

L

# THE SHADOW ON SHANDY HALL;
## OR, "WHAT LOVE COSTS AN OLD MAN"

Thou shalt not covet; thou shalt not cast an eye of desire; out of the heart proceed *murders*;—these dreadful realities shape themselves from so filmy a medium as thought!                              J. SHERIDAN LE FANU: *Wylder's Hand*.

ONLY once before in the course of my protracted literary pilgrimage have I ventured to cross the Irish Channel. Not that there is in Ireland an insufficiency of crime, for indeed the criminous harvest of the Emerald Isle is plenteous, but because, somehow or other, the crop did not appeal to me; so I have hitherto refrained, save in a single instance, from joining the labourers therein. The exception was a most attaching case, namely, the trial and conviction of William Burke Kirwan, for the murder of his wife by drowning, at the island quaintly known as Ireland's Eye, off Howth, in 1852.[1] It had long been with me a favourite, by reason of the strange and striking circumstances, the picturesque, unusual setting, and the curious characters of the chief actors in the tragedy. I know of no other murder that offers such peculiar attractions, and I hope and believe that I did justice to its many merits.

And now here is another Irish death-drama to which my attention has been drawn, providentially as I am in such matters apt to believe, by the acquisition of a full report of the affair, printed in the contemporary local Press. Often have I had occasion gratefully to admire the care and foresight of bygone collectors of newspaper cuttings, whereby my labours have been so agreeably lightened, and forgotten or otherwise unreported cases preserved for the benefit of the posterities. If I have done little else to earn my cake, I have at least done

---

[1] See "The Secret of Ireland's Eye," in my collection of cases *The Fatal Countess* (Edinburgh: 1924).

my best to carry on in this regard the good work. The blessed volume in question, a stalwart quarto, contains many interesting cases, including that of Mrs. Adelaide Bartlett, indicted for the poisoning of her spouse with chloroform, thereby establishing a toxicological record, a lady of whom I have elsewhere written.[1] It, the volume, bears upon the fly-leaf: "From the Library of Sir R. C. Tichborne, Bt." and is indexed and annotated by its former owner. I wish I could think that this was no less a person than The Claimant; the handwriting resembles his, and as he was released in 1884 and survived till 1898, it is not impossible. Be that as it may, the collector had a pretty taste in crime.

To my mind the pick of his basket is the trial of Dr. Cross, reported under the title of "The Coachford Poisoning Case," and illustrated by relative woodcuts and a photograph, of which there will be more to say. Unfortunately from my point of view, but not from the reader's, two earlier writers have already, in their different ways, given some account of the case—unfortunately, I say, because I like to work in virgin soil. First in the field was Dr. Leonard Parry, who deals with it in his book: *Some Famous Medical Trials* (1927). His account is adequate but necessarily brief, looking to the extent of ground he is otherwise called upon by his scheme to cover. The second is Miss Winifred Duke, who devotes to it the opening chapter of her admirable studies in crime: *Six Trials* (1934). As an experienced novelist she brings to her task those vivid gifts of characterization, atmospheric effect, and knowledge of human nature in its darker aspects, by which her fictions are so notably distinguished. Miss Duke has paid me the compliment of dedicating the book to me; to her, in small return, I would dedicate these impressions of the Cross case, which she has handled so fully and to such excellent purpose.

[1] " The Luck of Adelaide Bartlett," in *The Rebel Earl* (1926).

# I

I am drawn to Dr. Cross on account of his marked resemblance, in more respects than one, to my old acquaintance, Dr. Pritchard.   Each of these medical miscreants—the phrase is used by both the writers above mentioned—slew a devoted wife by slow poisoning, and in doing so was actuated by sexual motives.   Dr. Cross compassed his wife's death to enable him to marry his mistress, the governess of his own daughters.   Dr. Pritchard, having successfully seduced his children's nurse, had promised to marry her, if and when he became a widower—though I find it difficult to believe that so cunning a rogue would have contracted such a mésalliance. Anyhow, he certainly killed his long-suffering spouse with every circumstance of cruelty.   Each specialist employed, in the practice of his nefarious art, two poisons: Dr. Cross used arsenic and strychnine; Dr. Pritchard, antimony and aconite. Each treated the patient in his professional capacity, "nursed" her himself to the exclusion of skilled aid, and called in consultation a retired physician, who was, conveniently, a relative.   Each gave palpably false, misleading, and inconsistent descriptions of the nature of the illness, and signed mendacious death certificates.   But perhaps the most extraordinary parallel of all is the fact that each, upon the consummation of the crime, forthwith proceeded to enter in his diary, in similar shocking terms, a blasphemous and hypocritical prayer for the repose of the departed victim!   Both, needless to say, prided themselves above all things on their possession of that cardinal Victorian virtue : Respectability. Finally and satisfactorily, both were well and truly hanged.

It is surprising how these qualified slayers bungle their homicides.   Even I, in such matters a mere layman, if I wished to poison anybody, having studied so many relevant cases, could make, unless I flatter myself, a better job of it. But the incompetence of these skilled practitioners really passes belief, the inexpertness of the expert is inexplicable.

Dr. Lamson and his Dundee cake, flavoured with aconitine; Dr. Neill Cream, with his pink pills for pale prostitutes, the basis whereof was strychnine; Dr. Webster, Professor of Chemistry, who, despite his command of deadly drugs, preferred a bludgeon; Dr. Smith of St. Fergus, who, dispensing his own medicines, chose a pistol. Dr. Palmer, a wholesale poisoner, was content to confine himself to strychnine, Dr. Smethurst employed arsenic; both "household remedies," so far as concerns the gentle art of poisoning. Dr. Crippen, it is true, shewed more originality in administering hyoscine, but with the game in his hands, threw it away by bolting with his robust paramour "disguised" in a boy's ready-made suit! Well is it for their fellow-beings that relatively few members of the Faculty are found capable of attempting such crimes; still more, that those who essay them, by their rashness and stupidity, so often court detection.


## II

Philip Henry Eustace Cross, according to the obituary notice published after his accelerated departure from the scene of his activities, is said to have resembled his deceased father. "Both were ardent sportsmen, and their wild extravagance in this and other pastimes secured for them the reputation of being eccentric." Justly so, at least as regards the old gentleman, for when his will was read it was found to contain a clause bequeathing his body to the dogs and his soul to the Devil. His executor must have had difficulty in carrying out the testator's last wishes. As a lad preparing for his future profession, Philip Cross is described as of a very reckless disposition, and many tales were told of his pranks at the paternal abode, Shandy Hall, Dripsey, County Cork. A sketch of the house shews it an unpretentious dwelling of two storeys, standing amid trees in a garden, the front railings of which bordered the road to Coachford. No explanation is given of its attaching name, but doubtless it was built by an admirer of Sterne, who borrowed the nickname of the Cox-wold parsonage. "Though his father was no great stickler for the proprieties, it was quite a relief to him when Phil entered the army."

As Surgeon-Major Cross, he was for many years attached to the 53rd Regiment, and served in the Crimea, Canada, and other foreign stations. He does not appear to have been popular while in the army, although it is recorded that his courage was indomitable, and that with fearless bravery he repeatedly saved the lives of others at the peril of his own. In 1869, being then forty-five, Dr. Cross wooed and won, despite the opposition of her parents, a well-born and attractive young lady, eighteen years his junior, Miss Mary Laura Marriott, daughter of an English family of good social position. The couple were married in London on 17th August of that year, at St. James's Church, Piccadilly, and after a term of service overseas, the doctor retired, and they began their life partnership at Shandy Hall, some twelve miles from Cork. No settlement was made at the time of the marriage, and when the lady's father died in the 'seventies, Dr. Cross succeeded to her fortune of £5000. He occupied his time as a gentleman farmer, and, like Nimrod, was a mighty hunter. This led to trouble with the neighbouring farmers, and the doctor suffered the current local penalty of popular disapproval: boycotting. But he was not a man to take things lying down. Attacked with stones by roughs at a coursing meeting, he made such good use of his riding-whip —without which he seldom appeared in public—that his assailants were soon glad to beat a retreat. The Master of the 20th Hussars' hounds, with which he was wont to hunt, moved by agricultural threats, appealed to him to sacrifice his own pleasure rather than spoil the sport of his fellow-huntsmen; but the doctor refused to do so, and wrote to the Press, complaining that Her Majesty's officers aided and abetted blackguards who engaged in boycotting. As he persisted in hunting, whenever he put in an appearance at the meets, the hounds were drawn off and the hunt abandoned.

The episode, while confirmatory of his pluck and obstinacy, goes some way to explain the unfavourable feeling to which the state of his domestic affairs was later to give rise: it was the proverbial case of a dog with a bad name.

### III

At the time with which we are concerned the household at Shandy Hall consisted of Dr. Cross and his wife, their family of five, two sons and three daughters, the eldest being sixteen, and a staff of four servants. The boys were at an English school. Two of the girls were delicate, and in October 1886 Mrs. Cross decided to get for them a governess. Within two miles of Shandy Hall lived a Captain and Mrs. Caulfield who were parting with their children's governess, and on the 29th Mrs. Cross engaged her to come to the Hall in that capacity. The new inmate proved to be a beautiful and fascinating girl of twenty-one. She was cheerful, good-tempered, and most efficient in the performance of her duties. The whole family fell in love with her, and, as the phrase is, thought the world of her. With one exception: Dr. Cross was unaffected by the charms of the bewitching governess; he was sixty-four, had never been a ladies' man, and often expressed his aversion from what he termed "chattering females." So, for a time, everything went on smoothly in the doctor's house. But it was the calm that precedes a storm.

By what strange transformation the crusted misogynist became wildly enamoured of this young girl, and what attraction she found in his sexagenarian advances, we know no more than we do the siren's Christian name, which, oddly enough, was never mentioned at the trial: like that sinister governess Miss Jessel in *The Turn of the Screw*, she is always, simply, "Miss Skinner"; but the fact of their mutual infatuation is indisputable. Presently Mrs. Cross, observing the change in her husband's demeanour to the stranger within his gates, of whom at first he had taken no notice, spoke to him of his attentions. He resented her interference and denied that his interest in the girl was other than paternal. For three months the wife's suspicions continued to grow stronger, until finally she insisted that the governess should be dismissed, which despite the doctor's vigorous protests, greatly to the relief of Mrs. Cross, was done. The subject remained a sore one, and the domestic atmosphere was thundery.

In ordinary matters, as we have seen, Dr. Cross was not a man to be thwarted with impunity, and he now experienced the aggravation of an interrupted passion. Two things followed: his manner to his wife became harsh and threatening; he was heard to curse her and wish her in hell; and secretly he kept in touch with the banished fair one. In the spring of 1887, so often as opportunity could be had, they lived together as husband and wife, under a false name, at an hotel in Dublin. Miss Skinner had taken another situation at Carlow; Mrs. Cross kept her eye upon her husband's movements. In these circumstances the intrigue could only be carried on by means of constant vigilance, and involved the guilty pair in perpetual risk and worry. Dr. Cross perceived that something must be done to put an end to so discomfortable a state of things. How he proposed to remedy it will presently appear.

## IV

Mrs. Cross was a strong, healthy woman of forty-six. Dr. Cross and his sister—a lady who did not stick at trifles to save a brother's neck—represented her as having "a very delicate stomach," but there is no other evidence that her health was not quite good, or that she had ever been ill in her life. Suddenly, however, the unhappy woman was stricken by serious illness and developed most alarming symptoms. She complained of burning pain in her stomach, and was violently and continuously sick. Her husband alone attended her. At last, to save appearances, he called in a medical cousin, who obligingly concurred in the doctor's diagnosis: a bilious attack. To others Dr. Cross represented her case as one of heart disease.

Early in the morning of Thursday, 2nd June, Mrs. Cross, after a few weeks' illness, died in agony. Only her husband was present. He told a friend that "she died screaming." One of the maids was awakened by these terrible cries, which remind one of the three screams, heard across the water by certain witnesses, at the time that Mrs. Kirwan met her death on Ireland's Eye. Dr. Cross certified the death typhoid fever; and buried his wife with indecent haste at 6 a.m. on Saturday, the 4th. His conduct throughout and at the end of the illness caused, one is not surprised to hear, unfavourable comment in the district. When the echo of those last dreadful screams was scarce faded, the doctor, a man of method, proceeded to write up his diary. "Mary Laura Cross departed this life June 2nd. May she go to heaven, is my prayer. Buried 4th." [1] Such was the poor lady's epitaph. The bereaved husband gave her a five-guinea funeral. A fortnight later he married Miss Skinner.

The ceremony took place on 17th June, at St. James's Church, Piccadilly, where, you may remember, on 17th August 1869, his first marriage was celebrated. He seems to have liked the service. After a short and somewhat superfluous honeymoon, Dr. Cross brought his unblushing bride home to Shandy Hall, and installed her in the dead woman's room and place—not without further local comment. Their homecoming proved to be the last straw. The authorities took action, the body of the dead lady was exhumed, and an inquest was held. Analysis of the internal organs shewed the presence of arsenic and of strychnine; no vestige of food

---

[1] It is of interest to recall the terms of the entry before referred to, made by Dr. Pritchard in the same sad circumstances:—"March 1865. 18 Saturday. Died here at 1 a.m. Mary Jane, my own beloved wife, aged 38 years. No torment surrounded her bedside [oh, Dr. Pritchard!] but like a calm, peaceful lamb of God, passed Minnie away. May God and Jesus, Holy Gh., one in three, welcome Minnie. Prayer on prayer till mine be o'er; everlasting love. Save us, Lord, for Thy dear Son." Dr. Pritchard's style is more florid than that of his fellow-worker of iniquity, but their sentiments are similar.

was found in the stomach, nor were there any signs whatever either of heart trouble or of typhoid fever. It appeared that the patient had been slowly and regularly poisoned with arsenic, and the finishing stroke given with strychnine—which doubtless caused the characteristic screams heard at midnight by the maid. In these suggestive circumstances Dr. Cross, protesting his innocence of his wife's blood, was arrested and brought to trial.

## V

The trial of Dr. Cross for the alleged murder of his wife by poison began before Mr. Justice Murphy, presiding judge at the Munster Winter Assizes, on Wednesday, 14th December, 1887. Immense interest was taken in the proceedings; admission to the court was by ticket, and for such there were several thousand applications. Throughout the four days' hearing every available inch of space was occupied, a great number of "ladies," so-called, having secured seats. The Attorney-General (the Right Hon. John Gibson, M.P.), with George Wright, Q.C., and Stephen Ronan, conducted the prosecution. John Atkinson, Q.C. (later, as Lord Atkinson, a famous Lord of Appeal), assisted by Richard Adams, appeared for the defence. "Dr. Cross than entered the dock," says our reporter. "He looked nervous as he saw the crowded court facing him. In appearance he has little altered since the date of his committal last September. He wore the same spotted tweed suit as on that occasion. Around his neck hung loosely a long blue woollen scarf, and on his hands were black mittens." He pleaded Not Guilty to the charge.

The learned Attorney-General, in stating the case for the Crown, described the circumstances of the crime as painful and unusual. "If they [the jury] were satisfied of the prisoner's guilt, he was guilty of one of the most brutal and cowardly murders which had ever disgraced their common humanity." Counsel then outlined the facts, with some of which we are already familiar. The prisoner was a gentleman of means, residing at Shandy Hall. He had married many years ago a lady of good social position, Miss Mary Laura Marriott, a member of a well-known English family. The couple went to Canada with the 53rd Regiment, in which the accused was serving as Surgeon-Major. On their return to England they settled at Shandy Hall. Counsel then set forth the engagement of Miss Skinner as governess, who lived with them for three months from 29th October, 1886, until she left in circumstances which would be afterwards proved. She went to another situation at Carlow. The next they heard of her was on 27th March, 1887, occupying the same bedroom with Dr. Cross at the North-Western Hotel, Dublin. "Did this young lady come fortuitously from Carlow and throw herself at the prisoner's head? Was it the reckless act of a foolish girl brought by accident to town?" He would shew that from the time she entered Shandy Hall there was a marked change in the accused's demeanour to his wife. It would be for them to say whether this wicked intrigue did not begin in the prisoner's own house. A young girl did not sacrifice herself in a moment to a man of the accused's age: she must have been already his when they were found as married people at the hotel. On the 29th the couple disappeared for three weeks, turning up at Euston Station Hotel, London. On 21st April they revisited the Dublin hotel, where they stayed the night, Dr. Cross going home alone next morning.

Mrs. Cross was at this time in perfect health. On the 29th an old school friend, Miss Jefferson, came to Shandy Hall on a visit. This lady kept a diary, which was of the greatest importance from the Crown point of view, for in that diary was recorded the whole story of Mrs. Cross's illness, with all the symptoms of slow poisoning by arsenic, until the last flickering sparks of life were finally extinguished. She had no nurse; her husband was with her all the time. He remained alone with the dead body throughout the night, and in the morning announced to the maids, with callous levity, his loss: "Get up, girls; the Missis is gone since past one last night." Why had he not called his sister, why had he not called Miss Jefferson? Why give no explanation of the four minutes of screaming in the night? His wife was dead, and he certified her death as due to typhoid fever, the duration of her illness, fourteen days. She died at one o'clock in the morning of Thursday, 2nd June, and was buried at 6 a.m. on the 4th. Who were at her funeral? Only Cross, the husband and, as the Crown said, the murderer; Griffin, a publican; and the driver of the hearse. Dr. Cross wrote to his brother-in-law, Mr. Marriott, that he was going to England, to break the sad news to his two sons at school; he did go, but it was to rejoin his paramour and to make her mistress of Shandy Hall in place of the poor lady who was gone. To one brother-in-law he ascribed the death as due to heart disease; to another, typhoid fever. Counsel then referred to the entry in the diary, and to "the modest sum" expended on the funeral. Dr. Cross went to London on the 9th; stayed at Euston from the 10th to the 13th with an unidentified woman of whose identity they could have little doubt; and on the 17th married his mistress in the very church in which his first marriage was celebrated. On the 19th he took her back to the Dublin hotel, where they had cohabited in April, under the name of "Mr. and Mrs. Onslow." Why the false name? That was all very well when he was living there as an adulterer; but why should this husband and wife return "to the same shrine" under a false name? Again they parted; Dr. Cross went back to Coachford alone, and some days elapsed before Shandy Hall received its new mistress.

After reviewing at length the medical evidence to be called as to the finding of arsenic and strychnine in the body, and the absence of any sign of natural disease, counsel said it would be for the jury to say whether this woman's life was not destroyed by slow degrees with murderous doses, and whether that poison was not administered by the man in the dock. "He rushed frantically from the presence of the corpse to a woman much younger than himself, the partner in his crime." What killed his wife? was it heart disease, or typhoid, or was it poison administered by him? The case was divided into two parts: first, the history of the prisoner's house and his conduct during his wife's last fatal illness; and second, the actual proof of the cause of death, which would be laid before them. If they were satisfied of the accused's guilt, it surpassed in wickedness, brutality, and cowardice any crime that he (counsel) had ever heard of. "The husband murder his wife in his own house, the doctor murder his own patient, in order to fly back to the girl he had seduced and to put her in the place of the woman he had slain!" These formed a combination of circumstances without parallel. He was sure they would carefully consider the evidence and pronounce a verdict in accordance with it.

# VI

The first witness for the Crown was an old friend and neighbour, Mr. Colthurst, who stated that one day in the end of April he met Mrs. Cross in the fields near Coachford. She said she was quite well, and certainly seemed so. A week before she died Dr. Cross told witness he need not be surprised at any minute to hear that she was dead.

Mrs. Caulfield, an intimate friend of Mrs. Cross, described the engagement by her of Miss Skinner as governess. Witness called at Shandy Hall on 25th May. She found Mrs. Cross laid-up in bed. Captain Caulfield, who accompanied his wife, stated that during their visit the clergyman, Mr. Hayes, called to see the invalid. Dr. Cross's unchristian comment was: "Damn Hayes!" Both witnesses spoke to a curious incident which occurred the day after the doctor's return home from his honeymoon. Mrs. Caulfield had heard from the mother of her former governess that she was married to her late employer; so when the doctor called, she greeted him with the arresting question: "How is Mrs. Cross?"

Obviously taken aback, he tried to treat the matter as a joke. "Who is spreading these absurd rumours?" he asked Captain Caulfield. "There's no use in your denying it," replied the captain; "I know you are married," adding with greater significance than he then imagined: "*Murder will out!*"

The Rev. Richard Hayes stated that on 25th May he went to see Mrs. Cross. She was in bed, and seemed very weak and poorly. On the 30th he called again, but Dr. Cross would not let him see her, saying that she must be kept quiet. On the 31st he tried once more, but was prevented by Miss Cross from seeing the patient.

Miss Caroline Kirchoffer stated that she lived at Dripsey and was a close friend of the deceased. She saw her in bed on 25th May. She looked very ill and said she was suffering from diarrhœa. "Phil tells me I have disease of the heart," she explained. She said she had no one to attend to her at night except her husband, who slept on the other side of the room and could not hear her when she called for aid. Witness returned on the 31st and saw Dr. Cross. He said his wife was "as bad as she could be with typhoid fever." Witness naturally asked why she had not a nurse, to which he replied: "We are all nurses here, and Miss Jefferson is a professional nurse." (This, you may remember, was the visitor who kept a diary.) He also said that his wife had a gastric attack.

Dr. Godfrey stated that he lived next door to Shandy Hall and was a relative of Dr. Cross. Ten days before the death the doctor asked him to call and see his wife, who was suffering from diarrhœa. He did so and saw her for fifteen minutes, Dr. Cross being present. Witness formed the opinion that it was a bilious attack. He prescribed three or four grains of calomel and an aperient for the following morning. He was not asked to call again. The date of his visit was 24th May. When he examined the patient she presented no symptoms whatever of typhoid fever. By the Court—Witness had considerable experience both of typhoid and typhus.

Miss Margaret Jefferson stated that she and Mrs. Cross were school-mates. Witness was an associate of a sisterhood, The Sisters of the Church. On 29th April she arrived at Shandy Hall on a visit to her friend. Dr. Cross occupied the same room as his wife. Her hostess was then in her usual good health and spirits; a fortnight later she became unwell. She had spasms of the heart, accompanied by cramps, vomiting, and purging. From the 11th to the 14th of May she was confined to bed, suffering from these symptoms. She became easier and got up, but on the 16th and 17th was as bad as ever. On the 18th she was a little better and took a walk with witness along the Coachford road. On the 19th, being Ascension Day, she was able to drive to church. Sunday, the 22nd, was the last time she was out of the house. On the 24th she was back in bed with all the former symptoms in aggravated form. On the 26th she grew still worse, and witness began to be alarmed about her. It was untrue to say that witness was a professional nurse; but as a Sister, visiting the sick, she had seen many cases of typhoid. Mrs. Cross's illness presented no symptom of typhoid. It had been arranged that her visit should terminate on Saturday, 4th June; but Dr. Cross suggested that Thursday, the 2nd, would be more convenient. He attributed the illness of his wife to a gastric or bilious attack, "and hinted at typhoid fever." On 27th and 28th May, the patient's eyes became inflamed and her sight was affected: she could not see things distinctly. Dr. Cross gave her such food and the medicine as she required. The last time witness saw her alive was at 10 o'clock on the evening of Wednesday, 1st June. Miss Cross was then in the room. Her head had to be supported when she was given nourishment. She seemed quite clear, and able to describe her state. At 6.15 next morning witness was told by Mary Barron, one of the maids, that Mrs. Cross had died in the night. She went into the death-chamber at 7, and left Shandy Hall at 9. At breakfast she expressed her sympathy to Dr. Cross on his loss. "He said nothing special," but, with reference to the funeral arrangements,

DR. CROSS AND MISS SKINNER

(*From a photograph taken before the murder*)

remarked that Saturday was too soon and Monday too late.

Witness next saw Dr. Cross on 14th June when he called upon her in London to tell her that in three days he was to be married to Miss Skinner. She asked him as to the circumstances of her friend's last moments—thinking, presumably, that as he was so soon to replace her, he would now be sufficiently composed to discuss the matter. He said "that she died screaming; that she dozed off, and then died straight away." Her death was due to heart disease.

Cross-examined by Mr. Atkinson—Witness admitted that she made in her information no mention of cramp; she would have done so had she been asked. Since Mrs. Cross's death she had read in a book about arsenical poisoning. She saw therein nothing about cramp. She had no conversation on the subject with anybody except with one or two of the Sisters. By the Court—She had no conversation with anyone, particularly with no medical man, from whom she derived information regarding the symptoms of arsenical poisoning.

There followed the evidence of the four maid-servants. Jane Leahy only saw her mistress thrice during her illness; she complained first of a cold, and then of suffering from fever. Four days before her death her sight failed, and she could not read a newspaper. Two days before, "she was very bad." Mrs. Cross was not a delicate woman, though she was subject to fainting. Mary Buckley stated that the invalid's meals were taken to her either by Dr. Cross or by Mary M'Grath. She could swallow only liquid food, such as milk, cornflour, and chicken broth. On the night of the death witness was awakened by screams coming from her mistress's room: "It lasted four or five minutes, and I made nothing of it." Mary must have had strong nerves; this cry in the night would have aroused most sleepers to action. At 6 a.m Dr. Cross informed the servants that his wife had died during the night. Witness never heard screams on any other occasion. Mrs. Cross used sometimes to complain of her heart. Mary M'Grath gave similar evidence. She had seen her mistress sick after being given by the doctor some chicken broth and also chlorodyne. The patient complained to him that it, the chlorodyne, made her sick, but he did not reply. The bottle of chlorodyne produced was not the one which she had seen on the mantelpiece in Mrs. Cross's room. She did not see there any bottle but the one from which the dose was given. By the Court—No particular person attended to the patient at night. "If she rang her bell, I would answer it." Witness did so on three occasions; Dr. Cross was then asleep in his own bed. Each time what the patient wanted was a drink.

Mary Barron stated that she was parlourmaid at Shandy Hall. Dr. Cross was away from home for five weeks in March; after his return Mrs. Cross became ill. The persons who attended Mrs. Cross during her illness were witness, the doctor, Miss Cross, and Mary M'Grath. The invalid objected to having her bed made, as it caused her pain. Milk, lemonade, and toast and water were kept beside her bed. On the evening of her death, witness was in her room for an hour from 5 to 6 o'clock. Mrs. Cross was continuously sick all that time. Dr. Cross came to the maids' room next morning and told them to get up as "the mistress was no more." Cross-examined—Before her last illness witness had known Mrs. Cross to faint: "She would just go off in a weakness and get quite stiff." She used to say her heart was weak "and it would jump." Re-examined—The faints would last five minutes. Witness never saw Mrs. Cross sick until her last illness. By the Foreman of the Jury—It was no one's special duty to take the invalid her meals; sometimes the housemaid did so, sometimes witness.

It is obvious from the evidence of the servants that the poor lady was shockingly neglected. Although alleged by Dr. Cross to be dangerously ill from typhoid fever, not only had she no trained nurse, but nobody had the duty of waiting upon her, and her wants were but perfunctorily supplied. Her food and drink were put at her bedside to take or leave as she chose; and if she rang her bell, it might or might not be answered. In such scandalous circumstances, apart altogether from any question of poison, Dr. Cross, as her husband and medical attendant, deserved to be indicted for manslaughter. It is also very remarkable that with four servants, his sister, and his wife's oldest friend all at hand, the doctor should have summoned none of these women to help him in the distressing final scene.

Captain Woodley, a neighbouring friend, stated that, before the death of Mrs. Cross, he was invited by the doctor to lunch at Shandy Hall on Monday, 6th June. At luncheon he asked Dr. Cross of what his wife had died; "he said she had fever, but the immediate cause of death was heart disease." Witness suggested angina pectoris, and Dr. Cross concurred.

William Poole, manager of the London and North-Western Hotel, Dublin, being shown a photograph of Dr. Cross and Miss Skinner taken before their marriage (reproduced herewith), stated that he recognized the persons in that photograph as the accused and his present wife. They came to the hotel together at the end of March, and occupied the same bedroom, No. 3. They left by steamer for England the next morning. They returned to the hotel in June, occupying room No. 12 from a Sunday till the following Tuesday. They came back on Friday of the same week and stayed till Sunday evening. Beatrice Handcock, book-keeper at the hotel, identified the entries in a book as relating to "the persons in the photograph." These entries were in her own handwriting. The couple were twice in the hotel: on 29th March they arrived and asked for a room. They gave no name, being entered as "Mr. and Mrs. ——." They left next morning. On 21st April they came back; the accused asked for the same bedroom they had before. They stayed the night. He gave the names of "Mr. and Mrs. Osborne." In room No. 3 there was only one bed. Mary Smythe, chambermaid, identified the accused as having, along with the lady in the photograph, occupied room No. 3 in March and April. She saw them there again later, but could not fix the date. Arthur

Johnson, hotel porter, corroborated. He took the parties'
luggage to the Holyhead boat. The accused had a large
portmanteau with a white cross on it; the lady had only a
small hand-basket. They were back in June, when the
accused gave him a telegram to send to Dripsey, asking that
a vehicle be sent to meet him, Dr. Cross, at Cork at 2 a.m.

Dennis Griffin, postmaster, Dripsey, stated that letters
used to come for Dr. Cross at the post-office, marked to be
left till called for. This was after Miss Skinner left Coachford. Dr. Cross himself collected the letters. There were
initials on them, which witness could not decipher. Cornelius
M'Carthy, post messenger, stated that he delivered and up-
lifted the Shandy Hall mail. He got other letters personally
from Dr. Cross on the road. These were addressed: "Miss
Skinner, Killanure, Tullow, County Carlow." This was
after she had left the Hall. They were fifteen altogether.
Asked whether he had ever heard any quarrel between Dr.
and Mrs. Cross, witness replied: "Yes; I heard him say to
her he wished the Devil would take her out of the house.
And another day he said to her: 'The Devil crack your neck
or your leg.'" These were the only "rough things" witness
had heard him say to his wife. Cross-examined—Witness
had been in Dr. Cross's employment for five years. The
expressions he had quoted were used while Miss Skinner was
at the Hall. He was not discharged; "I left because Dr.
Cross had my wages in his pocket and kept it there."

District-Inspector Tyacke stated that he arrested the
prisoner in Cork on 27th July. He said: "My God! My
God!" He then said: "To think that a man at my time of
life should commit murder!" and finally: "There is a God
above, Who will see the villainy of this." There was. He
asked to speak to his sister, but was told he could have no
conversation with anyone except his solicitor. During the
inquiry in the Grand Jury Room accused gave witness a letter
which he wished sent to the Press; he was told that it must
go through the governor of the jail. The letter was produced and read:—

Sir—In your impression of the 29th, commenting on Dr. Cross and the charge against him relative to his late wife, I beg to inform you that the statement: "The prisoner attended his wife during her illness and allowed nobody to see her or attend the funeral" is not quite the fact. She was also attended and prescribed for by Dr. Godfrey, uncle to the prisoner. She was nursed and cared for during her illness by an old school friend and school-fellow, Miss Jefferson, a Sister of Mercy at Kilburn, a guest in the house for weeks before her death; by her servants; and by her sister-in-law, Miss Cross, at whose suggestion and that of Dr. Godfrey the funeral took place before 7 a.m. instead of 11 a.m. that day. For this reason the funeral was advertised private; being held at 11 would make it appear as if it was not intended to be so. Any friend who wished to see her had free access to her room, and the funeral was attended by several neighbours. As your article has the unintentional effect of creating prejudice against the prisoner, may I trouble you to insert this?

Well, we have heard the evidence, which scantly supports the accused's allegations. After the arrest, continued the Inspector, he went to Shandy Hall and took possession of certain drugs, a measuring glass, a chlorodyne bottle, and the doctor's diary. He found in a cupboard a paper labelled "Strychnine," also a packet marked "Dog Poison." In the accused's pocket-book, when arrested, he found a hotel bill for two persons at the Euston Station Hotel, for the dates from 10th to 13th June.

Sergeant Higgins stated that at the inquiry he heard the accused say to Miss Cross: "Did you see the little bottle about the length of my finger with the white powder in it?" and Miss Cross said: "Yes, yes. I destroyed it with the other things."

James Kiloh, assistant to Messrs. Golding, chemists, Cork, stated that on 2nd September, 1886, Dr. Cross bought one pound of arsenic, for, he explained, sheep-dipping. He signed the register of poisons, as produced:—

2/9/86. Name of purchaser—Dr. Cross. Address of purchaser—Shandy Hall, Dripsey. Name and quantity of poison sold—Arsenic, 1 lb. Purpose for which required—Sheep-dipping. Signature of purchaser—Philip H. E. Cross, Surgeon.

Mrs. Madras, a friend and neighbour of the deceased, stated that she met that lady on three occasions in May. She looked

ill, and on Ascension Thursday she looked worse; but Mrs.
Cross said she felt much better. Witness afterwards called
twice to inquire, but did not see the invalid; "Dr. Cross said
she should be kept very quiet." Witness called again on
the evening before Mrs. Cross died. The doctor and his
sister met her at the door. "They said she was very ill, and
was suffering from vomiting, and was very weak." Witness
suggested champagne and offered to send some, but Dr. Cross
said it was no use. In January Dr. Cross had told witness in
Cork that his wife was ill, and he would not be surprised if
she were dead when he got home. He said she had a heart
attack.

## VII

The chief medical witness for the Crown was Dr. Charles
Yelverton Pearson, who having stated his qualifications and
experience—he was Professor of Materia Medica in Queen's
College and Lecturer on Forensic Medicine—said that on
23rd July he performed a post-mortem on the body of the
deceased in the Court House at Coachford. He was assisted
by Dr. Crowley. The internal organs were well preserved,
particularly the stomach and intestines, in which there was
no sign of putrefaction. But for the presence of arsenic, as
afterwards ascertained, these would undoubtedly have exhibited such signs. There was no food in them. There
was no evidence of typhoid fever, nor any appearance of
inflammation of the stomach, but the lower end of the gullet
was inflamed. He described the several organs removed
for further examination; these were placed in separate vessels.
The larynx and lungs shewed putrefaction. The heart was
healthy. There was no appearance in the body of natural
disease; not the slightest sign of typhoid or heart trouble.
Certain parts of the lining or membrane of the stomach were
eaten away, and divers white particles were present. These,
on analysis, were found to consist of crystals of arsenic.
Witness used three independent processes in testing the white

particles, and each was conclusive of arsenic. The result of a quantitive analysis of one half of the stomach was 1·14 grains of white arsenic. The other half yielded strychnine, but not in weighable quantity. That analysis was confirmed by taste: the characteristic bitter taste of strychnine. The inflammation of the gullet was due to arsenic and must have caused considerable pain. In the liver was found 1·74 grains of white arsenic. The total quantity found was sufficient to destroy life: 2 grains had been known to cause death. The arsenic found in the body must have been administered three or four days before death. By the Court— He could not estimate how large a dose had been given. "You would certainly not find on analysis the entire dose." Witness then minutely described the symptoms of arsenical poisoning, all of which were present in this case, as set forth in the evidence. In his opinion the death of Mrs. Cross was due to arsenical poisoning: it might have been accelerated by strychnine. Two packets of pure strychnine were found in Dr. Cross's house and the minim measure produced contained traces of chlorodyne. Half a grain of strychnine had been known to destroy life. Witness could not form a satisfactory opinion as to the death screams of Mrs. Cross.

Cross-examined by Mr. Atkinson—Witness had attended cases of arsenical poisoning, but none of them was fatal. He admitted that he had formerly mis-stated the amount of arsenic found in the liver. "The explanation of my mistake is that I had not my notes with me at the inquest or inquiry; they were locked up at Queen's College, and I could not obtain them. The moment I discovered the mistake I notified the Crown solicitor of the error." This matter was made the occasion of much brow-beating, but as regards the methods and results of his analysis the witness's evidence remained unshaken.

Dr. Timothy Crowley concurred, and corroborated his colleague as to the result of the analysis. He stated that he was dispensary doctor at Coachford. On 2nd June Dr. Cross came to him for the purpose of registering his wife's death. The entry was as follows:—

> Mary Laura Cross, female, married, aged 49, lady; certified cause of death, typhoid fever; duration of illness, fourteen days. Signature, address, and qualification of informant—P. H. E. Cross, widower of deceased, occupier of Shandy Hall.

Witness could say, from attending the post-mortem, that Mrs. Cross did not die from natural causes, and that there were no appearances of typhoid fever. At the date in question there were no cases of fever in the district.

## VIII

On the third day of the trial the reporters noted that the accused shewed for the first time that the ordeal through which he was passing had told upon him. "His demeanour for the first two days was that of a man unmoved, and not deeply concerned by the position in which he stood. This evening, however, he looked flushed and somewhat excited, and displayed signs of nervousness and anxiety."

Mr. William Tyndall, a brother-in-law of the prisoner, stated that he lived in London. On 3rd June Dr. Cross wrote to him as follows:—

> Dear Mr. Tyndall—You will be sorry to hear that poor dear Laura passed away at 1 a.m. Typhoid fever debilitated the poor dear, I wonder how she ever lasted so long. Pray break this to her pet, Gussie. It will be a hard test for me to do the same to those little ones at school.—P. H. E. X.
>
> PS.—Owing to Sunday being the pet Papist Day I am sorry I must bury her on Saturday [4th June].

Witness saw Dr. Cross in London on the 17th—the day of his second marriage. Asked particularly as to the circumstances of his late wife's illness, Dr. Cross said it was due to angina pectoris, from which she had suffered for the last three days of her life.

Mr. Humphrey Marriott, of Abbott Hall, Essex, stated that he was a brother of the dead lady. On her father's death she received £5000. Witness allowed his sister £40 a year. The first intimation of her illness was a letter from Dr. Cross of 29th May, saying that she had an attack of typhoid fever. The writer added (falsely): "The medical men here say they have an unusual lot to do." (Dr. Crowley swore that there was then no case of fever in the district.) On 2nd June Dr. Cross wrote again, with reference to breaking the sad news to his boys at school. He said that his wife's heart "failed from exhaustion, as I knew it would many a long day ago." (The other doctors, you will bear in mind, described her heart as undiseased and normal.) One recalls in this connection the letters, equally hypocritical and mendacious, which Dr. Pritchard wrote to *his* brother-in-law with reference to his wife's illness and death, thus furnishing another link between these two detestable practitioners.

An official from the Registrar-General's Office produced the death certificate in the accused's handwriting: "Primary cause of death, typhoid fever; secondary ——; duration of illness, fourteen days." The case for the Crown was thereupon closed.

# IX

At 11.15, amid the breathless silence of his crowded audience and with the keen attention of his client fastened on his every word, Mr. Atkinson rose to state the case for the defence. At the outset he denounced the scandalous rumours and reports—"false as the Father of Lies himself"—which had been circulated to the prejudice of his client. These must have aroused the indignation of the jury, and there was great danger that their verdict might be one not of their minds, but of their passion. Black and revolting as was the crime with which the prisoner was charged, a crime as horrible and as dangerous to society would be committed by them if they allowed extraneous matters to influence their minds in deciding an issue of life and death. He, counsel, was not there to defend the accused's infidelity to his wife or his lack of taste in regard to the treatment of her remains. He would neither excite sympathy for him nor defend his acts, save in so far as they affected the charge against him. The Crown gave the accused credit for craft and cunning, yet they had proved him acting, if he were guilty, like a madman. His learned friend, searching for a motive, suggested that it was unbridled lust that made Dr. Cross sacrifice the wife who stood in his way. But the Crown had established the fact that her presence at Shandy Hall was no impediment to his intimacy with Miss Skinner. The case for the Crown was that this man waited to carry out his terrible crime until the arrival at his house of his wife's faithful school companion, *a trained nurse* and a most intelligent lady, and then in her presence, and in the presence of the servants, not at night but in the day-time, proceeded to poison his wife with arsenic in her food and medicine, and that he waited until the night before the faithful companion's departure to administer a finishing dose of strychnine. "Dr. Cross might be false to his wife, he might be a hypocrite to his friends, he might be the greatest liar that ever drew breath; but he was not a fool." Only a madman or an idiot would wait to terminate his horrible design until he had the presence of Miss Jefferson, who would be the best witness against him and the best protector of his wife. The evidence shewed that Dr. Cross believed her to be suffering from some febrile complaint: either bilious, gastric, or typhoid fever. Sometimes he called it one, sometimes another; but he always stated the ultimate cause of death as heart failure. There was no secrecy, no indecent haste as regards the funeral. He did not call the servants, but had he been guilty he would have done so, and have wept sham tears over the body of the woman he had murdered. Would Miss Cross, herself a woman, have entered into this diabolical conspiracy to do to death the wife, in order that her brother might have freer scope for indulgence of his passions? No doubt he married again. Counsel did not seek to defend that, either from the moral or the delicate standpoint; but if there were one thing to set tongues wagging and to raise suspicion, it was that marriage. It was the one thing that, in the circumstance, a criminal would have avoided. It was nonsense to suggest that he felt bound to marry this girl; the visit to Euston Hotel before the marriage disposed of that. It was proved that Dr. Cross bought a pound of arsenic in 1886. Was it suggested that before he had ever even seen Miss Skinner, he had determined to do away with his wife? And what was the poison used? Arsenic, which preserved the body, and which even the tyro-analyst Dr. Pearson was able to discover! A narcotic was plainly the poison to have used for one who had a weak heart. After discussing at length the medical evidence, counsel said that the strychnine theory was obviously based on the screams heard by one of the servants. (The Attorney-General— "The evidence of the servant girl was given on 8th August; the analysis was made in June.") Mr. Atkinson maintained that whether he was right or not, a more preposterous proposition was never submitted to a jury. Was Dr. Cross a madman to give her a poison that would make her for hours an incarnate proof of his guilt? If they rejected Dr. Pearson's evidence the whole case collapsed like a house of cards. Were they bold enough, on the evidence of such a medical tyro, to pronounce a verdict that the man in the dock should be strangled? The peroration was greeted with applause by a few persons in court; and his Lordship said if the police could find the offenders he would commit them to prison.

Mr. Atkinson ended on an interrogative note, and indeed, as reported, he put to the jury more questions than he answered. His rhetorical appeal would have had greater effect had it been justified by the proved facts. But the truth seems to be that so bad was his case, he was reduced to making a rude and unwarranted attack upon the chief medical witness for the Crown. If Dr. Pearson was wrong in his conclusions, other experts could have been called to confute him, but the defence called no medical evidence whatever. It is surprising that Mr. Atkinson should have founded on Miss Jefferson being "a trained nurse," seeing that lady had sworn expressly that she was not, and that to say so was untrue. The sole statement to the contrary was the false representation of his own client.

# X

Miss Henrietta Maria Cross was then called for the defence. She stated that she was a sister of the accused, and had lived at Shandy Hall for the last two and a half years. Dr. Cross and his wife were on very good terms. She was a delicate little woman, with a weak heart and a delicate stomach; she used very often to vomit. After a visit to England in 1886 she came back in very low spirits, "and grieved to have to live in Ireland." Witness slept at the end of the corridor on the same floor as Mrs. Cross and often gave her drinks. "The heart was what she always complained of." On the evening of her death witness took her some sago; later, as she had not touched it, witness took it away. She went to bed at half-past ten. During the night she was roused by a scream from Mrs. Cross's room. She heard other screams, and then her brother going downstairs and returning. "After that he came to my room and said something to me," in consequence of which she rose and went into Mrs. Cross's room. "She appeared to have just passed away." There was a bottle of brandy on the chimney-piece. Next day witness opened the dead lady's private press, which she always kept locked, and found a bottle with some rouge in it and a little vial with some white powder. Witness shewed the vial to her brother. She afterwards threw the contents amongst other rubbish in the fireplace and left the empty bottle on the chimney-piece. It was taken downstairs later by Mary Barron to be washed. There were two chlorodyne bottles used during the illness; the second was that produced. The minim glass was also on the chimney-piece. As the "cross" is instructive, I give it in "question and answer."

Cross-examined by the ATTORNEY-GENERAL—Did you ever hear Dr. Cross swear at Mrs. Cross? He might sometimes use strong language.

You were on good terms with Mrs. Cross? Yes.

When did you first hear of your brother's intention to marry Miss Skinner? He never told me.

When did you first hear of it? I heard it from Mrs. Caulfield first.

Do you remember the late Mrs. Cross complaining of her husband having gone away with her governess and remaining away for three days? No.

Was there any such conversation in your presence? No.

Where did your brother stop in Dublin? At the Hibernian Hotel.

Were you aware that Miss Skinner was stopping at the same hotel? Yes.

By the COURT—For three days! Did that strike you as improper? No.

*Cross-examination continued*—And did you never hear it made a subject of complaint on the part of the wife that her husband had spent three days in a hotel with a handsome young woman? No.

Did Miss Skinner leave Shandy Hall to go to a new place? She did; to go to Carlow.

Direct? No; she was to stay in Dublin for a night. There was a great difficulty in the trains. Mrs. Cross gave her money to pay her hotel bill.

Did you correspond with Miss Skinner after she went? Yes. I remember that Mrs. Cross was confined to bed with a gastric attack before her last illness. I can't fix the time.

Was she vomiting while your brother was in England in March? I think so.

Was what she was always suffering from a gastric attack? Yes; stomach attacks. She vomited from it.

Did you ever say a single word before about vomiting from gastric attacks or tell Mr. Deyos [the accused's solicitor] about it? I don't remember.

Did you think it a matter of importance? (No answer.)

Did you? (No answer.)

Did you? I wasn't asked. I don't think there was anything important in it.

Did you think Mrs. Cross was in danger? I did not think she was in danger; my brother never told me.

He was telling it to people five miles away and he did not tell you? (After considerable hesitation) I heard him say she might pass away any moment from her heart.

When was that? That was not during her last illness.

Had you any conversation with your brother about the terrific and painful agony she was passing through? Of course we knew she was very ill.

(Question repeated.) He said she had a low fever of a typhoid type.

When was that? I don't know the day.

Have you any idea what caused the vomiting? No.

Used she to complain of thirst? She used.

The day before she died you were out driving? Yes.

When you returned you found her vomiting? Just recovering from it.

What happened to the brandy bottle? I don't know.

Was it there in the morning? It was not.

What did you do with the bottle containing the white powder? I said to my brother: "What's this?" "Is it labelled?" he said. "If not it's rubbish; you had better throw it away." I did so.

Did you think there was arsenic in the bottle you emptied? I did not think about it.

Did the idea cross your mind that it might contain arsenic? Not then.

By the COURT—Did you think so at any time? I have thought since that it might be arsenic.

*Cross-examination continued*—Did you think your sister-in-law was taking arsenic? I have thought since that she might have taken it for her great delicacy.

Now look at the jury, Miss Cross. Did you say to the District Inspector: "Poor Laura, she was always dying; and if there was arsenic in her, she must have taken it for her complexion?" Possibly I did.

But your answer to me was that it was for delicacy, not for vanity. What did you believe arsenic would be good for as a medicine? It is taken for fits.

When did you first think that there may have been arsenic in that bottle? At the time the conversation overheard by Sergeant Higgins took place.

What occurred then? Dr. Cross said: "Do you remember the two little bottles with the white powder in them. They were amongst that rubbish." I said I did. He said: "Is it possible that that could have been arsenic?"

What was your answer to him? That I emptied them.

Will you swear that you did not say that you destroyed them? Perhaps I did say it.

How did you know about arsenic? I read about it in a book of my brother's.

When? Within the past three years.

When did you first think the arsenic was used by your sister-in-law for her complexion? Was it before or after the inquest? I can't say. I don't know.

Did you ever hear Dr. Cross say he gave his wife arsenic as a medicine for fits? Never. The rouge bottle is still at home.

Did you ever see your unfortunate sister-in-law rouge herself? I saw two bright spots on her cheeks.

And you suspected it was rouge? I thought so.

By the COURT—Dr. Cross did not take his clothes off at all the night Mrs. Cross died. She just passed away as I entered the room. I think her eyes were open.

Miss Cross was—naturally enough, in any view of the case—a most reluctant witness. If she told the truth, it was clearly not "the whole truth and nothing but the truth." I leave it at that.

## XI

Mr. Adams, in his closing address for the defence, renewed the attack on the Crown analyst. "If Pearson made a mistake, and the jury relied on Pearson's evidence, God help Dr. Cross!" Were they to set up the eminent Cork scientist, Pearson, in order to hang Dr. Cross? The wife might have committed suicide—he did not say she did, although the theory was as probable as that her husband poisoned her; but he maintained that if poison was found in this unfortunate woman, which he did not believe, it was never administered by the prisoner at the bar.

Mr. Wright, in the final speech for the Crown, protested against the unfair attack upon Dr. Pearson, and contended that his analysis proved unmistakably that a fatal dose of arsenic had been administered to Mrs. Cross. Dr. Cross was tired of his wife, he was carrying on an intrigue with another woman, he prevented his wife being seen by her friends and her clergyman during her last illness, and he lied as to the cause of her death. The Crown case was unassailed and unassailable, and pointed conclusively to the guilt of the prisoner, by whom his wife was done to death in order to make room for his paramour. These speeches are but briefly reported. It is unlikely, however, that counsel had much more of import to say on either side. The Court then rose.

Next morning, being the fourth day of the trial, Mr. Justice Murphy charged the jury. His Lordship started at eleven o'clock and spoke for four and a half hours. On the conclusion of his review of the evidence it is recorded: "It was now half-past three, and the man whose fate was in the balance was apparently not so much concerned about the verdict as he was about his lunch." Indeed it appears that from first to last the accused seemed strangely insensible to his position.

His Lordship pointed out that they were not trying the prisoner on a charge of immorality or adultery, but on that of causing his wife's death. Yet it was impossible not to take into serious consideration the circumstances connected with the relations between the prisoner and his former and his present wife, which might supply a motive for the crime. His Lordship then described the position of the dead lady: as wife, mother, and head of the household, entitled to the most anxious care and attention; no expense, no forethought spared to guard and preserve her life. Was that done? It was not from lack of means, from ignorance, from over-confidence in her staying power. "Consider his relations with this person Skinner. Did his late wife get a fair chance for her life? She appeared to be an uncomplaining creature, but was it right to leave her in a condition, according to Dr. Cross himself, so eminently and imminently perilous? Was it right to leave her to the casual attentions of servants, on the chance of their hearing her bell rung in the night?" They were not trying the prisoner for his neglect, his utter disregard of his wife during her illness, but they were bound to consider those circumstances as bearing on the charge against him.

His Lordship then went through the distressing symptoms which for weeks the patient suffered. "Why was no doctor summoned from Cork, only twelve miles distant? Why not have someone to sleep in her room? There were tender husbands who spent sleepless nights in watchful attention on their wives. Was the prisoner such a one? His adulterous relations with Skinner threw a lurid light on this subject. Mary Barron goes up one night to answer the bell of the suffering wife, and finds the loving husband asleep in the other bed." His Lordship then dealt with what he termed "the appalling scene" on the night of the death: the husband alone with the dying woman in the bedroom, the dreadful scream heard and heard again, and the sister, according to her own account, summoned to the death-chamber when all was over. The wife of eighteen years was dead; her only attendant was her husband. If his love had turned to indifference or to hate, he had no right to be there. "No alarm that night by the husband or the sister; no wail of grief for the calamity that had overtaken the household." Was the death a surprise to him? Did he grieve of sorrow for it? When Laura Cross was gone, the marriage, if marriage it could be called, was celebrated within as short a time as the law allowed. If Laura Cross's death was hastened, whether by heart failure induced by a drug, or by slow poison, who on earth could have administered these but the prisoner at the bar? "Arsenic for the complexion! Arsenic for fits! Rubbish—altogether rubbish!"

Now as to the evidence of Dr. Pearson, it was said that the jury should not hang the prisoner to set up or sustain Dr. Pearson's reputation; but on the other hand they were not, without proof, to suppose that Dr. Pearson, a medical man of established reputation, chosen for a high office in succession to the eminent chemist, Dr. O'Keefe, was an ignorant pretender, talking on a subject of which he knew nothing. Why was no specialist produced to controvert his findings, if fallacious, and to say that his tests for arsenic were wrong? His report on his analysis was there and could have been examined by any skilled person whom the prisoner's advisers might select. His evidence and that of Dr. Crowley made it clear that there was no sign of typhoid fever, not a trace of evidence of death from natural causes. The particles of arsenic found in the body were produced in court and could be examined by anyone on behalf of the accused.

It was pressed upon them by Mr. Atkinson that the prisoner must have been mad to act as he is said to have acted. That would be to assume that persons who commit great crimes are people of foresight and forethought; but experience of detected crimes shewed that the contrary was the case. What was the meaning of that conversation, spoken of by Sergeant

Higgins, about the two little bottles containing the white powder? Was that the conversation of an innocent man, who thought his wife had committed suicide by taking arsenic? If they were satisfied that the facts proved were not consistent with the prisoner's innocence; if they were convinced that Laura Cross met her death by foul play at the hands of her husband; then a hideous crime had been committed, and should it be their duty to find this man guilty of that crime, let there be no faltering in their verdict. "If you believe that Laura Cross was done to death by poison you must find the prisoner guilty."

## XII

The jury retired, and after an hour's deliberation returned at 4.30 with a unanimous verdict of Guilty, which, looking to the nature of the evidence and the tone of the judge's charge, is not surprising. "The prisoner," we are told, "was the only person unmoved by the terrible announcement. He appeared either wholly unconscious or entirely unconcerned." Asked whether he had anything to say, Dr. Cross rose and quietly replied: "I am innocent of the charge, and I will give my reasons if I am allowed." In common with counsel and his Lordship, he used largely the interrogative form, which for all I know may be characteristic of Irish eloquence. "Is it likely I would select arsenic—a poison that of all others would be found ten years after in her body, and if not, in the earth beside her? . . . Is it likely I would go and use strychnine at the same time? . . . Is it likely that having poisoned my wife, I would go and marry another young woman? . . . If I had not done wrong to her, do you think I would have married her? No fear!" And with reference to his fatal marriage he concluded: "See what it has brought me to; see what it has brought me to!"

The forty minutes of this rambling statement must have been very painful for those who heard it. One is reminded of the inconsequent and incoherent remarks made in similar adverse circumstances by M. Chantrelle, who was convicted at Edinburgh in 1878—ten years before Dr. Cross—for the poisoning of his wife with opium. The irrelevant maunderings of these guilty men are in marked contrast to the statements respectively made on conviction of murder by Jessie M'Lachlan in 1862 and by Mrs. Maybrick in 1889. But then these ladies had, as I hold, the advantage of being innocent, an inestimable asset for such as chance to be accused of crime.

Mr. Justice Murphy, in passing sentence, was much more moved than the man in the dock. His Lordship expressed his entire concurrence in the verdict: indeed no intelligent jury could have found any other. The evidence demanded it from them. "And that verdict has been given finding you guilty of this foul and terrible crime, by which, by the slow torture of a lingering death, you deprived of life one who had been fond and true to you." The sentence of the law was that Dr. Cross be taken back to prison and there, on Tuesday, 10th January 1888, be hanged by the neck until he was dead: "And may the Lord have mercy on your soul." The condemned man displayed not the least emotion. After speaking to his agent for a few moments, he was removed from the dock, and the trial was over.

## XIII

At the appointed hour and place Dr. Cross paid the utmost penalty of the law. The refusal of the Lord Lieutenant to interfere with the sentence was intimated three days before that fixed for the execution. "As an instance of Dr. Cross's coolness it may be mentioned that on Saturday he made a complaint about the quality of the toast supplied to him for breakfast."

The services of James Berry of Bradford, the English executioner, were requisitioned; that expert duly arrived at Cork, performed his dreadful office, and returned forthwith

to England.   His failure to attend the Coroner's inquest on
the dead man was highly resented by the jury; the proceedings were three times adjourned, and on 25th January a
summons was issued for the attendance of the hangman.   In
this connection that gentleman addressed to the Coroner the
following letter, which was communicated to the Press (the
orthography is the writer's):—

ENGLAND, *January* 12, 1888.

Mr. M. J. Horgan, Coroner.

SIR,—Re Dr. Philip Cross hanged for murder at H.M. Prison,
Cork, Ireland, in reference to the above I beg to explain that the
reason I left the prison is because I never attend inquests either in
England or Scotland or Ireland.   I have been in Ireland several times,
but never attends the inquest unless something goes wrong, and in
the case of Dr. Cross I never carried out a better execution in my
experience as an executioner.   He walked with a firm step and stood
erect.   When the drop fell he never moved a musle or a limb.   The
reason the delay of letting the reporters up was in consequence to the
religious ceremony be read after death by the chaplain of the prison.
Certainly it took up a little extra time, and I am sure, Mr. Coroner,
you will agree with me that that is the spiritual right to be read over
the dead.   There is a great many prisons in England where reporters
is not admitted, and in most cases only one.   Trusting this letter will
gratify yr morbid curious jury, I am, Sir, yours truely,

JAMES BERRY.

PS.—I have executed 113 convicts, and only attended to one
inquest, and that was at Norwich, County Norfolk, England, where
the convict's head was separated from his body, and I had to explain
how the unfortunate accident occurred.   If I attend the inquest which
is adjourned until the 20th inst. I shall be paid all expenses and my
time in coming to give evidence, as if anything had gone wrong I
should have stayed until the inquest was over.   Therefore if you like
to forward me £10 I will attend Cork Male Prison on the 20th inst.
to give evidence as you may require upon the question before
mentioned.

The Coroner replied that if he did not so attend, a warrant
would be issued for his arrest.   The result of the contro-
versy is not recorded.

The singular fortitude with which the convict faced his
end, thus earning the commendation of the hangman, is
borne out by the evidence of the prison doctor at the inquest.
Dr. Moriarty there said: "I have seen many executions, but

never such bravery as exhibited by Dr. Cross. He was a grand old man. He walked erect and without faltering to the scaffold." Although Dr. Cross made no confession of his guilt, he ceased, we are told, to protest his innocence after learning that his petition for mercy had been refused.

.    .    .    .    .    .

My benefactor of the press-cuttings furnishes, by way of epilogue, two items of news. First, under date 29th December 1887, that "Mrs. Cross, *née* Skinner, was delivered of a son on Friday at Shandy Hall." The second is more surprising.

In January 1888, Mr. Coroner Horgan, having just finished with Dr. Cross, held at Coachford an inquest on one Simon Crooke, aged 70, who had died after a week's confinement to bed. It is interesting to note that the widow, formerly Miss Jane Cross, of Gronody, was a first cousin of the subject of the former inquest. It appeared from the evidence that Mr. Crooke during his illness was grossly neglected by his wife; no one attended to him or gave him food, except a labouring man, who looked in occasionally of an evening and brought him—a consumptive—whisky, arrowroot biscuits, and cheese, for which the invalid gave him money to pay. The household staff consisted of a boy and girl, the latter testifying that she never made the patient's bed or washed his linen during his illness, "because they were too dirty"! "The room and bedclothes were in a terrible state" when seen by the police. No doctor was called in, and Simon Crooke was left to die like a dog. Our acquaintance, Dr. Crowley, and Dr. White, were instructed to perform a post-mortem. They found the body very much emaciated, and no vestige of food in the stomach or intestines. The immediate cause of death, in their opinion, "was starvation, in a man previously reduced by chronic pulmonary disease." With proper attention he might have lived for a considerable time. The Coroner, in addressing the jury, said it was for them to say, having heard the evidence, what was the cause of the death of Mr. Crooke, "whom they all knew very well." Of course, if they did not wish to, they need not incriminate anybody; but it was apparent that this unfortunate man was not properly looked after by those who were nearest to him and whose duty it was to have done so. The whole facts were certainly most extremely suspicious as to the treatment of the deceased by his wife. They had conclusive medical evidence that the cause of death was starvation. He supposed it could not be alleged by Mrs. Crooke that she was unable to procure for her husband the ordinary nourishment necessary to sustain life.

The jury returned the following verdict: "That the deceased was found dead at Dirreen on 15th inst., and that the death resulted from starvation, from want of proper medical attendance, and from neglect by his wife, Jane Crooke." Whereupon the Coroner issued a warrant for the arrest of Mrs. Crooke, *née* Cross, and that lady was apprehended on the charge of wilful neglect and starvation of her husband. She was admitted to bail; but, provokingly, I have no report of the subsequent happenings.

That this strange death should have occurred five days after the hanging of Dr. Cross; that the same Coroner should hold the inquest; that the tale of the two deathbeds should be so startlingly alike; and that the accused woman was a cousin of the murderer—these are indeed singular coincidences. Members of the Cross family were plainly ill-cast as ministers to the sick.

Caledonian United Service Club,
Edinburgh.

15ᵗʰ Sep. 33.

Dear Mr Shepherd,

Thanks so much for
your letters. I shall read
the M.S. of your article on
the first opportunity and
return it to you safely.

I am glad to hear
that you like the etchings
they are indeed delightful.

"Thanks awfully",
as my boys would say,
for your very kind invitation
to your hospitable roof,
which one day I hope
to accept, though I am

not, as a rule, given to visiting, preferring, at my age, to the most alluring salons, my Axis foresilo.

But even then I hope that you and your husband will dine with us at Belgrave Crescent some evening, when I shall Inclose to you all the Secret places of my Chamber of Horrors.

Meanwhile,

with best regards,

Yours sincerely,

William Roughead:

# KATHARINE  NAIRN

# KATHARINE NAIRN

Paolo and Francesca in Angus.—ANDREW LANG.

WHEN douce Mr. Thomas Ogilvy brought his young bride home to Glenisla his mother doubtless hailed the event as of happy augury for the house of Eastmiln. Hitherto fortune had frowned upon her family. Her eldest son "grew delirious and hanged himself in '48 in a sheepcot." As the length of the drop was insufficient, "he came down and delved below his feet to make it proper for him," which shewed considerable force of character. His brother William "went on board a man-of-war carpenter, and was crushed to death 'twixt two ships." Her husband, who under his chief, Lord Ogilvy, had been out in the Forty-five as a captain of the Prince's army, after the defeat of Culloden was confined in Edinburgh Castle, and, having lain a prisoner in that fortress until 1751, fractured his skull in attempting to escape over the walls "by a net tied to an iron ring." Thomas, the third son, prudently eschewing politics, became by virtue of these calamities laird of the paternal acres. Of her remaining sons, Patrick, sometime lieutenant of the 89th Regiment of Foot, was but newly invalided home from the East Indies, his career eclipsed, while the youngest, Alexander, then prosecuting at Edinburgh his studies in depravity and physic, had just redeemed a nominal celibacy by marriage with a woman of the lowest rank. When therefore, Thomas, at the responsible age of forty, wooed and won Miss Katharine Nairn, a damsel of nineteen, the beautiful daughter of Sir Thomas Nairn of Dunsinnan, old Mrs. Ogilvy (by Scots courtesy Lady Eastmiln) may have believed herself entitled to sing the Song of Simeon. How far she was justified in the event the following tale will shew.

The marriage, which took place on 30th January 1765,

would seem to have been on both sides one of affection. The bride, of a family more rich in ancestry than in money, was better born than her husband, who was but a "bonnet laird." Marrying against the wish of her relatives she brought him at least youth and beauty, whereas Eastmiln (so named by Scottish custom) was a man of small means who had, moreover, anticipated the modern malady—too old at forty. His health, as we shall see, was bad; he was somewhat of a valetudinarian. Mr. Spalding of Glenkilry, the husband of Katharine's sister Bethia, at whose house Thomas Ogilvy probably met his future bride, quaintly described him as wearing "a plaiden jacket and a belt round his middle, much broader than ever he saw another wear, with lappets of leather hanging down his haunches, and a striped woollen nightcap upon his breast, the lower end of which reached near his breeches." His change of state must have proved beneficial, for Mr. Spalding adds, "upon his marriage he took off these happings."

At this time the inmates of the house of Eastmiln were the dowager, her son and his young wife, Patrick the lieutenant, and three female servants. From the date of the marriage until the first of March ensuing all was apparently well with the family. But on that day—ominously enough a Friday—there arrived upon the scene one who was to prove the evil genius of the house and the harbinger of dishonour and death. This was Anne Clark, "aged thirty and upwards," a cousin of the laird. Her private character and professional pursuits, if known, would necessarily have excluded her from decent society, while as a guest she laboured under the further disadvantage of being "a notorious liar and dissembler, a disturber of the peace of families, and sower of dissension." Her relatives in Angus, however, knew nothing of all this, and she was received by them "without suspicion, and treated as an equal and a gentlewoman." Miss Clark came ostensibly upon a visit of reconciliation from Edinburgh, where she had been associated with her cousin, Alexander Ogilvy, in the sowing of his wild oats. Jealousy was not among her numerous failings, for after his marriage she had lived with his wife's father. By his alliance with "the daughter of a common porter" Alexander had given great offence to his family, and Katharine in particular had not concealed her opinion of his conduct. Hence the appearance of Anne in her maiden rôle of peacemaker. But it was later alleged that she was actuated by a motive less lovely. Both Eastmiln and Patrick, his heir-presumptive, were in ill-health; on their death, should the marriage of the elder prove childless, Alexander the needy would reign in their stead. The first step towards the attainment of this end was to effect an estrangement between the newly-married pair. If such was indeed her scheme, Anne had no time to lose. Her mission, genuine or not, had failed. Alexander's entry in the family black books was indelible.

Miss Clark must have had a winning way with her, inviting to confidence. She and young Mrs. Ogilvy had never met before, yet within a fortnight of her coming Katharine told her she disliked her husband, "and said if she had a dose she would give it him." Nor was this a mere isolated indiscretion, for Miss Clark states that thereafter "Mrs Ogilvy did frequently signify she was resolved to poison her husband." She even consulted Anne as to the best means of procuring the requisite drug—whether "from Mr. Robertson, a merchant in Perth, or Mrs. Eagle, who keeps a seed shop in Edinburgh, upon pretence of poisoning rats." Anne considered this classic formula open to objection, as being apt to bring the purchaser "to an untimely end," but she generously offered to go herself to Edinburgh "and get her brother, who lived there, to buy the poison." Although a woman with many pasts, Anne, as the cousin of the proposed victim, seems at first sight an unsuitable confidant, but such is her own version of the facts. There for the time the matter rested.

Anne Clark had not been long established beneath that hospitable roof when an ugly rumour concerning Mrs. Ogilvy and her young brother-in-law began to trouble the house of Eastmiln. Anne charitably warned her hostess "to be upon her guard as to her conduct and to abstain from the lieutenant's company." Her well-meant hint, however, proved ineffectual, for on Sunday, 19th May, according to her own account, she obtained indisputable proof of a liaison between them. Katharine, although at once apprised of the discovery by her considerate kinswoman, continued in her evil course with cynical, nay lunatic, effrontery. Anne would fain have supported her story by the testimony of her aunt, but old Lady Eastmiln, who enjoyed the same facilities for seeing and hearing what Anne alleged to have occurred, noticed nothing, despite the fact that her attention was specially called to the matter by her niece at the time. She consented, however, to communicate Anne's "suspicions" to Eastmiln.

It happened that at this time a dispute arose between the brothers "about the balance of a bond of provision resting owing to Patrick Ogilvy," as to which the latter considered himself aggrieved. On Thursday, 23rd May, in the course of a discussion of this vexed question, the laird lost his temper, referred to Anne's allegations, and ordered his brother out of the house. Patrick, indignantly denying the charge, left that afternoon and went to stay with a friend at Little Forter, about three miles distant. That Katharine, whether innocent or guilty, was in the circumstances considerably upset is not surprising. Eastmiln warned his wife that she would injure her reputation "by intermeddling in the differences betwixt him and his brother," which hardly looks as if he took the matter seriously; but the servants swore that they overheard him tell her "that she was too great with Lieutenant Ogilvy, and that they were as frequent together as the bell was to ring on Sunday." Anne says that the laird proposed to leave his own house so as to give the young people a clear field, and that she urged Mrs. Ogilvy to agree, "as she was little prospect of harmony between them," which, so long as she remained their guest, was no doubt likely enough. Be that as it may, Katharine, with singular imprudence, wrote to the lieutenant begging him to return, which he wisely declined to do. According to Anne's story Mrs. Ogilvy, who had become impatient at her delay in procuring the poison from Edinburgh as promised, told her, after the lieutenant's departure, that "with much difficulty" she had prevailed upon him to furnish it. That same day Anne had an unexplained conversation with a surgeon of Kirriemuir as to the properties and effects of laudanum and the amount of a fatal dose. Whether she shared Rosa Dartle's passion for information or made the inquiry on behalf of Katharine, does not appear.

It is admitted that by the following day husband and wife were so far reconciled that Eastmiln himself wrote to his brother asking him to come back. He sent the letter by a neighbour, to whom he first read it, telling him of Anne Clark's reports, "but that for his [Eastmiln's] part he did not believe them." Patrick, however, still refused to return. He visited various friends in the neighbourhood, and while at Glenkilry, the house of Mr. Spalding, Katharine's brother-in-law, he received from her another letter, the contents of which we do not know, unless it be the one produced later at the trial.

On Friday, 31st May, Patrick entertained his brother officer, Lieutenant Campbell, and a friend, Dr. Carnegie, to dinner at an inn in Brechin. He afterwards stated that before he left Eastmiln, Katharine asked him to send her for her own use some salts and laudanum, of which he told her he had a quantity in his sea chest, then at Dundee. Unfortunately for him, Dr. Carnegie proved that at this dinner he delivered to Patrick at his request "a small phial glass of laudanum and betwixt half an ounce and an ounce of arsenic," which latter "he wrapt up in the form of a penny worth of snuff under three covers." Patrick's reason for wanting the arsenic was, he said, "in order to destroy some dogs that spoiled the game" —which was open to the objection previously taken by Anne to Katharine's hypothetical rats. After paying Dr. Carnegie a shilling for these commodities, Patrick accompanied Lieutenant Campbell to Finhaven as his guest for the week-end.

On Monday, 3rd June, Patrick rode to Alyth to visit his kinsman, Andrew Stewart, who had recently married his sister, Martha Ogilvy. Mr. Stewart had brought the lieutenant's sea chest from Dundee to his own house, and on this occasion he saw Patrick "working among some salts" in the chest. Next day Elizabeth Sturrock, one of the servants at Eastmiln, came to Alyth upon some household matter, and delivered to Patrick a letter from Katharine, to which he returned an answer by her. Mr. Stewart having announced his intention of visiting Eastmiln the following day, Patrick gave him "a small phial glass, containing something liquid which he said was laudanum, and also a small paper packet, which he said contained salts," together with a letter for Mrs. Ogilvy, all of which he requested his brother-in-law to put into her own hands.

Meanwhile Miss Clark states that Katharine told her she had heard from Patrick, who had "got the poison the length of Alyth," and would send it by Andrew Stewart next day. Anne, ever zealous for the family honour, very properly exhorted her to abandon her nefarious purpose, dwelt upon the consequences likely to ensue "both in this world and the next," and asked her reasons for "this strange resolution." These were that Mrs. Ogilvy did not love her husband, and that he had used the lieutenant ill upon her account. "How happy," said she, "could they live at Eastmiln, if there were none there but the lieutenant, she, and the deponent [Anne]!" That experienced spinster at once pointed out that in no circumstances could Katharine marry her brother-in-law, but was met by the suggestion that they might live abroad. Still, Anne thought it "a dreadful thing to crown all with murder." Mrs. Ogilvy desired "to be let alone, for the conversation was disagreeable to her." Now all this could have been no news to Anne Clark in June, for on her own shewing she had known since the middle of March both the nature of Katharine's feelings towards her husband and her fell design.

In the forenoon of Wednesday, 5th June, a chapman (hawker) called and demanded from Eastmiln the price of some cambric, of which Anne was then making ruffles for the lieutenant. As he had been told that Patrick himself supplied the material, the laird was justifiably annoyed, and repudiated

liability for the account. Later in the day Andrew Stewart
arrived at the house of Eastmiln and privately handed to
Katharine the lieutenant's parcel, which she placed unopened
in a drawer in the spare bedroom. But Anne was on the
alert, and waylaying him, asked if he had brought anything
from Patrick. Mr. Stewart, "because he considered Miss
Clark as a person given to raise dissension in families," at first
denied that he had done so; but, being persistently pressed
by her, he finally admitted the fact. Whereupon Anne said
"they were black drugs," and that Mrs. Ogilvy meant to
poison her husband. Stewart, shocked at the suggestion, was
"very much displeased" with her, the more so that she proposed to her aunt to warn Eastmiln of his danger. But "the
old lady said it would be improper," being, as appears, a
stickler for etiquette.

That night the four relatives supped together—a strange
company—at a public-house in the Kirkton of Glenisla. Eastmiln told his brother-in-law, Andrew Stewart, that he had not
been well for some time past, and was thinking of consulting
Dr. Ogilvy of Forfar. He further said that he was seized
with illness the day before, and "had swarfed [fainted] on the
hill," for which reason he could drink no ale. So he called
for a dram, "which he took, and thereafter seemed hearty and
in good spirits." But Miss Clark's conscience, a tender plant,
still troubled her, and she unobtrusively left the board in
quest of ghostly aid, or, in her own words, "with a view of
being advised by the minister what was fit to be done in
such a case." The minister of Glenisla was from home, so
she rejoined the supper-party without the benefit of clerical
counsel, the nature of which, in a situation so delicate, one
would like to have known. On the way home Stewart
escorted his sister-in-law, the laird following with Anne, who,
availing herself of the opportunity, warned him that his life
was threatened by his own wife, and begged him to leave
home. Eastmiln said he was then too busy to do so, but
promised to take nothing from Katharine's hands. It is
probable that he was not much impressed by his cousin's

solitude; that he disliked and distrusted her is certain. Apparently the hour was favourable for confidences; Katharine at the same time was telling her companion that she lived a most unhappy life with her husband, and "wished him dead, or, if that could not be, she wished herself dead." This statement, chiming as it did with Anne's suspicions, somewhat startled Mr. Stewart. When they reached the house, and after Eastmiln and his wife had gone to bed, he proposed to Anne Clark and the old lady "that they should either take Mrs. Ogilvy's keys out of her pocket or break open her drawers at the back, so as to see what were the actual contents of the packet. To neither of these practical suggestions could Anne by any means be brought to agree, which is the more remarkable in view of the urgent anxiety expressed by her earlier in the evening. But when Lady Eastmiln, who had gone up to listen at the door of the connubial chamber, reported "that there was then more kindness between them than usual," Mr. Stewart was confirmed in his opinion "that there was no foundation for Miss Clark's fears."

Next morning, Thursday, 6th June, breakfast was earlier than common—"betwixt eight and nine"—as Mr. Stewart was returning that day to Alyth. All the members of the family were present except the laird, who, having been unwell in the night, was still in bed. Katharine poured out a bowl of tea from the teapot, put sugar and milk in it, and, telling the old lady and Stewart that she was taking it up to Eastmiln, left the room. While she was upstairs the party was completed by the appearance of Anne, to whom Katharine, on re-entering the parlour, remarked "that the laird and Elizabeth Sturrock were well off that morning, for they had got the first of the tea." Upon which, Anne says she exclaimed in alarm, "What! has the laird got tea? and on Mrs. Ogilvy answering that he had, the deponent said nothing"—like the parrot in the tale. An hour and a half afterwards, according to Mr. Stewart—Anne says half an hour—Katharine announced that the laird "was taken very ill." Anne ran upstairs to the bedroom, and on returning significantly re-

KATHARINE NAIRN

(*From an engraving in the British Museum*)

ported that "Eastmiln had got a bad breakfast." Stewart then went up himself to see what was the matter, and found his brother-in-law suffering from sickness and other distressing symptoms. The laird expressively said that "he was all wrong within." Mr. Stewart proposed to Mrs. Ogilvy to send for Dr. Meik of Alyth, but she would not consent, saying that "he [Eastmiln] would be better; and she would not for any money that a surgeon should be called, as the consequences would be to give her a bad name from what Miss Clark had said of her." Later, Mr. Stewart persuaded her to let him summon Dr. Meik, "a discreet person," and thereafter set out for Alyth.

Katharine's forecast was so far justified that Eastmiln presently rose "and went first to the stables to see his horses fed, and then to the Shillinghill, where he conversed with some of his tenants." On returning to the house he became violently sick in the kitchen, and had to be helped upstairs to bed. Katharine attended to her husband during the forenoon, but from midday until his death Anne Clark was in possession of the sickroom. She states that Mrs. Ogilvy refused to remain there unless she (Anne) was dismissed, to which the laird would not agree. Anne and some of the servants represent that Katharine tried to exclude people from the room, but it is proved that, apart from those in the house, Eastmiln was visited by at least five persons, including his brother-in-law, Mr. Spalding, and the local precentor, who was summoned by Katharine to pray with him. The symptoms exhibited by the dying man were admittedly vomiting, purging, "a burning at his heart," pains in his legs, restlessness, and persistent thirst. Anne gave him repeated draughts of water and of ale, none of which he could retain; but on her trying him with "a glass of wine and a piece of sugar in it," the sickness ceased for about an hour. On cross-examination, she had to admit that she got the wine from Mrs. Ogilvy. That the laird had become convinced that his wife had poisoned him is clear. When Anne Sampson, one of the maids, brought him a drink of water in the same bowl in which Katharine had given him the tea, he cried out, "Damn that bowl! for I have got my death in it already." He said in the hearing of Elizabeth Sturrock, another servant, "that he was poisoned, and that woman [his wife] had done it." Lady Eastmiln reproved him for saying so, to which he answered "that it was very true, and his death lay at her [Katharine's] door." Anne, on the other hand, says that the old lady blamed him for taking anything from his wife, when he replied, "It is too late now, Mother; but she forced it on me." He told Andrew Stewart that "he had what would do his turn"; to his friend and neighbour, Mr. Millam, he remarked, "I am gone, James, with no less than rank poison!" At midnight the unhappy man was dead. It was but four months since his wedding-day.

Dr. Meik arrived from Alyth two hours later; it does not appear when he received the summons. He had an interview with the widow, who was apparently "in great grief and concern." She made the remarkable request "that whatever he might think to be the cause of her husband's death, he would conceal it from the world." Patrick Ogilvy, sent for by Mr. Spalding from Glenkilry, where he had been that gentleman's guest, was then in the house, and conducted the doctor to the death-chamber. He struck Dr. Meik as being, like Mrs. Ogilvy, "in great grief and concern." After a brief examination the doctor departed, having, as it appears, come to no conclusion regarding the cause of death.

That morning (Friday, 7th June) the servants, probably at the instigation of the thoughtful Anne, applied certain scientific tests to the fatal bowl, in which they said they had noticed "something greasy in the bottom." The results were negative. They filled the bowl with broth, which was given to a dog, "who eat it up, but was nothing the worse of it." Anne Clark recounts a curious conversation had by her with the lieutenant on his coming from Glenkilry. She told him "she knew the whole affair of the poison," whereupon Patrick admitted sending it to Katharine, but said "he did not think she had so barbarous a heart as to give it."

The funeral was fixed to take place on Tuesday, 11th June,

the lieutenant, as his brother's heir, remaining at Eastmiln to make the requisite arrangements. Mr. Millam, the late laird's friend, tells us that when "the mournings came home" Miss Clark complained to him "for want of a mourning apron, adding that she would make it as dear to them [Katharine and Patrick] as if it was a gown!" This was short-sighted parsimony indeed; Anne's silence was worth many aprons' purchase. On Monday, the 10th, Mrs. Ogilvy dismissed her dangerous kinswoman, giving her money in presence of Mr. Millam, both of which facts Anne afterwards denied on oath. Anne further swore that before she left the house she did not communicate to anyone, "by letters or otherways," her belief that Eastmiln had been poisoned. Yet early in the forenoon of Tuesday, the 11th, her old flame Alexander Ogilvy arrived from Edinburgh, and dramatically stopped the burial on the ground that his brother had not died a natural death. The widow resented her brother-in-law's action—reasonably enough in any view of her conduct—and "behaved very ill, weeping and crying, and wringing her hands and tearing herself." Mr. Millam, hearing what had happened, strangely advised Patrick "to make his escape, if guilty"; to which the lieutenant replied, "That God and his own conscience knew that he was innocent." Next morning, at the request of Alexander Ogilvy, Dr. Meik of Alyth and Dr. Ramsay of Coupar-Angus arrived to make a post-mortem examination of the corpse, Katharine and Patrick offering no objection. Alexander, however, refused to allow the body to be opened until Dr. Ogilvy of Forfar, who had been desired by the Sheriff to attend, was also present. The two surgeons, therefore, merely inspected the corpse and left, refusing to wait for Dr. Ogilvy. After they had gone the latter arrived, but declined to open the body in the absence of the other surgeons, on the ground that the autopsy might be attended with personal danger. He, in his turn, made an inspection and departed. We shall see later the result of their several observations.

On Friday, 14th June, Katharine and Patrick were apprehended upon the signed information of Alexander Ogilvy, and, having been examined before Mr. George Campbell, Sheriff-Substitute of the county, were consigned to Forfar Jail. That day Miss Clark returned in triumph to Eastmiln, to assist her old friend Alexander in taking possession. On the 17th, the erstwhile medical student, confident in the assumption of his lairdship, "rouped the stocking upon the farm," *i.e.* sold by auction the cattle, etc., on the false pretence of an authority from Patrick, and appropriated the proceeds of the sale.

On 21st June the prisoners, having been removed to Edinburgh, were examined there before Mr. Balfour of Pilrig, Sheriff-Substitute of Edinburgh—the kinsman of Stevenson's David Balfour—and were committed to the Tolbooth to await their trial. It is said that when they landed at Leith, Katharine was with difficulty rescued from the fury of the populace, so strong was the feeling against her by reason of the rumour of her misdeeds.

It may be convenient here briefly to consider the purport of the prisoners' judicial examinations, so far as these relate to the question of the poison. In her first declaration at Forfar Mrs. Ogilvy deponed, "That before Patrick Ogilvy left his brother's house she asked him, any time he was at Alyth, to buy for her and send to Eastmiln two doses of salts and a little laudanum, as she slept very ill. . . . That she took one of the doses of salts on the Friday after her husband's death and the other on the Saturday; and on the Sunday and the Monday nights she took the laudanum each night, and as she did not use the whole laudanum she delivered back the glass and the remainder of laudanum to the said Patrick Ogilvy on his return to Eastmiln after his brother's death"—which, as regards the laudanum, was afterwards proved to be true. She admitted giving her husband the bowl of tea, which "she carried straight from the low room, where they were at breakfast, upstairs to her husband's room." She further declared that Elizabeth Sturrock got the remainder of the bowl of tea, as Eastmiln "did not drink it out." Patrick Ogilvy the same day declared, "That the said laudanum and salts he brought from the East Indies with him, as a remainder of what he

used when his health was bad there and on his passage home.
. . . That within these two weeks he was at the town of
Brechin, and in company with James Carnegie, surgeon, of
that place, *but that he received from him no laudanum or any
other medicine whatever*." He corroborated Katharine's account
of her request for the drugs.

While in Forfar Jail, Patrick learned from a friend that
Dr. Carnegie had disclosed the purchase of the laudanum and
arsenic, "upon which the lieutenant seemed to be under some
concern," and expressed a desire to see the Sheriff and amend
his declaration upon that point; but this could not be done.

When examined before Sheriff Balfour at Edinburgh upon
lengthy interrogatories both prisoners, by advice of their
counsel, declined to answer the various leading questions put
to them, Katharine refusing even to sign her declaration.

On 1st July, Sheriff Campbell of Forfar proceeded to the
house of Eastmiln to search the repositories (which since the
laird's death had been locked up by the scrupulous Alexander), and found two letters obviously written by Katharine
to Eastmiln before their marriage, and later so described in
the indictment. These were produced at the trial as proof of
her handwriting, with reference to an unsigned, unaddressed
letter alleged to have been written by her to Patrick on an
unknown date, in the following terms:—

> Dr Captin,—I was sorrie I missed you this day. I sat at the
> water side a long time this forenoon; I thought you would have
> comed up here. If you had as much mind of me as I have of you, you
> would have comed up, tho' you had but stayed out-by, as there was
> no use for that; there is more rooms in the house then one. God
> knows the heart that I have this day, and instead of being better its
> worse, and not in my power to help it. You are not minding the thing
> that I said to you or [before] you went out here, and what I wrote for.
> Meat I have not tasted since yesterday dinner, nor wont or you come
> here; tho' I should never eat any, it lyes at your door. Your brother
> would give anything you would come, for God's sake come.

This letter was not recovered by Sheriff Campbell on his
search of the premises, but was sent to him later by Alexander
Ogilvy. How it came into that gentleman's doubtful hands
does not appear. By a curious oversight, Hill Burton, in his

narrative of the case, assumes that all three letters were written by Katharine "to her alleged paramour," and even quotes from the two former as such.

The trial commenced before the High Court of Justiciary at Edinburgh upon the 5th of August 1765. The judges present were the Lord Justice-Clerk (Sir Gilbert Elliot of Minto), Lords Auchinleck (Alexander Boswell, father of the immortal Bozzy), Alemore (Andrew Pringle), Kames (Henry Home), Pitfour (James Ferguson), and Coalston (George Brown). The Lord Advocate (Thomas Miller of Barskimming, the pawky Sheriff Miller of *Catriona*), the Solicitor-General (James Montgomery), Sir David Dalrymple (the future Lord Hailes), and two juniors conducted the prosecution. Alexander Lockhart (afterwards Lord Covington) and the great Henry Dundas appeared for Mrs. Ogilvy; David Rae (later the eccentric Lord Eskgrove) and Andrew Crosbie (Scott's Counsellor Pleydell) represented Lieutenant Patrick Ogilvy. The first day was occupied in the usual debate upon the relevancy of the indictment, which was duly found relevant to infer the pains of law. On the following day there was presented to the Court a petition in the name of the pannels regarding Anne Clark, then in custody in the Castle. The movements of this exemplary female since we left her reinstated at Eastmiln are uncertain. Although in her private capacity of friend and relative of the prisoners she had told extra-judicially everything she could against them, and made a formal statement before the Sheriff, she is said to have shrunk from the painful necessity of swearing to her story in the witness-box. She therefore disappeared from the ken of the Lord Advocate until the eve of the trial, when she communicated with his Lordship as follows:—

> LORD ADVOCAT,—Upon my coming to town, I am informed that you have been searching for me. It would never bread in my breest to keept out of the way had it not been for terror of imprisonment; but houping you will be more favourable to me I shall weat upon you tomorrow morning at eight of the clock.
>
> ANNE CLARK.
>
> Sunday evening, eight of the clock.

Despite her "houp," Miss Clark was lodged in the Castle, along with the three women servants from Eastmiln who were to be witnesses in the case. The petition stated that "as she was in a combination to ruin the pannels and, as far as she could, to deprive them of their lives as well as their reputations," it was obviously unfair to them that she should have an opportunity of tampering with the other witnesses. It was accordingly craved that she should be separated from them. This was granted by the Court; but it afterwards appeared that Anne was only removed for one night, and was then replaced in the same room with them as before, by order of Lord George Beauclerk, Commander-in-Chief of the forces in Scotland, who considered "that the room in the gunner's house she was by desire put into, was by no means a place to keep a prisoner in safety."

At seven o'clock in the morning of Monday, 12th August, a jury was empanelled, and the examination of witnesses began. It was the practice of those times that after a jury was once charged with a pannel the Court could not be adjourned until the jury was inclosed, *i.e.* till they withdrew to consider their verdict. The hardships thus entailed upon all concerned where the case was of any length are evident. In the present trial the proceedings up to that stage lasted for forty-three consecutive hours, the jury not being inclosed until two o'clock in the morning of Wednesday, 14th August.

The purport of most of the evidence adduced for the Crown has been given in the foregoing narration, but certain points remain to be considered. With regard to the proof of a criminal intrigue between the pannels, the prosecution relied mainly upon the testimony of Anne Clark—"whose evidence," as Hill Burton well observes, "is always suspicious"—corroborated to some extent by that of the servants, Katharine Campbell, Elizabeth Sturrock, and Anne Sampson. No doubt their memories had been much refreshed by Anne's reminiscences while in the Castle. To Campbell, the most damaging witness of the three, it was objected that she had been dismissed by her mistress for theft, which she practically admitted, and had sworn revenge. The Court, however, allowed her to be examined. When Anne Clark was called, Dundas, for the defence, strongly objected to her admission on the grounds of her infamous character and lurid past; that, in confederacy with Alexander Ogilvy, she herself had propagated the false reports which led to the pannels' arrest; and that she had expressed deadly malice against them, and threatened to bereave them of their lives. Sir David Dalrymple, in reply, did not attempt to whitewash his fair witness, but contended that general proof of character was incompetent; that the crimes charged were occult crimes, only provable by witnesses who lived in the family, "be their character what it will"; that until the evidence was closed it could not be said whether the reports spread by Miss Clark were false or not; and that the pannels must prove the cause of her alleged ill-will. The Court admitted the witness, reserving the question of malice. Anne Clark's examination occupied eight hours. We cannot here discuss the infragrant details of her evidence, though these present many singular and suggestive features—the case was heard with closed doors, from which let the gentle reader, like the stranger admonished by Mrs. Sapsea's epitaph, "with a blush retire"; but in reference to the proof upon this part of the case it may be generally remarked that the behaviour of the prisoners, as described by Anne Clark and her attesting nymphs, exhibits a reckless disregard of consequences which well-nigh passes belief, while the corroborative evidence of undue intimacy is to a large extent discounted by what we know of the coarseness of speech and manners pervading Scottish society in those days. The acts of familiarity upon which the prosecutor relied to support Anne's tale were said to have occurred in public and before third parties, some even in presence of the husband himself. The very limited capacity of the house of Eastmiln has also to be borne in mind. It appears from an unpublished sketch-plan, prepared for the use of Crown counsel, that the house consisted of two storeys; upon the ground floor there were but two rooms, kitchen and parlour, one on either side of the entrance hall or passage; on the flat above were two bedrooms corresponding to the rooms below, with a small closet between them over the lobby. A garret in the roof was used as a store-room. We learn from the evidence that the servants slept in the kitchen, beneath the west bedroom occupied by the laird and his wife; that the east bedroom, above the parlour, was assigned to the lieutenant; and that Anne Clark and old Lady Eastmiln shared a "box-bed" in the parlour. So homely and primitive were then the habits of the Scots gentry that a family of five persons and three servants were thus "accommodated" in four small rooms. It is also in evidence that the kitchen ceiling was unplastered, and that the conversation of the laird and his wife in their bed in the room above was clearly audible in the kitchen below. The partition walls, too, were of lath and plaster, which enabled Anne Clark to overhear from the staircase all that went on in the lieutenant's room. Verily the house of Eastmiln was ill adapted to purposes of stealthy intrigue. If Anne Clark's astonishing tale be true the guilt of the pannels on this count must be accepted; but one hesitates at which the more to marvel—the baseness of Anne if forsworn, or Katharine's unblushing impudence if guilty.

The proof of the murder is in a different case. The ground of the prosecution was that Eastmiln died of poison. This, strange as it may seem, looking to the subsequent verdict, the medical evidence entirely failed to establish. Dr. Meik, who first saw the body, found "the nails and a part of the breast discoloured and his tongue swelled beyond its natural size and cleaving to the roof of his mouth." He was "unacquainted with the effects of poison," but having been told by Alexander Ogilvy that poison had been administered in this case, he "conjectured" it to have caused the death. Dr. Ramsay concurred as to the post-mortem appearances, with this addition, that the lips were "more discoloured than by a natural death," and, upon the same information, agreed with Dr. Meik. Both admitted having seen similar symptoms in cases of death from natural causes. Dr. Ogilvy, who had inspected the corpse at the request of the Sheriff, deponed "That the breast was white and the lips pretty much of a natural colour. . . . That the face, the arms, and several other parts of the body were black and livid, and that the nails were remarkably black." Manifestly the condition of the corpse, which when seen by the surgeons had lain unburied for six summer days, was due to putrefaction. This Dr. Ogilvy practically admitted, by stating that "he could draw no conclusion as to the cause of the defunct's death." The only appearance that struck him as peculiar was the condition of the tongue, which was "such as occurs from convulsions or other strong causes."

In view of the negative testimony of these experts as to the cause of death, the evidence regarding Eastmiln's general health becomes important. Anne Clark and the three servants represent him as a strong man, sound and hearty until the last day of his life. His mother, a valuable witness on this as upon many other points, was called by neither party— which affords matter for reflection. Mr. Spalding, his brother-in-law, swore that for some years past Eastmiln had been in bad health, "complaining often of a heart-cholic or pain in his stomach, attended with a short cough which was not continual but seldom left him." That some years before he had suffered from an "ulcerous fever" (as was otherwise proved to be the fact), and was never the same man again; also that on one occasion, being seized with illness at the house of Glenkilry, Eastmiln "got hot ale and whisky with a scrape of nutmeg in it, and was put to bed without any supper"—a curious remedy for gastric inflammation. Mr. Spalding further stated that in February, the month after the marriage, he wrote to Katharine's mother, Lady Nairn, advising "that infeftment be taken in favor of Mrs. Ogilvy upon her marriage contract," owing to the unsatisfactory state of her husband's health. His brother-in-law, Andrew Stewart, deponed that Eastmiln was "a tender man," whose sister, Martha Ogilvy (Stewart's wife), used to say that he would not be a long liver. He repeated what Eastmiln had told him, as already mentioned, about "swarfing on the hill." James Millam, his friend and neighbour, said that four days before Eastmiln died he complained to him "of a gravel and a cholic, and that he could not live if he got not the better of it." On the Tuesday before his death he became unwell at the deponent's house. He had a fire lit to warm him, though the night was not cold, and got heated chaff applied to ease his suffering. He remarked to the witness "that he was fading as fast as dew off the grass; that he could not get peaceable possession of his house for Anne Clark; that he wished her away; and he got from the deponent a ten-shilling note for the expense of her journey." But that faithful spinster was not so easily disposed of. Five witnesses from Glenisla proved that the day before his death Eastmiln had been attacked by severe internal pain while visiting his tenants; that he had to lie down upon the ground; that he said he had not been so ill for six years; and that "he behoved to get Dr. Ogilvy to give him something to do him good." It should be remembered that at this time there is no suggestion of his having been poisoned by his wife, who, if she had the will, had not then the means to do so, and it is difficult to reconcile the evidence of these relatives and friends with the laird's rude health, as sworn to by Anne and the accusing maids. To poison a person in such a condition seems, to the lay mind, a superfluity of naughtiness.

What told most heavily against the lieutenant undoubtedly was his deal in arsenic with Dr. Carnegie at Brechin, of the purchase and disposal of which no satisfactory explanation was offered. But, curiously, it was not even proved that the substance sold was in fact arsenic; all that Dr. Carnegie could say was that he had bought it as such long before, and had "heard from those he sold it to that it had killed rats." So much for scientific testimony in 1765! With regard to Katharine, Anne Sampson, one of the maids, swore that on the morning of the day of Eastmiln's death, having followed her mistress upstairs on some domestic errand, she saw her in a closet adjoining the bedroom, "stirring about the tea with her face to the door," but did not see her put anything in the tea. Mrs. Ogilvy made no attempt to conceal what she was doing, and spoke both to the servant and to a lad employed in the house, who was also present at the time. Elizabeth Sturrock deponed that her mistress had tried to induce her to say she (Sturrock) had drunk the remainder of the tea. She admitted that Mrs. Ogilvy brought her tea that morning, when she was ill in bed, but she denied it was what had been left by Eastmiln. That Katharine did take salts—she being then in a delicate state of health—Anne Clark admits, and is corroborated by Elizabeth Sturrock, who says she "got a part of them." The incriminating letter from Katharine to Patrick produced by Alexander, if genuine, leaves little doubt as to their intimacy. One sentence only can be held to refer to the poison: "You are not minding the thing that I said to you or [before] you went out here, and what I wrote for." This might equally be referable to the salts which she says she had asked him to send her. As already pointed out, this letter was without either date or signature, but the indefatigable Anne, presumably an expert in handwriting, swore that it was written by Mrs. Ogilvy. Yet when shewn an undoubted letter of Katharine, addressed to Eastmiln, "she did not know whose handwriting it was."

The case for the prosecution was closed at three o'clock on Tuesday afternoon, and the exculpatory proof and addresses to the jury occupied till two o'clock on Wednesday morning. Of the sixty-four witnesses cited for the Crown twenty-four were examined; a hundred and eight witnesses had been summoned for the defence, but for reasons that will presently appear, only ten of these were called. The contemporary report of the trial unfortunately does not include the speeches of counsel, but we read in the *Scots Magazine* that "the evidence was summed up by the Lord Advocate for the King, by Mr. Rae for Lieutenant Ogilvy, and by Mr. Lockhart for Mrs. Ogilvy." Ramsay of Ochtertyre, who was then at the Scots bar, says of Lockhart's performance on this occasion: "He never failed to shine exceedingly in a very long trial, when defending criminals whose case appeared to be desperate. Mr. Crosbie told me soon after, that in the trial of the Ogilvies, which lasted forty-eight hours, he stood the fatigue better than the youngest of them. He took down every deposition with his own hands, but no short ones, when he went out to take a little air. In answering Lord Advocate Miller, who was perfectly worn out, he displayed such powers of eloquence and ingenuity as astonished everybody. To save the life of his unhappy client he gave up, with great art, her character; but contended there was no legal proof of her guilt, though enough to damn her fame."

At four o'clock on the afternoon of Wednesday, 14th August, the jury, "by a great plurality of voices," found both pannels guilty as libelled. Lockhart at once entered a plea in arrest of judgment in respect of certain irregularities in the proceedings. We cannot here deal fully with this interesting debate, which throws an extraordinary light upon the judicial procedure of the day—how in the course of the trial the jury repeatedly "dispersed into different corners of the house," eating and drinking as they pleased, and talking to the Crown witnesses and the counsel for the prosecution; how between three and five o'clock on the Tuesday morning only one of the judges remained upon the bench, "the rest retiring and conversing in private with sundry of the jury and others"; how, "when the evidence on the part of the pannels began to be adduced, several of the jury shewed a very great impatience and insisted that that evidence which the pannels thought material for them should be cut short, and some of them particularly disputed the relevancy and propriety of the questions put by the counsel for the pannels with great heat, insomuch that some of the judges and other jurymen were obliged to interpose, in order that the exculpatory proof might go on; and the counsel for the pannels were obliged to pass from many witnesses, in order to procure attention from those assizers. Hence, though thirty-three hours were spent in hearing calmly the proof adduced for the prosecutors, yet the proof for the pannels, after being heard by those jurymen with great impatience, was put an end to in about three hours." Finally, how, contrary to an Act of Charles II, whereby the prisoner's advocate was to have the last word,

Lord Kames, one of the judges, addressed the jury upon the whole case after counsel had done so for the defence. This is the first recorded instance in Scots criminal practice of the familiar charge to the jury by the presiding judge. The Court, in respect of the "regularity and accuracy" with which the trial had been conducted, repelled the plea. But Lockhart had still another card to play; he alleged that his client was pregnant, and in her case judgment was superseded until her condition should be reported upon by five professional ladies. Sentence of death was then pronounced against Patrick Ogilvy, to be executed on 25th September, and the Court rose, doubtless with much relief.

Next day the jury of matrons, which included Mrs. Shiells, a local practitioner eminent in her art, of whom we shall hear again, reported that they could give no positive opinion on the subject of the remit. The Court therefore delayed pronouncing sentence against Mrs. Ogilvy till 18th November, to give the five ladies the opportunity of arriving at a definite conclusion.

Meanwhile the friends of the prisoners were not idle in their interests. Application was made to the King in Council for a respite to Patrick Ogilvy, not of favour but of right, until certain points of law should be determined:—(1) Whether in a capital case an appeal was competent from the High Court of Justiciary to the House of Lords? (2) Whether the proceedings at the trial were fair and legal according to the law of Scotland? and (3) Whether, if the first point were doubtful, the execution of the convict should be respited till that question was judged by Parliament, which was not then sitting? Prior to the determination of these questions, which were remitted to the decision of the Attorney-General for England and the Lord Advocate, Patrick received four reprieves—the three first for fourteen days each, the last for seven days only. He is said to have been a great player on the violin, and the interval between his condemnation and execution was, we are told, "exclusively devoted to his performance on that instrument."

While the young lieutenant's fate yet hung in the balance, the judicial dovecot of the Parliament House was fluttered by the publication in certain Edinburgh journals of an "opinion" by an English counsel, one Mr. M'Carty, upon the points at issue. This gentleman, writing from London on 14th September, animadverted upon the conduct of the trial, holding that the prisoners were prejudiced by being tried for two entirely different crimes upon one indictment. He was of opinion that if the crimes charged were considered separately and the evidence produced to support one crime taken singly, without the assistance of the other, no jury in England would have found the prisoners guilty. "The intrigue was supposed to be certain, because the husband was supposed to have been poisoned; and, on the other hand, the man was believed to be poisoned, because there was a supposed proof of intrigue." After criticizing the peculiar features of the evidence with some freedom and to excellent purpose, Mr. M'Carty saw neither law nor reason why the proceedings of the Court of Justiciary might not be subject, as well as those of the Court of Session, to review by the Supreme Court. These views on the subject of criminal appeal gave great offence to the College of Justice. The publication of the opinion was held to be contempt of Court, and, upon the complaint of the Lord Advocate, the publishers of the *Edinburgh Weekly Journal*, where it first appeared, and of the *Courant*, *Caledonian Mercury*, and *Scots Magazine*, in which it was reprinted, were haled before the Court of Justiciary to answer for their offence. They severally expressed sorrow for the wrong they had done, and the Court, while dwelling on the "high indignity" which it had thereby sustained, dismissed them with a rebuke.

The law officers of the Crown having reported in the negative upon the questions submitted to them, Patrick Ogilvy was executed in the Grassmarket on 13th November, pursuant to his sentence. Chambers states, so popular was the lieutenant with his regiment, which was then quartered in the Castle, that it was judged necessary "to shut them up in that fortress till the execution was over, lest they might attempt a rescue."

A letter from his colonel, giving him an excellent character, is printed in the report of the trial. In "An Authentick Copy" of his dying speech, published at the time, we read, "As to the crimes I am accused of, the trial itself will shew the propensity of the witnesses, where civility and possibly folly are explained into actual guilt; and of both crimes for which I am now doomed to suffer I declare my innocence, and that no persuasion could ever have made me condescend to them. I freely forgive every person concerned in this melancholy affair, and wherein any of them have been faulty to me I pray God to forgive them." The newspapers of the day record a shocking incident at the execution. After he was "turned over," the noose slipped and he fell to the ground. The wretched man, "making what resistence he could," was again dragged up the ladder by the hangman and others, "who turned him over a second time, and he continued hanging till dead." For assisting the law on this occasion, a member of the Society of Tron-Men (chimney-sweeps) was expelled from that association and banished to Leith for five years—a grievous punishment for an Edinburgh citizen.

On 18th November the professional ladies were at length enabled to report that Mrs. Ogilvy could not in humanity be hanged for several months, and the Court further delayed sentence until 10th March. Upon 21st November Katharine presented a petition to the Court, praying that a judicial factor should be appointed to administer the estates of the deceased laird in the interests of her unborn child. Alexander Ogilvy, his brother's heir-presumptive, did not meantime oppose the application, but in his answers he indicated that if occasion arose he meant to contest the succession. A factor was duly appointed.

On 27th January 1766, in the Tolbooth of Edinburgh, Mrs. Ogilvy gave birth to a daughter. When the Court met on 10th March to pronounce sentence of death, a physician and two nurses deponed that she was not yet strong enough to be brought up for judgment. The diet was therefore continued for a week. At seven o'clock on the night of Saturday the 15th, however, the interesting invalid summoned sufficient energy to burst her bonds. Her escape, which is said not to have been discovered till the Sunday afternoon, was, as we shall see, probably collusive. The contemporary accounts are suspicious. It is said that, being indulged with "the quiet and privacy which the nature of her illness required," she dressed herself in man's clothes, and, the door of her room having been at her request "left open for the benefit of the air," she naturally walked out. Perhaps the turnkeys and sentries were still celebrating the New Year, old style. On Monday the 17th the Lord Justice-Clerk granted a warrant for her arrest, and the magistrates of Edinburgh issued a notice offering a reward of one hundred guineas for her apprehension. She is described as "middle sized and strong made; has a high nose, black eye-brows, and of a pale complexion"—a description which seems wilfully at variance with the received accounts of her beauty. She "went off on Saturday night in a post-chaise for England by the way of Berwick; and had on an officer's habit and a hat slouched in the cocks, with a cockade in it." On the 22nd the Government announced in the *London Gazette* an additional hundred guineas reward for her recapture. It is therein stated that Mrs. Ogilvy, disguised as a young gentleman, very thin and sickly, muffled up in a greatcoat, and attended by a servant, had passed through Haddington on Saturday at midnight, and had pushed on with four horses, day and night, from stage to stage, towards London. The *Gentleman's Magazine* records "that information was received at Mr. Fielding, the magistrate's, office, that on the Wednesday following she was at Dover in the dress of an officer, endeavouring to procure a passage to France"; and in a later report, that having failed to do so, she "returned from Dover to London, took a hackney coach to Billingsgate, got on board a Gravesend boat, with a gentleman to accompany her, agreed with a tilt boat there to take them over to France for eight guineas and a guinea a day for waiting for them four days in order to bring them back; which tilt boat landed them at Calais, but is since returned without them." This, of course, was a device to gain time and baffle her pursuers.

But tradition gives a more probable account of Katharine's escape from the prison. Her uncle, Mr. William Nairn, a well-known and respected member of the Scots bar, was at that time Commissary Clerk of Edinburgh. He was raised to the Bench in 1786 with the judicial title of Lord Dunsinnan, and in 1790 succeeded to the baronetcy, which, on his death in 1811, became extinct. His lordship is said to have contrived his niece's freedom. Sir Daniel Wilson, in his *Memorials*, states, upon the authority of Charles Kirkpatrick Sharpe, that Katharine walked out of the Tolbooth "disguised in the garments of Mrs. Shiells, the midwife who had been in attendance on her and added to her other favours this extra-professional delivery." James Maidment, in *Kay's Portraits*, tells the same story, with the additional particular that Mrs. Shiells had feigned toothache for some days before, and muffled her head in a shawl. The doorkeeper, according to Chambers's *Traditions*, knowing what was afoot, gave the fictitious nurse a slap on the back as she left the prison, and bade her begone for "a howling old Jezebel." Sharpe owed his own introduction to the world to the good offices of this benevolent dame, who, as Chambers notes, was still practising in Edinburgh so late as 1805.

There are various accounts of Katharine's adventures after she had successfully "broke prison." Sharpe says that in her confusion she "risped" at Lord Alva's door in James's Court, mistaking the house for that of her father's agent, when the footboy who opened the door recognized her, having been present at the trial, and immediately raised an alarm. As the case was heard *in camera*, this lad must have been exception-ally privileged. Her uncle's house was in a tenement at the head of the Parliament Stairs, the site of which is now occu-pied by the Justiciary Court-room. Thither, says Sharpe, Katharine fled, and was concealed in a cellar by Mr. Nairn till the hue and cry was over, when his clerk, Mr. James Bremner, afterwards Solicitor of Stamps, accompanied her to the

Continent. Maidment, on the other hand, states that on the night of her escape a carriage was in waiting at the foot of the Horse Wynd, in which she and Mr. Bremner at once left the city. In view of the contemporary evidence there is little doubt that this is the correct version of her flight. She probably assumed the officer's dress *en route*. Chambers says that the coachman had orders, if the pursuit waxed hot, to drive into the sea so that she might drown herself. The contingency, fortunately for her fellow-traveller, did not arise. Thus Katharine vanished from the ken of her contemporaries, and history knows nothing certain of her fate.

"Was she guilty, was she innocent, and, if innocent, why did Lieutenant Patrick Ogilvy buy arsenic at Brechin?" asks Mr. Andrew Lang; and indeed these are "puzzling questions," which every reader must answer for himself.

Wilson states that Mrs. Ogilvy went from France to America, married again, "and died at an advanced age, surrounded by a numerous family." Maidment says she was afterwards "very fortunate, having been married to a Dutch gentleman," with satisfactory results, as above. Alternatively, she took the veil, and, surviving the French Revolution, died in England in the nineteenth century. Chambers marries her happily to "a French gentleman," and credits her with the usual large family. Similar vague surmises are still current regarding the aftermath of Madeleine Smith.

The only fresh light which the present writer has been able to discover is derived from the following sources:—a paragraph in the *Westminster Magazine* of 1777—"Mrs. Ogilvie, who escaped out of Edinburgh Jail for the murder of her husband, is now in a convent at Lisle, a sincere penitent"; and an unpublished MS. note in a contemporary copy of the trial—"Catherine Ogilvie or Nairn did not marry a French nobleman as was at one time reported. She entered a convent and remained there until the troubles consequent upon the French Revolution compelled herself and the other inmates to fly to England, where she died. My informant, Mr. Irvine, lawyer of Dunse, tells me that a friend of his saw her tomb,

with the name 'Catherine Ogilvie' upon it; and that upon
inquiry the superior mentioned that of all the females in the
convent she was the most exemplary in every respect."

Of the others concerned in the tragedy, the unconscious
infant died in the Tolbooth within two months of her birth.
She is said to have been "overlaid," but by whom is not
recorded. The mother was then in France. It is satisfactory
to learn that Alexander Ogilvy took no benefit from the
child's death, for on 1st March 1766, the anniversary of Anne
Clark's arrival at Eastmiln, that bold spirit was arrested for
bigamy, and was in his turn committed to the Tolbooth. One
might have expected that Anne would be the redundant bride,
but from his indictment it appears that the favoured lady was
a Miss Margaret Dow, daughter of an officer of the Royal
Highlanders, unlawfully espoused by him so lately as 24th
February. Upon his trial on 4th August, Alexander pleaded
guilty to the charge, and was banished for seven years. He
was allowed, however, to remain two months in Scotland to
settle his affairs, which he effectually did in the following
manner: while leaning over the window of a house in one
of Auld Reikie's towering *lands*, he lost his balance, fell out,
and was killed on the spot. Thus only Anne Clark and old
Lady Eastmiln withstood the changes of that eventful year.
"Their conversation must have been rich in curious reminiscences," like that of Lady Bothwell and her first love,
Ogilvy of Boyne, when they came together at the end of
the chapter.

The case of Katharine Nairn is one of the most attractive in
our criminal annals, and should this imperfect summary be
the means of sending a stray reader to the report of the trial
itself, he will not go unrewarded.

## Postscript

The matter of this chapter was collected so long ago as 1913. The seed fell on good ground: see *The Laird*, by Winifred Duke (London: John Long, 1925), in which that well-known Scots novelist has clothed agreeably the dry bones of fact with the living garments of fiction.

Since the above essay was written I have edited a full report of the case: *The Trial of Katharine Nairn*: in the Notable British Trials series (Edinburgh: 1926), containing the official record of the evidence and many illustrative documents from original sources.

# KEITH OF NORTHFIELD

# KEITH OF NORTHFIELD

In perusing this trial, a very material defect in the evidence must immediately occur. No proof has been brought sufficient to satisfy us that Mr. Keith of Northfield died a violent death.                                    ADVERTISEMENT.

SOCIETY in Scotland had a sufficiency of scandal to furnish topics for many tea-tables in the summer of 1766. In March of that year, the beautiful Katharine Nairn, then under sentence of death for the murder of her husband, made her picturesque escape from the Heart of Midlothian, not without suspicion of her uncle's connivance, himself being a Senator of the College of Justice, and successfully fled to that *plaisant pays de France*, where they order some matters better, as Mr. Yorick remarked. The Douglas Cause, that huge, unwieldy lawsuit, was at length well under way, and the portentous pleadings began in July their three weeks' course before "the Fifteen" at Edinburgh, amid the intense excitement of a per-fervid people, bets to the amount of £100,000 being laid upon the result. That same month provided a fresh sensation: Mrs. Keith of Northfield, in Banffshire, and her son William were, on the information of the laird, her stepson, arrested for the murder of his father ten years before within the house of Northfield.

"The singular circumstances of this case," observes a contemporary pamphleteer, "the atrocious nature of the crime, the great distance of time since that crime is said to have been committed, together with the doubtfulness and uncertainty of the evidence, have excited the curiosity of the public"— and incidentally inspired his pen. And though the world has long since ceased to concern itself as to whether the widow and her son were cold-blooded assassins or the innocent victims of family spite and medical ignorance, their trial may still be read with interest, as affording a quaint picture of the Scottish life of its day, and as an instructive problem in the niceties of presumptive proof.

Alexander Keith, the late laird—old Northfield, as he was termed at the trial, to distinguish him from his son and successor—was born in 1692, and was thus "three score and three years when he died" on 21st November 1756. Some twenty years before his death, Northfield, a widower with a son and daughter, had married a girl named Helen Watt, the daughter of a fisherman at Crovie, a village in Banffshire, who bore him several children, and with whom, as she afterwards alleged, he always lived very happily. Their union, however, had other and less pleasing results, for the marriage was deeply resented by the family of the first wife, whose brother "thought it a most disgraceful one." It led to a complete estrangement between old Northfield and George Keith, his son and heir, who quarrelled with his father on the subject, and left home in consequence, nor were they ever reconciled during the old man's life. The laird's brother and sister, John and Anne Keith, who lived "about three rig-lengths distant," continued upon friendly terms with their relatives at Northfield. The daughter of the first marriage later made her own experiment in matrimony, so that in the month of November 1756 the household consisted, in addition to the servants, of the laird and his second wife and their five children—William, aged 17; Henrietta, 15; Elizabeth, 13; Alexander, 10; and Helen, 7. Old Northfield, it was alleged, had early in life contracted a habit of excessive drinking, which gradually impaired his health, and being persisted in for a long course of years, at length ruined a constitution naturally sound. Be that as it may, there is evidence that during the autumn of 1756 the laird's health was in a critical condition. His brother, John Keith, deponed "that he had been long in a valetudinary way," and considered himself "a-dying"; while his medical attendant, Dr. Chap, surgeon in Old Deer, stated that he professionally visited the laird, who was suffering from "an asthma, attended with a high fever," until the week before his death, when he found him so ill that he also "thought him a-dying." The doctor, who seems to have been an easy-going practitioner, added that in these circumstances he desired Mrs. Keith not to send for him again unless her husband "grew better," and took his departure, leaving the patient to the care of Providence.

Old Northfield, having thus had his own belief that his days were numbered fortified by the expert opinion of the Faculty, prepared like a prudent man for the inevitable end. In view of the attitude adopted from the first by his eldest son George towards his father's second wife and family, and of the unforgiving temper which that young man had since exhibited towards himself, the laird well knew that he could trust little to his heir's generosity or good feeling in regard to the future of his widow and younger children. In order, therefore, to secure for them some provision after his death, he decided to make a will settling upon them certain small sums of money, by no means beyond what his estate could easily bear. Accordingly, a few days before his death, Northfield sent for his old friend the Reverend James Wilson, minister of Gamrie, who at his request wrote out for him a short document embodying this intention, which was duly signed by the testator in presence of his neighbour, Mr. Garden of Troup, and his own servant, William Taylor, who subscribed the deed as attesting witnesses. It was admitted that the execution of this will was the voluntary act of the laird, and that the provisions therein contained were equitable, and such as his estate could well afford. Nevertheless, as afterwards appeared, the granting of these sums, small though they were, gave great offence to his successor.

In the evidence led at the trial we have glimpses of the old man on what was to be his last day in this world. Mr. Wilson, the minister, called in the afternoon to see the invalid, and found him looking better. Northfield, who appears to have borne his bodily infirmities with a cheerful spirit, talked to his reverend visitor "in his usual jocose manner." The minister thought him "to be past danger." William Taylor, the servant who had witnessed the will, having finished his day's work, went up to ask for his master. The laird, though confined to his room, apparently did not keep his bed; he was "sitting in the chair with one leg above the other, and a pinch of snuff between his finger and thumb," and remarked that he was feeling better. George Gelly, a friend, afterwards looked in before dark to inquire for him, and saw him "sitting in the chair, and not very well." They talked together for a while, and Northfield laughed several times in the course of the conversation. The last caller, one James Manson, shoemaker in Gardenstoun, came that evening as usual to shave the laird, who "was sitting in his night-gown, not well." That night Northfield, as seems to have been his custom during his illness, supped in his bedroom with his wife and their five children. We are told that he took "a very little supper, either of aleberry or kail-brose," which, in view of his condition, is not surprising. What little he did eat seems to have disagreed with him, for he complained of feeling worse, and asked to be put to bed. The bed was accordingly made ready, "a blanket was warmed and put about him," and the old man was helped into bed by his wife and her eldest son, William. The supper dishes having been removed by the servant, the laird "desired his children to go to bed, for that he wanted to be quiet." The two eldest girls, Henrietta and Elizabeth, then bade their parents good-night and went to their own room.

As to what afterwards happened we have no information except the declarations of the widow and her son, emitted later with reference to the charge of murder brought against them by George Keith. In considering these, it has to be kept in view that although they were made ten years after the event, by two persons, suddenly seized and separately examined upon the most dreadful of charges, they are nevertheless strikingly uniform and consistent. The laird having told his wife that he was afraid he would die in the night, she insisted that the boy William should remain in the room, to be at hand in case his father grew worse, and the old man "desired him to lye down at his back to see if he could gather any heat." Mrs. Keith then went to bed herself, along with her two youngest children, Alexander and Helen, "in a bed at the end of the deceased's bed," and the lad, having "thrown off all his clothes but his breeches," blew out the solitary candle and lay down beside his father. He noticed that the old man's breathing was barely perceptible, and spoke to him twice, but received no answer. He then jumped out of bed, and "calling out hastily in surprise to his mother to rise and light the candle, for his father was either dead or dying," ran to the door to summon the two elder girls and the maid. They entered the room as Mrs. Keith was relighting the candle.

Meanwhile, as appears from her evidence, the servant, Elspeth Bruce, was in the kitchen immediately adjoining Northfield's bedroom, from which it was divided by "a timber partition." She said she heard no sound in the bedroom that night. After supper Henrietta Keith came into the kitchen and told her that the laird "was sitting ben yonder, and that he had taken two spoonfuls of brose to his supper"; and "in a little time after the cry came ben that he was dead." Elspeth then ran into her master's room, where she was joined by the two girls. The subsequent events as spoken to by her are, with the exception presently to be noticed, in accordance with the declarations of Mrs. Keith and her son. Neither Henrietta nor Elizabeth was called as a witness at the trial, and the children, Alexander and Helen, were too young to be examined. William declared that when the others came in and the candle was lighted, he looked at his father's face and saw "one eye shut and another open; his lips quivered a little, and he could just be observed to breathe." Mrs. Keith said that she herself did not then look at her husband, as she "expected he would come alive again," but that Henrietta did so, and told her that "she saw her father's lips moving." Elspeth says she looked at her master, "and found him in appearance dead in the bed." William states that he then sent her for William Spence—apparently one of old Northfield's men—"who was drying corn at the kiln," and that she returned with Spence forthwith, by which time "the deceased's breathing could not be observed, and the eye that was formerly open was partly shut." Elspeth says nothing of this incident, and Spence was not produced as a witness at the trial. Probably he was dead, for the prisoners' counsel afterwards, with justice, complained that the defence had suffered greatly by reason of the ten years' delay in bringing the charge, owing to the death of several witnesses "who would have been of the most material consequence in their exculpation." Elspeth, according to the story of the mother and son, was then dispatched to bring John and Ann Keith. the laird's brother and sister, who lived at hand, which, as she admits, she did. Mrs. Keith declared that when John Keith came they both looked at her husband, and John "said he did not think but he was dead." John Keith, though examined at the trial, was asked no question as to this night's doings, which is the more curious as Elspeth had stated that when she returned at once with the Keiths, she found the laird's body already taken out of bed and "streikit upon a deal"—laid out upon a board; whereas both Mrs. Keith and William declare that this was not done until after the arrival of Northfield's brother and sister. Anne Keith had died some years before the trial, and was not amenable to earthly citation, but John could have told what actually occurred. The importance of this point is, that while we have plenty of evidence as to the appearance presented by the body next day, there is none as to its condition on the night of the death.

Northfield breathed his last about ten o'clock on the evening of Monday, 21st November, and that night there was no suspicion whatever that he had not died in the natural course of his disease. It is therefore instructive to see from what quarter the first suggestion of murder came. We do not know where George Keith lived, but it must have been in the neighbourhood, for he had early information of his bereavement, and lost no time in coming to look after the inheritance. He entered the house of Northfield, to which he had been so long a stranger, on the morning after his father's death, and it is probable that not till then did he learn of the provisions of the will. Now the sole foundation for

the charge brought by him ten years later against the mother
and son was a certain discoloration of the skin upon the neck
and breast of Northfield's body, seen on the Tuesday and
Wednesday after his death.   He was buried, as we shall find,
on the forenoon of Thurdsay, and the "chesting" spoken to
by some of the witnesses probably did not take place till the
night before, as the coffin had to be made and the funeral
arranged.   The first we hear of the mysterious mark is in
the evidence of Elspeth Bruce, who depones "That when
George Keith, young Northfield, came next morning [Tues-
day] and took a look at his father's corpse, he expressed some
suspicion of foul play because of a blae [livid] mark round
his neck."   Elspeth, who obviously had heard no word of
this before, then went into the room and examined the body,
when she "saw a blae mark round the defunct's neck about
the breadth of two fingers, and a blae spot upon his breast,"
which she thought were "strange circumstances."   The
other evidence of those who saw the marks is as follows:
William Taylor, the late laird's servant, "saw a blue mark
about his neck about the breadth of three fingers, but whether
it went round the back part of his neck he cannot say, because
he did not see that part."   John Strachan, wright in Gardenstoun, who made old Northfield's coffin, stated that when the
body was being placed in it, young Northfield turned down
the grave-clothes "and shewed the deponent a mark round
the fore part of the defunct's neck, but whether it went round
he cannot say, because he did not see the back part of his
neck; that he also saw a mark upon the defunct's breast that
reached down towards the slot of his breast; and that the
marks were of a blackish blue, like the neck of a fowl newly
strangled."   James King, who assisted Strachan "to make
the coffin for the late Northfield, and to put him into it," said
that at young Northfield's request he looked at the body, and
saw "a black red mark round the neck, such as the deponent
never saw on any corpse before that time."   Alexander
Hepburn, in Cushnie, deponed that he inspected the body at
the "chesting," being desired to do so by young Northfield,

"who threw off or laid aside the dead cloaths from the upper part of the body." The first thing that attracted his attention was "some blue spots upon the breast"; the next thing he noticed was "a blue girth that went round his neck, like bruised blood; and on the back part of the neck he saw a mark like what is occasioned by a knot drawn strait."

The observations of Elspeth Bruce and William Taylor were each the result of a private view of the corpse, but the evidence of Strachan, King, and Hepburn has reference to one and the same occasion, namely, the "chesting," at which young Northfield, Mrs. Keith, the lad William, and apparently John Keith, were present. This seems to have been the first time that the widow's attention was specially called to the marks. Hepburn states that she appeared unwilling to have the body inspected, saying "that there was nothing unseemly to be seen there." Taylor, however, depones "That no person, so far as he knows, was hindered from looking to the corpse." The same witness adds that he asked Mrs. Keith, in presence of John Keith "and others," what was the meaning of that mark, and that she answered that it was occasioned by a string tied round Northfield's neck "for holding on a plaister." John Keith, when in the witness-box, says nothing about this incident. Such was the explanation given by Mrs. Keith at the time, so soon as she was asked about the matter. Ten years afterwards she and her son gave in their declarations a more particular account of the circumstance. Mrs. Keith declared, "That she did not look at the body that night [of the death], but next day she assisted to put on a shirt on the body, and then she observed something blue about the back part of the neck, but cannot tell whether that blueness was round his neck or not; That she heard a plaister had been applied to the deceased's back or his neck; but when she assisted to put on the shirt on the dead body, as above, she cannot tell whether the plaister was on the body or not, or whether there was any mark of a plaister upon the body or not; and that she can tell nothing more of her husband's death than is above mentioned." William is more specific: "Declares, that there had been a blistering plaister applied to the deceased's back; and after it was taken away, kail-blades [cabbage leaves] were applied to the place where the plaister had been; and in order to keep these blades in the proper place, they were tied on with the deceased's own garters, which went below the arm-pits, and round the farther side of the neck; and these kail-blades and garters continued in that situation after the deceased's death, until his grave-linen was made and put upon him. Declares, that he was present when the grave-linen was put upon the body; at which time some of the women who were there loosed the above garters, and took them away; and the declarant then observed a blue spot upon the left breast, about the breadth of three fingers, but did not observe anything about the neck, further than that there was a great swelling over his whole body. Declares, that from the time the deceased was put to bed the evening of his death, no person went near him until the declarant called to light a candle, as above; nor did the deceased make the least noise after he was put to bed."

Now someone must have helped to prepare the body for the grave, and whoever did so would be likely to notice this curious arrangement of the garters, which can hardly have been invented by William. But throughout the trial no other reference is made to these "women who were there," unless it be that one of them was Anne Keith, who had died some years before, and, as was alleged for the defence, would have confirmed the prisoners' explanation as to "the innocent and accidental cause of these discoloured appearances on the dead body, which are the frail and only foundation of this prosecution." That the plasters, at least, were no creation of the young man's fancy is proved by the testimony of Dr. Chap, who depones that when he withdrew from the case as hopeless, he "left two blistering plaisters to put upon his [Northfield's] back." When and by whom the plaster and "kail-blades" were respectively applied, tied on, and taken off, who took away the garters and what became of them, are matters upon which the evidence throws no light.

It appears that there were "words" between the widow and the heir "about naming a day for the late Northfield's burial," Mrs. Keith proposing Thursday and George Keith wishing the interment postponed till Saturday. The widow carried her point. John Mair, a neighbour, who mentions this difference, states that before the funeral "he heard the said George require Elspeth Bruce to acquaint him with the circumstances of his father's death; to which she made no answer, but turned about her back and wept. Upon which George said that as she would not tell then, she behoved to tell afterwards." Elspeth says nothing about this incident. Plainly, she had no suspicions till these were suggested to her by George Keith. William Taylor says in his evidence that George objected to the earlier date being fixed "before he had time to prepare matters for the burial"—not because he suspected foul play. Taylor, whose sympathies were evidently engaged in behalf of the prosecution, adds that on the night following Northfield's death he heard Mrs. Keith ask her son William what his brother George would get for his supper. Upon which William answered, "That a guidfull of the dog's meat was good enough for him; that he had no business there; and that, cursing his brother, he said that little hindered him to take a gun to shoot him." The lad may be excused this outburst of resentment against the new laird, who hitherto had ignored his existence, and now began their fraternal relations by accusing him of parricide. Neither is it surprising that the widow, after the insulting treatment she had received at and since her marriage, should resent the imputation of having murdered her own husband.

For what happened at the funeral, we have the account of the Reverend Mr. Wilson. "Being invited to the burial of the deceased Northfield, he was taken up to a room privately by the present Northfield, who intimated to him his suspicions that his father had not got justice in his death." Here, as in all the other instances, the first suggestion of foul play is made by the heir. It is evident that George Keith sought to involve the minister in the responsibility of openly charging his stepmother and brother with murder, for he desired Mr. Wilson "to look to the dead body and give him his advice how he should behave." The good man perceived the snare thus artfully set for him, and declined to examine the corpse, "excusing himself by his ignorance in these matters" —he was no expert in the science of forensic medicine as applied to post-mortem appearances. He gave, however, the practical and judicious advice that if George thought anything was wrong he ought to consult a physician. "Upon this he was told by young Northfield that he had wrote Mr. Finlay, surgeon in Fraserburgh, and had got for an answer that he could do nothing single, and advising him to take the assistance of the two physicians at Banff." Dr. Finlay, who, by the way, if actually consulted as George alleged, was not produced as a witness at the trial, shewed no anxiety to move in the matter; but why did not George, if he honestly believed that his father had been strangled, call in Dr. Chap, the local practitioner in charge of the case until a few days before the death, who does not even appear to have been invited to the funeral? During their secret conclave, the last arrangements had been going forward, and the minister states that George, at this point of the conversation, having looked out of window, "observed that the corpse was gone, at which both of them were much surprised." They then left the house in pursuit of the funeral cortege, the young laird on foot and the minister on horseback. The following reference to what occurred on this occasion is contained in the evidence of Taylor, who depones "That the present Northfield and Mr. Wilson, the minister, were in an upper room when the corpse was taken out of the house for the burial without acquainting them; that when they got notice that the corpse was removed, they followed; but it was a considerable time before they overtook the company; that Northfield was at the time in complete mourning; that the corpse was removed in the forenoon; and that the place of interment was at the distance of three or four miles." This incident is treated by the prosecution as affording one of the proofs of the pannels' guilt, but it is difficult to see what is its bearing upon the question whether old Northfield was or was not murdered. If the widow and her son guessed the purpose for which George Keith was then closeted with the minister, it is very natural that they should have allowed the funeral to proceed without them.

The only other evidence we have regarding George's attitude at this time is that of his uncle, James Gordon of Techmuiry, brother of the first Mrs. Keith. This gentleman exhibited a strong animus against the woman who for twenty years had occupied the place left vacant by his sister in the affections of Northfield. He stated that he saw little of the laird after his second marriage, which he considered "a most disgraceful one," and that he was last at the house of Northfield on the occasion of his niece's wedding, solely to witness that ceremony, "but insisted that Helen Watt, Northfield's wife, should not be admitted." The mistress of the house would doubtless appreciate to the full this courteous stipulation, and it need not surprise us that Mr. Gordon received no invitation to the next family function, his brother-in-law's funeral. He added that some time after the laird's death he received from his nephew George a letter, "signifying a strong suspicion that his father was strangled by his wife and his son William, and desiring the deponent's advice how he should behave." Once again young Northfield lacked the courage of his conviction. Mr. Gordon wrote in answer, advising him not to insist in any criminal prosecution unless he had clear evidence, which rather looks as if the uncle had not much faith in his nephew's detective genius.

There for the time this matter of the alleged murder rested; and not the least mysterious circumstance in the case is that George Keith did nothing further till ten years had elapsed, when he lodged the formal information against his relatives which resulted in their arrest. One would naturally expect that he was led to do so by the discovery of some fresh evidence which justified his former suspicions and at length warranted his making a specific charge, but such is not the fact. This point was well put by counsel for the defence in their pleadings at the trial:—"It is hoped the Gentlemen of the Jury will not be inattentive to these disadvantages under which, from the long delay of this prosecution, the prisoners must necessarily labour in making their defence. We hope they will not fail to observe that the present Keith of Northfield neglected to exhibit any information to the public prosecutor while witnesses were alive who had the best access to know the true state of this matter, and has brought it now after their death when, at the same time, he cannot allege that any new evidence has presented itself."

How the widow and her young family fared when they went out into the world, leaving the rightful heir in possession of the house of Northfield, and whether they ever received payment of the sums due to them under the will, we do not know, but uncertain glimpses of the mother and son may be descried in the evidence given at the trial. William, whose conduct as well before as after his father's death is said by his counsel to have been irreproachable, "employed himself in agriculture," and that with sufficient success to enable him at the time of his trial to support "a wife and a little family." He seems to have quarrelled with his mother, as we shall see from various angry scenes between them spoken to by the witnesses, and there is no doubt that Mrs. Keith's affairs, from whatever cause, were much less prosperous than those of her son. It appears from the evidence of James Duncan, in Whitefield, a shearer in William's employment, that in the harvest of 1761, five years after Northfield's death, his widow's circumstances were so far reduced that she "came to her son William and offered herself to him as a shearer, and that he rejected her services." We shall consider later the relations between William and his mother; in any view the picture thus presented is a pathetic one.

George Keith having for some inscrutable reason at last brought himself to denounce his relatives to the authorities, the mother and son were apprehended by warrant of the Sheriff and lodged in the prison of Banff. The prisoners were respectively examined on 7th and 8th July 1766, in presence of Mr. Alexander Dirom, Sheriff-Substitute of Banffshire, when they emitted separate declarations, and were duly committed for trial. They lay in Banff prison until 26th August, when they were removed to Aberdeen, where at a Circuit Court of Justiciary held by the Right Honourable Lord Kames, one of the Lords Commissioners of Justiciary, on Thursday, 4th September, "Helen Watt, widow of the deceased Alexander Keith of Northfield, and William Keith, eldest lawful son procreated betwixt the said deceased Alexander Keith and the said Helen Watt, pannels, were placed at the bar indicted and accused at the instance of James Montgomery, Esq., his Majesty's Advocate, for his Majesty's interest, for the crime of murder committed by them upon the person of the said deceased Alexander Keith, in manner mentioned in the Criminal Letters raised thereanent."

Henry Home, Lord Kames, a man of much learning and a voluminous writer, "who did more to promote the interests of philosophy and *belles lettres* in Scotland than all the men of law had done for a century before," was noted for his severity as a criminal judge. When at the bar he had acted as counsel for the unfortunate Captain Porteous; and he was one of the judges presiding at the trial of Katharine Nairn in the preceding year, on which occasion he introduced the practice of charging the jury at the conclusion of the speech for the defence, a custom since universal but till then unknown. Lord Kames, however, is now best remembered in legal traditions on account of his familiar use of that monosyllable which Mr. John Willet so reprehensibly called up the stairs of the Maypole six distinct times, to the grave scandal of the cook and housemaid. The "Procurators for the Prosecutor," or counsel for the Crown, were Mr. Cosmo Gordon, Advocate-Depute, and Mr. John Douglas, advocate; the "Procurators in defence," or counsel for the pannels, were Messrs. Alexander Wight, Alexander Elphinstoun, and Robert Cullen, advocates. Wight afterwards assisted Henry Erskine in the famous but unsuccessful defence of Deacon Brodie on his trial before the great Braxfield in 1788.

The indictment set forth that the deceased having executed the will to which we have referred, the prisoners became "impatient" for his death; that Mrs. Keith "was heard to express wishes to that purpose"; that she and her son "did treacherously and wickedly conspire to murder" Northfield; and that "in pursuance of this their wicked intention," they, in the circumstances already mentioned, "did wickedly murder the said Alexander Keith by strangling him in his bed either with their hands or with some cord or rope or napkin or in some other violent manner," as appeared from certain marks of discoloration afterwards seen upon his body, "which could not have proceeded from the effects of any natural disease, if the said Alexander Keith had died without violence." It was further alleged that Mrs. Keith, "conscious of her guilt in the premises," attempted to conceal the marks from observation, invented the whole story of the plaster, and "to prevent further discovery" caused the body to be buried with unseemly haste "in a most indecent manner."

Both pannels having pleaded not guilty, counsel for the defence stated that while it was not proposed to offer any objections to the relevancy of the indictment, as the prosecutor did not pretend to bring against the prisoners any direct proof of this alleged murder, but meant by a train of circumstances to infer their guilt, "it had become necessary for the prisoners, in justice to themselves, to state the facts which had given rise to this prosecution as they truly happened, and as it was expected they would appear from the evidence to be brought. That this, they hoped, would remove the impression created against them by the frame of the Indictment, and would prepare the Gentlemen of the Jury to attend equally to those circumstances which were to be proved in defence." Counsel then gave their clients' own version of the facts, from which we have quoted in the foregoing narrative. It was argued that in order to support the accusation there were two separate facts, of each of which it was necessary there should be clear and distinct evidence: firstly, that a murder had been committed, and secondly, that the prisoners were guilty of that murder. Was it clearly proved that Keith of Northfield died a violent death? To establish his case the prosecutor relied mainly upon the marks seen upon the body some time after the death, but the jury would bear in mind that the appearances of dead bodies are often so various and extraordinary "that physicians of the greatest abilities and most extensive experience have declared themselves unable to account for their causes, or to determine with any degree of certainty whether they proceeded from a natural or a violent death." Besides the general uncertainty of such post-mortem appearances there was in the present case the further circumstance, "which should make us still more cautious to infer from such discoloured marks that Northfield's death had been a violent one," namely, that the body was neither seen nor examined by any surgeon or person of skill, but that these appearances were now to be described ten years after the event by ignorant, inaccurate country folk, "by whom alone they are said to have been perceived." Physicians who admitted their own inability to determine the cause of such marks when seen by themselves would surely be less able to account for them from the description of ignorant and unskilful observers. The jury were cautioned against confounding the proof required regarding each of the two distinct questions before them. "They will reflect on the dangerous consequence of admitting circumstances tending to fix a crime on particular persons to supply the defective evidence of that crime's having itself existed. Circumstances of conduct in themselves the most innocent may, upon the supposition of a crime, assume a very suspicious appearance, which arises entirely from innocence that had rendered the conduct careless and unguarded. From circumstances, therefore, suspicious only upon the supposition of a crime's having been committed, to reason backwards and conclude from these that the crime truly was committed, is contrary to all just and fair reasoning, and surely inconsistent with that regular form of procedure which has been established for the protection and security of innocence." If, however, the jury came to the conclusion that a murder had been committed, they must carefully examine the evidence adduced to prove the prisoners guilty of that shocking crime. Upon this branch of the case counsel dwelt upon the injury their clients had sustained by reason of the ten years' delay in bringing the charge. Many important witnesses necessary to their defence had died, and in particular Anne Keith, Northfield's sister, the loss of whose testimony was a great misfortune for the pannels, "as she was the only person, besides the two prisoners, who was constantly near the bedside of the deceased." The motive alleged in the present case was, counsel maintained, absurd and incredible. Even if the prisoners were wicked enough to be influenced by such a motive, in view of Northfield's age and serious illness the story was still highly improbable. "Can we believe that when they foresaw his death to be so fast approaching, they would thus wantonly imbrue their hands in the blood of a husband and a father merely to attain a few days, perhaps a few hours, sooner the possession of that pittance which he had provided for them?" On the contrary, it was far more to the pannels' interest that Northfield should survive, for while he continued in possession of his estate they were much better off than they would be when reduced to live on the inconsiderable provision which he had secured to them. There was no suggestion that Northfield wished to alter his will, and the only person having any interest to induce him to do so was the heir, who lived at a distance and never approached his dying father. Counsel then made a powerful appeal to the jury on behalf of William Keith, pointing out the extreme improbability of a boy of seventeen, of previous good character, and "of all his other children the most beloved and favoured by his father," committing so atrocious and unnatural a crime. And when it was remembered that there was the greatest uncertainty whether any crime had been in fact committed at all, surely little doubt would remain concerning his innocence. If, however, the jury were satisfied he was innocent, they were bound to acquit his mother also; the two prisoners were the only grown persons in the room with the deceased at the time of his death, and if he were murdered, both of them must have been equally guilty of that bloody deed.

An interlocutor was pronounced by Lord Kames finding the libel relevant to infer the pains of law, and allowing the pannels to prove all facts and circumstances that might tend to exculpate them or alleviate their guilt. A jury consisting of local landowners and Aberdeen merchants was then em-panelled, and the trial proceeded. With most of the evidence adduced I have already dealt, excepting that which relates to certain incriminating expressions said to have been uttered by the pannels on various occasions before and after North-field's death, which we shall now consider. The first of these is spoken to by Elspeth Bruce, who says that the laird and his wife did not live comfortably together, but were often squabbling, "though she cannot say who gave occasion to their squabbling." On a certain day unspecified Mrs. Keith came "butt the house" in a passion and exclaimed, "God! that he [her husband] had broke his neck when he broke his horse's neck, and then she would not have got so much anger by him"—which hardly implies an intention to murder him herself. This is the only instance given by Elspeth, who of all the witnesses was the one most likely to know the facts. William Taylor deponed that a fortnight before his master's death Mrs. Keith said: "If God would not take her husband, might the Devil take him!" and that the reason of her saying so was that Northfield "liked a dram too well and was spending too much." The lady plainly had a sharp tongue and an unweeded vocabulary; but how the laird contrived to be extravagant in his sickroom does not appear. Taylor adds that some time afterwards he heard William address his mother in the following enigmatic and unfilial terms:—"That if it had not been her four quarters his father might have been living; that she never would get justice till she was hung up beside William Wast; and that he could be content to pull down her feet." On research I find that the gentleman referred to was executed at Aberdeen in 1752 for the murder of his wife, where his skeleton still hung in chains on the Gallowhill to give point to William's remark. Isobel Robertson stated that five or six years before, she, being a servant with Mrs. Keith, had occasion to know that William, who was then living with his mother and sleeping in the bed in which his father died, "was frightened with ghosts and apparitions," so that he got a lad to lie in the room with him for a night or two, and afterwards changed his bed. James Irvine, the lad in question, said that six or seven years ago his master, William Keith, complained that he could not sleep in his bed "because he was troubled," but did not say what he was troubled about. At his request the witness sat up with him in his room a whole night, after which William changed his bed. In cross-examination, Irvine admitted it was said that William was afraid of his brother George, but that he never heard that William was afraid of his father's ghost. James Boath, tailor in Banff, deponed that several years after old Northfield's death the pannels quarrelled in his house, "provoking one another by abusive language," when the mother said to the son: "Sir, I know as much of you as would get you hanged." Janet Watt, in Crovie, apparently a relative of Mrs. Keith, stated that once, after a quarrel between the pannels "about milking cows," William observed that his mother was a liar, a thief, and a murderer. John Duncan deponed that when William refused to employ his mother as a shearer, as already mentioned, William said that she would not get justice till she was hanged. Here ends this unedifying testimony. If mother and son did in fact share that fatal secret, it seems unlikely that they would thus twit one another in public with their mutual guilt; more probably when they afterwards fell out, they found in the old suspicions a handy form of recrimination. In any view, William's conduct scarcely warrants the encomiums of his counsel.

The medical evidence adduced for the Crown was confined to that of a single witness, Dr. Alexander Irvine, physician in Banff, who dogmatically deponed that he never saw in the course of his practice such marks as those described in the case of Northfield "that he could suspect was occasioned by any sort of disease, without external violence," and that such marks could not be occasioned by any known disease. This evidence would have immense weight with a local jury. Now, in the year of grace 1766, and for many a long year afterwards the ordinary country practitioner knew as much about the science of medical jurisprudence as he did of wireless telegraphy. Not until 1806, by the efforts of the great Andrew Duncan, was the study of that subject officially recognized by the University of Edinburgh, when the first chair in the country was there founded. To-day, any final year's medical student knows that one of the commonest of all post-mortem appearances is just such hypostatic lividity as was seen upon Northfield's body the day after his death, and that neither plasters nor garters were necessary to produce it. Nay, more, that had be been strangled, as was alleged, by the forcible compression of his throat with cord or handkerchief, the resulting mark would have been pale rather than blue, any livid appearance being above and below the line of constriction. Thus no competent medical man would nowadays peril his reputation by endorsing the scientific testimony of Dr. Irvine of Banff.

The Crown proposed to call as their last witness George Keith of Northfield, to whose evidence objection was taken in behalf of the prisoners that not only was he "the private informer and spring of the present prosecution," but he had likewise acted as an agent by assisting in the precognition— examination of witnesses—before the Sheriff, and had suggested questions to be put to the persons examined. The Court sustained the objection on proof of the fact, and refused to receive George Keith as a witness, which is a matter of regret; for while the prisoners took no benefit from his exclusion, his deposition would probably have made plain many points otherwise obscure. Only two witnesses were called for the defence, John Keith and Dr. Chap, whose

# TO MEET MISS MADELEINE SMITH:
## A GOSSIP ON
## A WONDER HEROINE OF THE 'FIFTIES

*Where there's a beautiful woman in the dock, it makes a Criminal Court trial so much more amusing!*

AUGUSTUS MUIR: *The Bronze Door.*

THEY say that even of a good thing you can have too much. But I doubt it. True, such good things as sunbathing, beer, and tobacco may be intemperately pursued to the detriment of their devotees; yet, to my mind, one cannot have too much of a good murder.

For example, my friend and criminous colleague, Mr. Edmund Pearson—I wonder, by the way, what has happened to the intervening "Lester" of his earlier title-pages?—told in his first and most excellent book in this vein, *Studies in Murder*, the attaching tale of the incomparable Lizzie Borden, a New England maiden, charged, in the 'nineties, with the unfilial massacre of her parents by means of an axe, and surprisingly acquitted by a sympathetic jury of her fellow-countrymen. And in later works Mr. Pearson has returned to the "charge," and given us further aspects of his favourite heroine's personality and unique achievement, manifestly to his own delight and to the equal joy of such readers as share his admiration for the gentle Lizzie.

So that although the story of Madeleine Hamilton Smith has often been, with more or less competence, set forth—the latest and best account being that by Miss Tennyson Jesse, in her admirable introduction to the Madeleine volume of the Notable British Trials series—and the name of that engaging fair one is become, for such as savour legal mysteries, familiar in our mouths as household words, I venture to think the subject not yet exhausted, and that in fact we can never have enough of her and of the Mystery of Blyths-wood Square.

Any time I chance to be in Glasgow with an hour or so to spare—which, in view of the grievously inadequate miscalled "connections" afforded by the railway companies to Clyde-bound travellers from the east coast, often happens—I make my way to that respectable and dignified enclosure, and pausing at the second basement-window in the by-street, round the corner of the Square, ponder awhile upon what the iron stanchions could tell me an they would. For this very window once gave light to the chaste mysteries of Miss Madeleine's bedroom, and the space between the sill and the pavement, below the level of the street, was used by the lovers as their letter-box. And it was through these rusty bars that the white hand of Madeleine was wont to proffer for the refreshment of her unpleasant wooer those midnight cups of cocoa or chocolate, of whose baneful effects he com-plained to his complaisant confidante, Miss Perry.

It is hard to account for the spell which even unto this day Madeleine Smith unquestionably casts upon her votaries. Hers was an unlovely nature: false, self-centred, wholly regardless of the rights and feelings of others, so far as these conflicted with her own desires; and her treatment of her blameless suitor, Mr. Minnoch, was flagrantly perfidious. Miss Tennyson Jesse, to whose recondite knowledge of the mysteries of her sex I respectfully take off my hat, has sought to excuse these shortcomings on the ground of the sex-suppressions by which Victorian virgins were cabined and confined. But it humbly appears to me that Madeleine was essentially, in the phrase of Andrew Lang, "other than a good one"; and that even in the wider freedom offered by this golden age of lipstick, cocktails, and night clubs, she would infallibly have gone wrong.

Professor Saintsbury, in his graceful preface to *Pride and Prejudice*, has wisely observed: "What is the good of seeking for the reason of charm? it is there." And he instances, from the novels of the last hundred years, five young ladies

with whom it might be a pleasure to fall in love. "Their
names are, in chronological order, Elizabeth Bennet, Diana
Vernon, Argemone Lavington, Beatrix Esmond, and Barbara
Grant. I should have been most in love with Beatrix and
Argemone; I should, I think, for mere companionship, have
preferred Diana and Barbara. But to live with and to marry,
I do not know that any one of the four can come into com-
petition with Elizabeth." For the benefit of would-be
admirers lacking his encyclopaedic acquaintance with our
fiction, I may mention that the shyest of these maids is to
be found concealed in the *Yeast* of Charles Kingsley.

In like manner I too have, in my own line of reading, my
darker favourites, who, following the Professor's order, I
name our Madeleine (1857), Jessie M'Lachlan (1862), Florence
Bravo (1876), Adelaide Bartlett (1886), and Mrs. Maybrick
(1889). Of three of the five I have elsewhere treated at
large; Miss Smith and Mrs. Maybrick are for me—figura-
tively speaking—virgin. Despite the superior social standing,
the richer hues and higher romantic value of Madeleine, I
give my vote, as a "case," for Jessie, whose attractions, though
physically inferior to those of her more brilliant rival, are
morally of much greater appeal. And yet Madeleine has
many "points" to which the humbler genius of Jessie can
make no claim. Her amazing correspondence—to Victorian
ears so outrageously outspoken; her equally astounding
courage, coolness, and seeming unconcern in a situation
fraught with such danger and disgrace; and more notable
than all in one of her age and sex, her complete lack of sensibility, her callosity of heart, in face of the ruin and devasta-
tion which she had wrought upon her hapless kinsfolk.

Apart from personal and professional feeling, I am moved
to return to this old tale by the circumstance that I have before
me a report of the case, which a former owner has "embellished" by the insertion of divers cuttings from the contemporary Press, relating to the nine-days' wonder of the
trial. These are of value as giving us some notion of how
the affair was regarded at the time. Although I have been

living with Madeleine—I hasten to add, merely in a literary sense—for many years, they are to me instructive "news"; so I have thought it worth while to give some excerpts from them for the benefit of readers like-minded with myself. They do not solve the mystery, but they lighten a little our darkness as to the reactions of her fellow-citizens to the startling features of her case.

While I have neither wish nor intention to journey over again the travelled road of the evidence, it occurs to me as possible—having regard to the precedent of a learned Judge's historic question to counsel: "Who is Connie Gilchrist?"—that some readers of this inconsiderable essay, whether by ill-luck, inadvertence, defective education, or other cause to the present writer unknown, may never even have heard of Madeleine Smith! Such ignorance is to be deplored, and so far as may be in the space at my disposal, remedied. I shall, therefore, furnish first an outline of the general question at issue, which will enable these benighted persons to appreciate the situation. Those acquainted with the facts and circumstances of the case need not read it, but it may prove of service to such as know not Madeleine.

## I

The daughter of an architect of position in Glasgow, Madeleine Smith at nineteen was a dashing damsel, accomplished and attractive, an ornament of middle-class society in that city. Her charms caught the roving eye of a young Frenchman, Pierre Emile L'Angelier, clerk in a commercial house, and he contrived through a common friend an introduction to her in the street. This ill-omened meeting occurred in 1855. Socially, of course, L'Angelier was impossible; but he was a good-looking little "bounder," and the girl fell in love with him. They corresponded constantly, with that amazing mid-Victorian voluminosity which, happily, is a lost art, and met as often as circumstances permitted. No one in

Madeleine's set knew of their intimacy; but a romantic spinster friend of L'Angelier, Miss Perry, acted as go-between, and one of the Smiths' maids connived at their clandestine meetings.

In the spring of 1856 the flirtation developed into an intrigue, the changed relations of the lovers being reflected in the tropical and abandoned tone of the fair correspondent. They addressed one another as "husband" and "wife," and there can be little doubt that in the belief of L'Angelier, as well as by the law of Scotland, they actually were married. An elopement was anticipated, but the gallant's official salary amounted only to ten shillings a week and the young lady was quite dependent on her parents, so the prospect was none of the brightest. In November 1856 the Smiths occupied a main-door corner house, No. 7 Blythswood Square. The stanchioned windows of Madeleine's bedroom in the basement, as I have said, opened directly upon, and were partly below the level of the pavement of the side street; it was the lovers' custom to converse at these, the sunk part formed a convenient receptacle for their respective letters, and when the coast was clear she could take him into the house.

In the flat above lived a gentleman named William Minnoch, who began to pay his charming neighbour marked attentions. Whether or not the copiousness of her draughts of passion had induced satiety, Madeleine was quick to realize that her position as the wife of a prosperous Glasgow merchant would be very different from her future with the little French clerk, so she gave her responsible suitor every encouragement. On 28th January 1857, with the approbation of her parents, she accepted his hand. Meantime her correspondence with L'Angelier was maintained at the accustomed temperature, till, early in February, she made an effort to break the "engagement," and demanded the return of her letters.

Rumours of Mr. Minnoch's attentions had reached L'Angelier; he suspected what was afoot, taxed her with perfidy, and refused to give up the letters to anyone but her father. The mere suggestion drove Madeleine well-nigh crazy. The letters were indeed such as no parent ever read and few daughters could have written. She poured forth frantic appeals for mercy and solemnly denied that she had broken faith; she besought him to come to her and she would explain everything. L'Angelier stood firm. He has been called blackguard and blackmailer; as I read the facts, it was neither revenge nor money that he wanted, but his wife. "I will never give them [her letters] up," he told his friend Kennedy; "she shall never marry another man so long as I live," adding with prophetic significance: "Tom, she'll be the death of me!"

A reconciliation was effected on 12th February, the correspondence was resumed on the old footing, and L'Angelier became again "her love, her pet, her sweet Emile." He told Miss Perry he was to see Madeleine on the 19th. That night he left his lodgings, taking the pass-key as he intended to be late; next morning his landlady found him writhing in agony on his bedroom floor, with all the painful symptoms of irritant poisoning. Whether the lovers had met or not is disputed, but in his diary, production of which at the trial was disallowed, L'Angelier wrote: "Thurs. 19. Saw Mimi a few moments—was very ill during the night." He recovered, but was never afterwards the same man.

At 4 a.m. on Monday 23rd, L'Angelier rang for his landlady, who found him suffering from another similar attack. The diary records: "Sun. 22. Saw Mimi in drawing-room —Promised me French Bible—Taken very ill." This meeting is otherwise established under Madeleine's own hand: "You did look bad on Sunday night and Monday morning. I think you get sick with walking home so late and the long want of food, so the next time we meet I shall make you eat a loaf of bread before you go out." L'Angelier said to Miss Perry: "I can't think why I was so unwell after getting coffee and chocolate from her [Madeleine]," referring, according to that lady, to *two* separate occasions. "If she were to poison me I would forgive her." He also told his friend Towers that he thought he had been poisoned *twice*, after taking coffee and cocoa.

Now, prior to the first illness, Madeleine had made an abortive attempt to procure prussic acid—"for her hands"—but no arsenic could then be traced to her possession. The day before the second attack, however, she bought from Murdoch, a druggist, *one ounce of arsenic*, "to send to the gardener at the country house"—Mr. Smith's summer villa, Rowaleyn, near Row, on the Gareloch.

On 5th March, L'Angelier, whose jealousy was reawakened, wrote insisting on knowing the truth about Mr. Minnoch. That day Madeleine purchased from Currie, another druggist, *a second ounce of arsenic*—"to kill rats in Blythswood Square"; and on the 6th she went with her family for ten days to Bridge of Allan. Mr. Minnoch was of the party, and the wedding was fixed for June.

L'Angelier, on sick leave, had gone to Edinburgh, impatiently awaiting Madeleine's return, when everything was to be explained. On the 19th he followed her to Bridge of Allan; but Madeleine had come back on the 17th, and next day she obtained from Currie *a third ounce of arsenic*—"the first was so effectual."

On the evening of Sunday 22nd, L'Angelier returned to his lodgings: a letter forwarded to him from Glasgow had brought him home in hot haste. He looked well and happy, and after a hasty meal hurried away, saying he might be out late. At 2.30 a.m. his landlady, aroused by the violent pealing of the door bell, found him doubled up with agony upon the threshold. He was put to bed and she sent for a doctor, who formed a hopeful prognosis. "I am far worse than the doctor thinks," cried the patient. He said nothing as to the cause of his sudden seizure, but asked to see Miss Perry. When that lady arrived upon the scene L'Angelier's lips were sealed for ever. In his vest pocket was found the last letter of a remarkable series:—

Why my beloved did you not come to me. Oh beloved are you ill. Come to me sweet one. I waited and waited for you but you came

not. I shall wait again to-morrow night same hour and arrangement. Do come sweet love my own dear love of a sweetheart. Come
beloved and clasp me to your heart. Come and we shall be happy.
A kiss fond love. Adieu with tender embraces ever believe me to
be your own ever dear fond MIMI.

The postmark was Glasgow, 21st March. A facsimile will be
found in Miss Tennyson Jesse's edition of the trial.

L'Angelier's half of the fatal correspondence was discovered;
Madeleine fled to Row, and was brought back by her fiancé;
an examination of the body pointed to poison, and she was
apprehended. In her declaration she said that she had not
seen L'Angelier for three weeks; the appointment was for
Saturday, 21st March; he came neither that night nor the
next; her purpose in making it was to tell him of her engagement to Mr. Minnoch! As to the arsenic, she used it all as a
cosmetic, on the advice of a school-friend. She admitted
giving cocoa to L'Angelier once, at her window.

Of the nine-days' wonder of her trial at Edinburgh in July
I have small space left to speak. No less than 88 grains of
arsenic were found in the body, and the defence made much
of the fact that this was the greatest quantity hitherto detected,
arguing that so large a dose indicated suicide rather than
murder. The unsoundness of this contention is proved by
two subsequent English cases,[1] where 150 and 154 grains
respectively were recovered. As regards the two first charges
—of administration—the Crown was handicapped by the
exclusion of L'Angelier's diary; and in the murder charge,
by inability to prove the actual meeting of the parties on the
Sunday night. There was proof that L'Angelier had talked
once or twice in a vapouring way of suicide, but none that
he ever had arsenic in his possession. The prisoner's account
of her object in acquiring arsenic was contradicted by her old
school-fellow, and the fact that what she obtained was, in
terms of the Statute,[2] mixed with soot and indigo, rendered
it strangely uninviting for toilet purposes. On the other
hand, the Crown doctors noticed no colouring matter in the
body, but to this point their attention was not then directed.

[1] *R.* v. *Dodds*, 1860, and *R.* v. *Hewitt*, 1863.  [2] 14 Vict. c. 13, s. 3.

On the question of motive, it was maintained that the accused had nothing to gain by L'Angelier's death if her letters remained in his possession. These, however, having neither address nor any signature except "Mimi," afforded little clue to the writer's identity. But surely it was his *silence* that was for her the supreme object, and how could that be ensured save by his death?

Lord Advocate Moncreiff's masterly address, strong, restrained, convincing, was then, as now, unduly eclipsed by the brilliant, emotional speech of John Inglis for the defence, held to be the finest ever delivered in a Scots court. The one appealed to the head, the other to the heart; each pledged his personal belief in the righteousness of his cause. Lord Justice-Clerk Hope's charge favoured an acquittal; the jury found the pannel Not Guilty of the first charge; the two others, Not Proven. In the popular verdict: "If she did not poison him, she ought to have done it," I am unable to concur.

The amazing self-command with which the prisoner faced her ordeal, no less than her youth and beauty, inspired the pens of contemporary scribes. During the trial she received many proposals, lay and clerical. Her fiancé was not an offerer. . . .

## II

Such is the abridgment of the case which I wrote for a chapter on Scottish poisonings in *Glengarry's Way*, a collection of essays first published in 1922. I make no apology for reprinting it here, because I am rather proud of it, as presenting in minimum compass the essential facts. The book was dedicated to my friend Mr. Hugh Walpole, who, in acknowledging the copy I sent him, thus referred to my inadequate treatment of Miss Smith:—

PENDRAGYN, CURY,
S. CORNWALL, *June* 1, '22.

MY DEAR ROUGHEAD,

I've just finished *Glengarry*, and I do congratulate you. I only wish it had been three times as long. I don't know what to pick out when it is all so good. But I think the "Locusta" chapter is perhaps the best, a really wonderful summary that must have been the Devil itself to do.[1] When I had finished it I swore I'd never eat porridge in Scotland again—a decision good for my figure, if I could only hold to it.

Any mention of my little pet and favourite Madeleine Smith always thrills me to the bone; but do you give her letters quite sufficient literary credit? They seem very fine compositions to me, and I would have been almost in L'Angelier's place might I have received them. And is it true that there is someone alive in Edinburgh today who saw the poor young man on the fateful night leaving Madeleine's window? . . .

Thanking you once more for your splendid book and the honour you did me in connecting my name with it,

Yours very sincerely,

HUGH WALPOLE.

I admit that I did not do justice to the pen-flowers of Madeleine's indefatigable culture, but to have done so was, in the circumstances, impossible: they would require a volume to themselves. The rumour that L'Angelier was seen at her window that Sunday night was current at the time and has persisted even unto this day. I have often heard it asserted, but have never been able to verify the fact.

Madeleine's letters are painful reading, as well materially as morally. She wrote the large, angular hand—I believe it was termed Italian—then affected by well-bred young ladies. Six to eight pages was her average allowance, half of which, in the damnable fashion of the day, she "crossed," with the result that her MS. presents at first-sight the appearance of a Chinese puzzle. And when we reflect that the unfortunate L'Angelier received, and presumably perused, no less than 198 of these cryptographic missives—I had almost written "missiles"—which an expert at the trial stated were so difficult to decipher that he had to use a magnifying lens, the theory of suicide suggested by the defence seems, after all, less untenable than it otherwise appeared.

To shew the versatility of Madeleine as a correspondent and the remarkable range of her epistolary gift, here is a letter

---

[1] *Author's Note.* It was!

written by her to her husband-elect, on parting from him at Bridge of Allan, *but five days before she wrote to her lover the impassioned appeal above quoted*. The contrast in style is not less striking than instructive. Posted at Stirling on 16th March, it is addressed to "William Minnoch, Esq., 124 St. Vincent Street, Glasgow," and runs as follows:—

MY DEAREST WILLIAM,

It is but fair, after your kindness to me, that I should write you a note. The day I part from friends I always feel sad. But to part from one I love, as I do you, makes me feel truly sad and dull. My only consolation is that we meet soon. Tomorrow we shall be home. I do wish you were here today. We might take a long walk. Our walk to Dumblane [*sic*] I shall ever remember with pleasure. That walk fixed a day on which we are to begin a new life—a life which I hope may be of happiness and long duration to both of us. My aim through life shall be to please you and study you. Dear William, I must conclude, as Mama is ready to go to Stirling. I do not go with the same pleasure as I did the last time. I hope you got to Town safe, and found your sisters well. Accept my warmest kindest love and ever believe me to be

Yours with affcn.,

MADELEINE.

MONDAY,
PROSPECT VILLA.

When "dearest William" read the letters she had written to his rival, as disclosed at the trial, he must have had his doubts concerning the mutual happiness promised by his fiancée, had their marriage gone through as arranged. As it was, he behaved with conspicuous loyalty; when the blow fell and she fled in panic to Row, he followed her at once, found her on board the Helensburgh boat at the Broomielaw, brought her back to her parents' house, and gallantly stood by her until the revelations of the trial. These, however, proved too much even for his generosity. In the last of her letters which we have, that written to the Edinburgh prison matron four days after her release—I shall later have occasion to quote it in full—she thus refers to the man who, despite the unspeakable wrong she had done him, treated her to the end like a gentleman: "My *friend* I know nothing of. I have

269

not seen him. I hear he has been ill, which I don't much care [*sic*]."

The only complete verbatim text of the famous letters in book form is to be found in the appendix to Miss Tennyson Jesse's definitive edition of the trial. Madeleine had destroyed her share of the correspondence, and of L'Angelier's letters we have only a few, of which he kept copies. But the cunning little cad carefully preserved every line she ever wrote to him. The full text thus for the first time made generally available— there is an American unexpurgated edition, issued in 1857 and much sought after by the curious—furnishes less lurid reading than the judicial fulminations would lead one to expect. Naïvely outspoken in matters sexual, while they may be termed indelicate, to class them as pornographic is absurd. The fault lies in their unconventional frankness; and the mid-Victorians deemed it unseemly to call a spade a spade. "Candour such as this," justly remarks Miss Tennyson Jesse, "was felt to be perfectly shocking from a young woman, and to do the spirit of the time justice it would probably have been felt to be just as shocking had the parties been married. Love-making was a mysterious arrangement on the part of Providence, which was necessary to gentlemen and which a good wife accepted as her bounden duty. It was not a pagan festival such as Madeleine found it."

If Madeleine's phraseology was upon occasion ungenteel, the sentiments expressed by her lover, so far as we are permitted to know them, were perfectly correct—indeed, surprisingly so in one of his age and race. For example, the so-called seduction took place in the garden at Rowaleyn one June night in 1856. After his departure, Madeleine, in a long letter to him dated, amazingly, "*Wednesday morning, 5 o'c,*" refers to the episode with engaging *épanchement*: "Tell me, pet, were you angry at me for letting you do what you did— was it very bad of me? We should, I suppose, have waited till we were married. I shall always remember last night. . ." To which L'Angelier, also at great length, very properly replied: "I was not angry at you allowing me, Mimi, but I am sad it happened. *You had no resolution.* We should indeed have waited till we were married, Mimi. It was very bad indeed. I shall look with regret on that night." The reproaching of Mimi for her moral weakness is a charmingly characteristic touch.

Although the Lord Justice-Clerk's strictures on the tone of the letters was as severe as the most acidulous virgin could desire, in charging the jury his Lordship dealt with the very formidable case for the Crown in a manner that, despite the dictum of a certain doctor of laws at Padua, somewhat strained the quality of mercy. But his lordship was apt to be lenient, as witness another *cause célèbre* on which he presided: the trial of Dr. Smith of St. Fergus in 1854, for the murder by shooting of a young farmer friend, whose life he had insured and by whose death he stood to profit to the tune of £2,000. Yet, notwithstanding most damning evidence against him, the Judge practically directed the jury to acquit him of the charge, which, to the extent of Not Proven, they obediently did. There is an irreverent tradition that the Justice-Clerk, besides being an able lawyer, was a good judge of feminine charms, and that Madeleine, being possessed of a neat foot and an undeniable ankle, was advised not to conceal those assets from the purview of the Bench, a display facilitated by the crinoline of the day. But no such tactics were available to the physician of St. Fergus.

Gratitude, as appears, was not one of Madeleine's strong points; she described the Lord Justice-Clerk, to whose charge she was so largely indebted, as "a tedious old man." As shewing the incredible coolness exhibited by her during the trial, where everyone else concerned was in a state of intense feverish excitement, it is recorded that on the conclusion of the Lord Advocate's deadly address for the Crown, she was asked what she thought of it. "When I have heard the Dean of Faculty I will tell you," she placidly replied; "I never like to give an opinion till I have heard both sides of the question!"

## III

There can, I think, be little doubt that the withholding by a majority of the Court—2 to 1—of L'Angelier's diary from the knowledge of the jury was the determinant factor in the case. Had they been allowed to see, under the dead man's own hand, the recorded fact of his meetings with Madeleine on the nights immediately preceding his two first seizures, it would probably have turned the scale against her. The last entry in the diary is of Saturday, 14th March; it was on the night of Sunday the 22nd that the Crown alleged he got from her his third and fatal dose. Morally, we can be fairly certain they did meet that night. He had come hot-foot from Bridge of Allan on her urgent invitation, he left his lodgings for that express purpose, he was seen in the near vicinity of her house; but, legally, there was no proof of their meeting. In like manner, on the occasion of the two first attacks, it was not proved that they had met. There the diary supplies the missing links.

It is idle to suggest that L'Angelier fabricated these entries with a view to inculpate Madeleine, for, as Miss Tennyson Jesse has acutely pointed out, he had only to breathe to his landlady during his last illness a suspicion that it was due to the attentions of his "intended," and the game was up. But he spoke no word as to the cause of his condition. Then, as regards the suicide theory, whoever heard of anyone taking three separate doses—on 19th and 22nd February and on 22nd March—as a means of self-destruction, of so agonizing a poison as arsenic? And his last words: "If I could only get a little sleep I think I should be well," are scantly indicative of a wish to take his own life.

Too little attention has been paid to Madeleine's other medicinal shopping: her attempt to procure, on an unspecified day in the second week of February, "a small phial of prussic acid," coinciding as it does with L'Angelier's first threats of exposure, and curiously anticipating the similar failure of Miss

Lizzie Borden to obtain the same death-dealing substance, whereby she was driven to adopt the more crude expedient of an axe. "She said she wanted it for her hands," says Madeleine's boy-messenger. In her declaration she does not state, as she did of the arsenic, that its use as a cosmetic was recommended to her by a school-friend; the matter is not mentioned. Yet the applicability of prussic acid to toilet purposes is so novel and startling as surely to call for some explanation. Madeleine's notions of beauty-treatment were, to say the least, peculiar.

It is sad to think that we possess no picture of those marvellous and compelling charms which she thus sought superfluously to enhance. The woodcut portraits published in the illustrated papers at the time of the trial are singularly unattractive, depicting a horse-faced female of repellent aspect. But from the correspondence it would seem that she was actually photographed, although unfortunately no copy of the result is known to exist. Writing to L'Angelier in November 1856 she says: "Emile, I know you won't look on my likeness with pleasure—it is so cross—but, love, when it was done I had been in the horrid man's place from 12 o'c., and I had it closed at 4 o'c. [sic]. I had had no food from the night before and I was very furious." So protracted a time-exposure on an empty stomach must have been a trying ordeal. The form of photography then in use was the daguerreotype, which was taken on glass. Most of us possess grim and ghostly presentments of our forebears, surrounded by gilt tin frames, commonly preserved in little velvet-lined leather cases. That Madeleine's was of this sort appears from her next letter, sending the portrait to her lover: "I have put up this likeness in an old book, so that it may not be felt to be glass." And in later letters she writes: "I hope ere long you will have the original, which I know you will like better than a glass likeness"; "Tell me what Mary [Perry] says of my likeness. It is horrid ugly." Finally, in February 1857, when she made her first attempt to break the bonds wherein she was entangled, she wrote to him: "I shall feel obliged by your bring me [sic]

S          273

my letters and likeness on Thursday eveng. at 7. Be at the area gate, and C. H. [the maid, Christina Harrison, who was privy to the intrigue] will take the parcel from you." But *this* appointment, at any rate, L'Angelier failed to keep, and the "likeness or portrait" was found in his repositories by the police on 31st March, and is included in the Crown list of productions (exhibits). What became of it afterwards I cannot tell. Probably the family applied for it and got it back.

My regret for the lack of a "likeness" was shared by Henry James, who, surprisingly in one of his delicate and fastidious taste, was fond of a good murder. I once presented him with a copy of the official report of the trial by Forbes Irvine (Edinburgh: 1857). In accepting my gift he made most interesting reference to the case, and his characteristic comments will be welcome to Madeleine's admirers. Here is his letter:—

21 CARLYLE MANSIONS,
CHEYNE WALK, S.W.
*June 16th,* 1914.

MY DEAR ROUGHEAD,

Your offering is a precious thing and I am touched by it, but I am also alarmed for the effect on your fortunes, your future, and those (and that) who (and which) may, as it were, depend on you, of these gorgeous generosities of munificence. The admirable Report is, as I conceive, a high rarity and treasure, and I feel as if in accepting it I were snatching the bread perhaps from the lips of unknown generations. Well, I gratefully bow my head, but only on condition that it shall revert, the important object and alienated heirloom, to the estate of my benefactor on my demise.[1]

A strange and fortunate thing has happened—your packet and letter found me this a.m. in the grip of an attack of gout (the 1st for 3 or 4 years, and apparently not destined to be very bad, with an admirable remedy that I possess at once resorted to). So I have been reclining at peace for most of the day with my foot up and my eyes attached to the prodigious Madeleine. I have read your volume straight through, with the extremity of interest and wonder. It represents indeed the *type* perfect case, with nothing to be taken from it or added, and with the beauty that she precisely didn't squalidly suffer, but lived on to admire with the rest of us, for so many years, the rare work of art with which she had been the means of enriching humanity.

[1] *Author's Note.* It didn't!

274

With what complacency must she not have regarded it, through the long backward vista, during the time (now 20 years ago) when I used to hear of her as, married and considered, after a long period in Australia, the near neighbour, in Onslow Gardens, of my old friends the Lyon Playfairs. They didn't know or see her (beyond the fact of her being there), but they tantalized me, because if it made me feel very, very old it now piles Ossa upon Pelion for me that I remember perfectly her trial during its actuality, and how it used to come to us every day in the *Times*, at Boulogne, where I was then with my parents, and how they followed and discussed it in suspense and how I can still see the queer look of the "not proven," seen for the 1st time, on the printed page of the newspaper. I stand again with it, on the summer afternoon—a boy of 14—in the open window over the Rue Neuve Chaussée where I read it. Only I didn't know then of its— the case's—perfect beauty and distinction, as you say.

A singularly fine thing *is* this report indeed—and very magnificent the defence. She was truly a portentous young person, with the *conditions* of the whole thing throwing it into such extraordinary relief, and yet I wonder all the same at the verdict in the face of the so vividly attested, and so fully and so horribly, sufferings of her victim. It's astonishing that the evidence of what he went through that last night didn't do for her. And what a pity she was almost of the pre-photographic age—I would give so much for a veracious portrait of her *then* face.

To all of which absolutely inevitable acknowledgment you are not to *dream*, please, of responding by a single word. I shall take, I foresee, the liveliest interest in the literary forger-man. How can we be sufficiently thankful for these charming breaks in the sinister perspective? I rest my telescope on your shoulder and am

Yours all gratefully,

HENRY JAMES.

The "forger-man," by the way, was that skilful penman known as "Antique Smith," of whose nefarious career I was then preparing an account;[1] but Henry James found him rather colourless, after his brilliant namesake—and no wonder.

Another literary friend of mine supplied a further reminiscence of Madeleine. Andrew Lang told me how he was at school with her brother, and that one day he and some of the other boys saw on a newspaper bill the striking announcement: "Arrest of Young Glasgow Girl for Murder." Whereupon, turning to his companions, Lang jokingly remarked: "That'll be Jim Smith's sister," which proved to be the truth!

[1] First published in the *Juridical Review*; later reprinted in *The Riddle of the Ruthvens*, 1919 (new edition, revised, 1936).

Once upon a time I thought I had secured the prize. A middle-aged young lady of my acquaintance advised me that her venerable mamma was possessed of a water-colour drawing of Madeleine Smith, executed from the life and given to her by the artist. She set no value on such things, and would doubtless let me have it for the asking. An appointment was made; I waited upon the lucky dowager, a frosty-faced and crusted person with a mischievous eye, and preferred my request. She replied that I would have been welcome to the sketch, had she not unfortunately, when clearing out some "rubbish"—save the mark!—committed it to the flames. When I was sufficiently recovered I took my leave, expressing my fears for the future welfare of one capable of committing such a crime, and withdrew, followed by the unhallowed chuckles of that malevolent old woman.

From another survivor of that dim epoch, who as a girl had seen Madeleine in the flesh at "parties" in Glasgow, I learned that she was ever the belle of the ball, extremely handsome, dark and dashing, alluring to the male; but in style and manner what the language of the day termed "bold." Which was just as well, looking to all she was later called upon to outface.

## IV

I have been a long time in reaching the Press-cuttings that I promised, but you will have noticed that I took the precaution to call these desultory gleanings a "gossip."

The earliest is from the *Glasgow Herald* of 3rd April 1857. It is headed: "Painful Event—Charge of Poisoning," and is the first blast of the trumpet against the fair fame of Madeleine Smith. "For the last few days the recital of an event of the most painful character has been passing from mouth to mouth, and has become the subject of almost universal excitement and inquiry. So long as the matter was confined to rumour and surmise we did not consider that we were called on to make any public allusion to it; but now that a young lady has been committed to prison on a most serious charge, and the names of the respective parties are in the mouths of everyone, any further delicacy in the way of withholding allusion to the case is impossible. At the same time we fervently trust that the cloud which at present obscures a most respectable and estimable household may be speedily and most effectually removed." The article proceeds to give a long and well-informed narrative of the facts, so far as then ascertained, and concludes: "Though she should be found pure and guiltless, as we trust may be the case, the family will have suffered deeply by having had one of their household even suspected of a crime so odious. We may add that Miss Smith, who, we understand, was judicially examined at great length before the Sheriff on Tuesday last, has comported herself throughout with perfect calmness." The *Glasgow Mail* also reports: "The utmost coolness is stated to have been manifested by the prisoner ever since she was placed in custody."

We learn from *The Times* that "The prisoner is grand-daughter of the late Mr. David Hamilton, the celebrated architect of Glasgow Exchange and Hamilton Palace"; and I have somewhere read, although I cannot recall the reference, that she was akin to the ducal house of Hamilton.

"All sorts of rumours are afloat," says the *Morning Advertiser*, "bearing on the character of Miss Smith and the young Frenchman L'Angelier, whom she is accused of having poisoned. It is, of course, out of the question to place any reliance upon these stories, but it is said that the evidence at the trial will be of a very startling nature—so much so indeed that it may be deemed advisable to conduct the case with closed doors." An unnamed correspondent, who had talked with Miss Smith on the day of L'Angelier's death, informed the journal "that the young lady was then as gay and fascinating as he had ever seen her."

"The trial is now fixed for the 30th of the present month [June]," says the *Mail*. "It may be premature and unfair to prejudge the case, but we cannot help remarking that we can see nothing for it but that the jury must bring in a verdict

of ' Not Proven.'  No one can prove that Miss Smith administered the poison; there is an hour at least unaccounted for
between L'Angelier's leaving her and reaching his lodgings;
circumstantial evidence, too frequently faithless, is all that the
prosecution can be based upon."  It is interesting to note that
the writer admits, *pace* the Dean of Faculty, the meeting of
the lovers on the fatal night.  He goes on to outline the
cosmetical defence; suggests that L'Angelier, on his way
home, may have fallen in with somebody, "who treated him
with infinitely less kindness than his *inamorato* [*sic*]"; and
concludes with the statement that the majority of Miss Smith's
fellow-citizens believe her to be entirely innocent.  And a word
of warning is uttered for the Judge and jury: to remember
"the maxim of our immortal dramatist," touching the quality
of mercy.  As we have seen, the Lord Justice-Clerk seems to
have taken the editorial hint!

After the trial, a public subscription was got up for L'Angelier's mother in Jersey, of whom he was said to have been the
sole support, and the *Herald* published an open letter from
her, invoking the blessing of the Almighty on the generous
contributors.  The amount raised was £89, 9s. 3d.  It is
stated by the *Sentinel* "that a few of the leading citizens of
Glasgow subscribed largely for the defence of Miss Smith.
We understand that a sum of not less than £5,000 was raised
for this purpose."  Thus substantially did the Glasgow public
back their opinion.

The *Courier* states that, after her discharge from the bar,
she left Edinburgh, unobserved, by train for Glasgow.  "Miss
Smith, on getting out at Stepps Station, near Glasgow,
immediately drove to Rowaleyn House, where she arrived a
little after ten o'clock.  We regret to learn that Mrs. Smith
(the mother) is in a very critical condition, and is rapidly
sinking under the calamity which has been brought upon the
family by the unfortunate daughter."

Only the pen of a Dostoevsky could describe the harrowing
scene of the unrepentant Magdalen's—I beg pardon, Madeleine's—return to the family bosom.  It was in truth a tragic

homecoming. She had cast down the Great Goddess Respectability, that idol of the Victorian home; she had blasphemed her worship and defiled her altars. We, with our looser bonds and less exalted standards, can hardly realize the devastating outcome of her sacrilege. But though the pen of the great Russian master of pain and sorrow is not available, we are fortunate to possess a first-hand account from that of the heroine herself. Four days after her release she wrote to the matron of Edinburgh prison a letter, which, as Miss Tennyson Jesse has justly observed, is "far more profoundly shocking than any of her violent epistles to L'Angelier":—

DEAR MISS AITKEN,

You shall be glad to hear that I am well—in fact I am quite well, and my spirits not in the least down. I left Edinburgh and went to Slateford, and got home to Rowaleyn during the night. But, alas, I found Mama in a bad state of health. But I trust in a short time all will be well with her. The others are all well.

The feeling in the west is not so good towards me as you kind Edinburgh people shewed me. I rather think it shall be necessary for me to leave Scotland for a few months, but Mama is so unwell we do not like to fix anything at present.

If ever you see Mr. C. Combe [the Foreman of the Jury] tell him that the "pannel" was not at all pleased with the verdict. I was delighted with the loud cheer the Court gave. I did not feel in the least put about when the jury were out considering whether they should send me home or keep me. I think I must have had several hundred letters, all from gentlemen, some offering me consolation, and some their hearths and homes. My *friend* I know nothing of. I have not seen him. I hear he has been ill, which I don't much care [sic].

I hope you will give me a note. Thank Miss Bell and Agnes in my name for all their kindness and attention to me. I should like you to send me my Bible and watch to 124 St. Vincent Street, Glasgow, to J. Smith.

The country is looking lovely. As soon as I know my arrangements I shall let you know where I am to be sent to. With kind love to yourself and Mr. Smith, ever believe me,

Yours sincerely,

MADELEINE SMITH.

*Monday, 13th July.*
ROWALEYN,
GARELOCH.

To comment upon this unconscionable missive were to paint the lily. A facsimile of it may be seen in Mr. Duncan Smith's edition of the trial.

But even more repellent is her letter to the prison chaplain, first published from the original MS. as communicated to the *Scotsman* on 15th June 1933:—

DEAR MR. ROSE,

After the kind interest you shewed me, I think it is but fair I should let you know of my safe arrival at home. I am very well, and my spirits are good. I found Mama far, far from well, but I trust she will soon be convalescent.

The feeling here is, I rather fear, strong against me, so I rather think I shall have to leave Scotland for a few weeks, but the poor state of Mama's health renders it impossible for me to make any arrangements at present.

I was not at all pleased with the "verdict," but I was charmed with the loud cheer the Court gave me. I got out of Edinburgh in the most private manner possible. I trust that painful, unhappy affair may tend to do us all great good—I see a different feeling pervades our family circle already. I am so glad that they all view it as an affliction sent from God for past errors and crimes, and if this be the means of drawing a family to the feet of Christ, I shall not grumble at the pain that sad event has cost me.

I may live to hear the family exclaim that it was the most blessed day of their life—the day I was cast into prison. God grant it may be so. I shall ever remember your kindness to me.

Receive my deepest, warmest, and heartfelt thanks, and with kind regards, believe me,

Yours sincerely,

MADELEINE SMITH.

*July* 15*th* '57.
ROWALEYN,
GARELOCH.

Again, comment is needless: the letter speaks for itself. But one would like to have known the nature of those "past errors and crimes," committed by *other* members of the family, that so merited Divine punishment.

## V

Resuming our newspaper researches, we find the reporter of the *Daily Express* giving a minute, but by no means flattering, portrait of the fair prisoner at the bar. Under the heading: "Personal Appearance of Madeleine Smith," he thus anticipates the methods of his modern journalistic successors: "The figure in the dock is small in stature, slight, and finely-formed, with the elasticity of youth and healthful upbringing. It is attired in a manner which shews how the most refined elegance may be united with the quietness of a Quakeress. Madeleine Smith, it is plain to every eye, is an artist in matters of dress. . . . But with her dress and figure admiration ends. Her countenance is striking, but not pleasant. A projecting brow, a long prominent nose, and a receding chin, impart to her sharp features a hawk-like aspect; and if her eye is large and lustrous, no spring of sensibility gleams from beneath those long, drooping lashes. . . . The brow is narrow and low; but the head, swathed in a profusion of dark brown tresses, swells upwards in the region in which phrenologists place the bump of firmness, and broadens behind to an extent that corresponds exactly with the mental weakness and moral depravity developed in her love epistles." But here, I think, our reporter is wise after the event; and how he was able to define her "bumps" beneath the "small, straw bonnet, trimmed with white ribbon, of the fashionable shape," does not appear. "Her mouth," he continues, "is significantly large, the upper lip projecting far over the one beneath, which, when she is moved, droops away from its companion, and has a tendency to reveal the rising tide of emotion, so that more than once she has been seen to catch her lips tightly between thumb and forefinger, to hide the feeling that she did not wish to shew. Her head embodies, more than we have ever seen before, the union of intellectual weakness with strong propensities and unbounded firmness." Our reporter is better at description than deduction, for the charge of "intellectual weakness" is grotesquely unfounded: Madeleine had the brains of a man, and a clever one at that. "Her eye, which fears to meet no other, and which is always the last to be withdrawn, is one which compels us to believe the statement she made in prison—that she never shed a tear." If this forbidding portrait be indeed a true "likeness," we can but exclaim with Dr. Faustus of immortal Helen—

> Was this the face that launched a thousand ships
> And burnt the topless towers of Ilium?

The reporter's unfavourable account, however, is confirmed by that of a brother scribe, who, under the style and title of "An Eye-Witness," furnishes his impressions of the trial. "Apart from the unhappy associations then, now, and there is too much reason to fear, alas! for ever likely to be inseparably connected with her appearance anywhere, the pannel was a decidedly handsome, lady-like figure, of fully average height and development for a female, with a very graceful carriage. Most erroneously, in some sketches, she has been called a 'little, slim girl.' Her countenance has been termed 'pretty' and 'beautiful,' and designated by other hackneyed phrases, but was not according to our taste in female beauty. From the brow to the chin, a very long face, very small features, nose prominent, but unclassable among any of the three chief varieties of that organic protuberance; splendidly rich, dark grey eye—physically considered—of pure and sparkling lustre, but to a degree unpleasing, nay forbidding in its expression; bad lips, mouth, and chin. We thought it fox-like, unattractive, cunning, deceitful, and altogether un-prepossessing."

The truth is that none of us would shew to advantage in the dock. It is a trying situation in which nobody looks their best. I have often noted how quite faceable, ordinary folk, viewed in that dread environment, take on a sinister aspect at once. Had a Cleopatra or a Mary Stuart sat within that narrow, railed-in pen, there would not have been lacking those who perceived flaws even in their loveliness. And, curiously, the accepted portraits of the Scottish Queen exhibit the same long face, prominent "organic protuberance"—I thank thee, "Eye-Witness," for teaching me that word—and oblique eyes, which seem to have been leading features of our Madeleine. Doubtless the charm of each resided in the play of their expression: a subtile smile, a swift-flashing glance, the rich tones of a fine contralto voice—such may have been the secret of their allure. But it is idle to speculate; I had better get on with my cuttings.

The *locus classicus* regarding the accused's demeanour during the trial is the oft-quoted description in the *Ayrshire Express*, which I have italicised: "In the midst of all this excitement, passing through the eager crowd from and to prison, seated at the bar with hundreds of eyes fixed steadily upon her, Madeleine Smith is the only unmoved, cool personage to be seen. From the first moment to the last she has preserved that undaunted, defiant attitude of perfect repose which has struck every spectator with astonishment. She passes from the cab to the Court-room—or rather, to the cell beneath the dock—*with the air of a belle entering a ballroom*. She ascends the narrow staircase leading into the dock with a jaunty air, an unveiled countenance"—(why, by the way, do reporters never say, "face"? Is there anything indecent in the word?) —"the same perpetual smile—or smirk, rather, for it lacks all the elements of a genuine smile; the same healthy glow of colour, and the same confident ease. . . ."

It is also recorded of her that day by day, when the Court rose for the luncheon interval, the prisoner refused either to leave the dock for the temporary privacy afforded by the cells below, or to take anything either to eat or drink, declining even a proffered packet of sandwiches. Immediately on the retiral of their Lordships, the official silence was broken and the tongues of the spectators were loosed. From the packed seats arose a continuous hum of many voices, discussing the evidence and commenting on such incidents as caught the popular fancy. Less abstemious than the accused, the eager crowd, with appetites whetted by excitement, munched steadily from paper bags or lunch cases, and athirst in the July heat of the stuffy Court-room, refreshed themselves, according to their degree, from surreptitious bottles or flasks. And amid this restless babel sits Madeleine Smith unmoved, calm and composed as if alone in her Mamma's quiet drawing-room in

Blythswood Square! Verily, whatever else we may think of her, we must applaud her prodigious pluck.

From a lively article, headed "Notes on the Trial," I take the reporter's thumb-nail sketches of one or two of the principal figures. "Of all the witnesses, 'dear' Mary Perry seemed the most general favourite, her indiscreet patronage of the young lovers notwithstanding. No one, when they saw her, could believe the stories of her that had come from Glasgow. Folks expected a dashing young creature, a second string to the bow of the facile L'Angelier. Fancy the surprise when a little old maid, in quiet black bonnet and brown dress, with an intellectual cast of countenance, and a pair of spectacles imparting quaintness to her face, entered the witness-box! For the young Jersey man she had evidently at first entertained an affection more than Platonic. Her case was probably one of those in which we so frequently find old-maid friendship crossing the borderland of mere friendship, and shading insensibly away into the region of something warmer and more endearing.

"Mr. William Minnoch was the witness whose appearance created most interest in anticipation. He is a man of apparently thirty-five years, though a fair complexion makes him look younger. He is short and slim, perhaps one of the best-dressed men on 'Change in Glasgow and with a keen-cut and more lady-like face than that of the woman to whom he was betrothed. His coolness in the witness-box was remarkable; all the symptoms of agitation which he displayed were an occasional cough, evidently to clear his throat when his voice was becoming husky, and a somewhat frequent appeal to a glass of water, which lay conveniently at hand, when his lips were becoming dry. But his coolness could not help to inspire the spectator with the notion that had he and Miss Madeleine Smith been married, they might have taken up house at the North Pole without much inconvenience to either." (It is elsewhere recorded that never once did he allow his eyes to light upon the figure in the dock, although she stared fixedly at him while he gave his evidence.)

"The youthful sister of the accused could not have been recognized as a relative from any family resemblance; her features were less prominent, and displayed much less force of character.

"Mr. Robert Baird, the young gentleman who introduced L'Angelier to Miss Smith, and was thus the most important actor in the first act of the tragedy, seemed to be about twenty years of age, and looked an ordinary enough specimen of young Glasgow—the best man in the world to cut a figure in Buchanan Street, or in any other fashionable promenade of the west country 'swells'; the last to shine in the most tragic Scottish tale of the nineteenth century."

# VI

Of the acting of the leading lady in the dramatic scene, the same writer gives us some enlightening glimpses, particularly as regards her reactions to the Lord Advocate's address. At first she leant forward on her elbow, the more favourably to mark his words and to watch the impression made by them upon the jury. But her interest soon relaxed, and while his Lordship was dealing with "the horrible and disgusting details which had been placed before them," she was gazing intently at a face that had attracted her attention in one of the galleries, and seemed not to hear the biting words in which her moral failings were described. "It was when the word *arsenic* occurred in the speech that she was most attentive. In whatever direction she might be looking, however intently she might be studying the motions of someone, the bare utterance of that word seemed to have a magic influence over her, and she at once turned round to the speaker from whose lips the sibilant came. But no sooner had the word passed out of use, than the smallest matter apart from the speech sufficed to secure her attention. . . . The first allusion to her letters made her eye dilate to its fullest extent, and so it remained through all the extracts from, and comments upon her extraordinary literary productions; and this dilation of the eye, which many remarked, although it increased the striking appearance of her countenance, did not by any means give it a more prepossessing effect."

The reporter gives a graphic sketch of the final scene, after the jury had retired to consider their verdict. "Every spectator has risen from his seat in the feverish expectancy of the moment. The Court is like a beehive with the buzz and hum of voices. Amidst all this, the prisoner sits calm and quiet, only at intervals you may note her lips tightly compressed. Her colour neither comes nor goes. . . ." A short half-hour passes, yet it seems an age; then the jingle of the jury-bell is heard: it sounds like the Last Trump. Solemnly the fifteen messengers of destiny file into the box; one is seen to smile, so the omens are propitious—though perhaps it is only due to nervousness. Then, in the breathless silence, the voice of the Chancellor [Foreman] announces an acquittal. So soon as the last "Not Proven" has issued from his lips, the decorum of the Court is shattered. "Loud cheers and huzzas and hand-clappings and ruffing rend the rafters, drowning the cries of purple-faced officers of court and deafening the angry Judges, who strive in vain to still the tumult." Friends gather round her to congratulate her on her escape; her law agent grasps one hand, the female warder the other. She smiles once—"a strange, sad, unlovely smile." But the great Dean of Faculty, to whose efforts she owes her freedom, remains seated at the table in the well of the Court, his head sunk in his hands. He neither looks at her nor smiles. The gate of the dock is thrown open, the trap-door is lifted, and for the last time Madeleine Smith, with her wonted elegant composure, slowly descends the stair, followed to the end by the eager gaze of the multitude, and so passed from the ken of her contemporaries.

Well do I recall being present at the finish of another famous trial thirty-six years later, namely, that of A. J. Monson, charged with the murder of Cecil Hambrough at

Ardlamont. Splendidly defended by that admirable advocate, John Comrie Thomson, the accused was acquitted in like manner to Madeleine, though the verdict was received with less enthusiasm. In beginning his address to the jury, Comrie Thomson made telling reference to the fact that, as a young counsel, he had listened in the same Court-room to the historic speech of John Inglis in behalf of Madeleine Smith, and quoted with much effectiveness the masterly opening words of that celebrated appeal: "Gentleman, the charge against the prisoner is murder, and the punishment of murder is death; and that simple statement is sufficient to suggest to you the awful nature of the occasion which brings you and me face to face."

I was struck by a further coincidence. When, upon the pronouncement of the verdict, Not Proven, the prisoner stood up, smiling, in the dock, his two junior counsel went forward to the rail and shook hands with him. Comrie Thomson left the Court without so much as a glance at his late client. The parallel is instructive.

## VII

In their joy at the triumph of innocence, and with intent further to whitewash the besmirched fame of the popular heroine, certain newspapers of the baser sort made a cruel and unwarrantable attack upon the behaviour of Mr. William Minnoch. That gentleman had, one would think, suffered sufficiently by reason of his connection with the case and might have been allowed to quit the stage without a hostile demonstration. But I am glad to see that one voice at least was raised in his defence. This well-founded protest was made by a correspondent of the *Northern Whig*, who addressed that journal as follows: "An article appeared in your columns of the 11th instant, censuring, in very strong terms, the conduct of Mr. Minnoch during the late trial at Edinburgh. I, therefore, take the liberty of writing to set you right on one or two points—or rather to lay before you facts that will induce you to alter your opinion of that gentleman. In the first place, you condemn him for consenting to appear as a witness at the trial. Upon Miss Smith's being arrested, so firmly was he convinced of her innocence that he declared his intention of marrying her as soon as she was acquitted. In the meantime he left Glasgow, giving up his business for a month, in order to avoid the chance of being subpœnaed [cited] as a witness; but it was represented to him that it would go against Miss Smith if he refused to give evidence. And, besides this, I think that you will allow that the situation in which he was placed—that of an accepted lover giving evidence against his affianced bride—was a most painful one, and not one that any man would willingly have courted.

"After he had given his evidence, he did not return home, as might have been expected, but remained at Edinburgh, and there awaited the issue of the trial; and as soon as Miss Smith was released he escorted her, not only back to Glasgow, but the whole way down to her father's country house, Rowaleyn.

"The next thing we hear of him is, that he has put down his name for £500 to a subscription which was got up for the purpose of defraying the expenses of the trial—a delicate way of testifying to poor Mr. Smith his esteem for him, and his sympathy with him during his affliction. What his private conviction with regard to Miss Smith's innocence may have been I am at a loss to say; but this is a point on which Mr. Minnoch has a right, and ought to judge. If he thought her guilty, it only renders his conduct all the more meritorious. The whole affair is involved in the deepest mystery, and forms a problem for moralists to speculate upon—a problem which will, perhaps, not be solved until the day when all things shall be made known."

The reader will remember that in her letter to the prison matron Madeleine says she has not seen her "friend" since her return; but she is by no means a reliable witness, and having taken her safely home, he may then have left her for good and all. Or it may be that the writer, though he seems to be otherwise well-informed, has confused this journey with the earlier one, when she fled to Rowaleyn and Mr. Minnoch brought her back. At any rate it would doubtless occur to him, as a man of affairs, that if his betrothed could do what she was alleged to have done to one whom she had so passionately loved, what might she not do in the end to one whom she had never loved and was marrying for his money?

# VIII

From the many notices of this extraordinary case published in newspapers and journals after the trial, I must content myself with quoting one or two extracts from a leading article in the *Saturday Review*, which seems to me the best of the lot: "The verdict in Madeleine Smith's trial is 'Not Proven.' It declares nothing. The case, then, as they say in Germany, shifts from the actual to the ideal. The guilt or innocence of the accused will henceforth be like Queen Mary's guilt or innocence—it will be a moot point for moralists. If we seem to assume the alternative of guilt, Madeleine Smith is to us only *nominis umbra*. She is an historical and debateable character, and an inquiry into her criminality becomes a question of purely moral and psychological interest. . . ."

Upon this assumption, the writer finds that in the matter of motive the chief interest of the case resides. "Yet it is not," he remarks, "any one single and simple passion—revenge, or lust, or avarice—which can end in such a catastrophe as this. It is in the mixture of motives, the complexity of passions, the conflict of sins—the seven devils wrestling with each other as well as with the victim—that the unearthly grandeur as well as horror of the deed with which she was charged consists. Passion leads many a man to murder his mistress; jealousy leads many a woman to murder her lover, even in the very frenzy of affection; cold-blooded ambition and interest prompt to murder, in order to get rid of an inconvenient obstacle to respectability and a fair standing with the world. But on the hypothesis of Madeleine Smith's guilt, we have each and all, and yet none of them, as adequate motives. The problem to solve—and it is inscrutable, because, as far as we know, absolutely without example —is the coexistence of that burning intensity of mere sexual passion which indisputably led Madeleine Smith to discard every restraint, even of common decency, that frailty so generally throws over the acts of sin, with a cool, settled malignity of self-possession, a deliberate hypocrisy in counterfeiting rapturous affection, which, for the credit of human nature, is unparalleled. And yet this must have been so, if she be guilty. The counsel for the defence never accounted for the fact—an indisputable one—that the letters to Minnoch and the last letters to her seducer (if that is to be the word), with all the old passion at least pretended, were of the same date. Whether Madeleine Smith poisoned L'Angelier or not, her parallel correspondence with him and with Minnoch in March is established; and this is the moral anomaly in presence of which the fact of murder is a mere sequence. . . . Madeleine Smith was not convicted because it was not proved that she and L'Angelier met on the night before his death. This single circumstance compelled the verdict."

Commenting on the Dean of Faculty's telling point as to the improbability of this burning, passionate girl being suddenly transformed into a cold, deliberate murderess,[1] the writer observes that the miracle might well have been worked by L'Angelier's character: "His was just the sort of mind to work this horrible change in Madeleine Smith. A meaner and more contemptible scoundrel it would be difficult to conceive; and probably his low, selfish character prompted

[1] "Gentlemen, I will not say that such a thing is absolutely impossible; but I shall venture to say it is well-nigh incredible. He will be a bold man who will seek to set limits to the depths of human depravity; but this at least all past experience teaches us: that perfection, even in depravity, is not rapidly attained, and that it is not by such short and easy stages as the prosecutor has been able to trace in the career of Madeleine Smith, that a gentle, loving girl passes at once into the savage grandeur of a Medea, or the appalling wickedness of a Borgia. No, gentlemen, such a thing is not possible."—*Speech for the Defence.*

that sort of unhappy popular sympathy with Madeleine Smith which seems to prevail, at any rate in Edinburgh. A profligate, vain adventurer, boasting of his *bonnes fortunes*, and trafficking with this *liaison*, as perhaps with others, as a means of advancement—this is what L'Angelier was. . . . We believe that as a further knowledge of his miserable character broke upon Madeleine Smith, the insight into the man who could hold this girl's shame over her, and who could resist the terrific pathos of her shuddering, shivering appeals for mercy—appeals unequalled in the whole range of tragic vehemence—may account for this moral change. The deep fountains of her passion were, on discovering her paramour's character, frozen up. She found that she had ventured everything upon an unworthy object; and the very depth of her love was changed, on the complete and perfect sense of utter loss, into the corresponding depth of hatred."

And the writer proceeds to argue, with skill and cogency, that such satisfied hate, such vengeance fulfilled, would explain the strange indifference of the prisoner, which so baffled all beholders—

> The deed is done,
> And what may follow now regards not me.

## IX

Every now and then, from that day to this, the fate of Madeleine Smith has furnished a paragraph for an all-wise and sleepless Press. She emigrated to America, Australia, and New Zealand; she lived her life in London, she settled in Staffordshire; she contracted divers marriages, with issue and without; she never married at all. *Enfin*, she frequently died and was as often resurrected. Amid such contradictory pronouncements it was difficult to discern the truth.

The earliest authentic account of her subsequent adventures appears to be that communicated by Mr. A. L. Humphreys to *Notes and Queries* (11 S. IV. Oct. 14, 1911). It begins, however, with the customary false report of her death, this time at Melbourne in 1893, on the authority of an obituary notice in the *St. James's Gazette* of 20th November. According to Mr. Humphreys, she married in the year of the trial a surgeon, named Tudor Hora, whom she accompanied to Melbourne. Four years later, the marriage having been dissolved—whether by natural or legal process is not stated—she returned to the old country, and in 1861 made a fresh matrimonial venture. Her second husband was Mr. George Wardle, an artist, then living at 5 Bloomfield Terrace, Pimlico, the bride's address being given as 72 Sloane Street, Chelsea. The wedding was celebrated at St. Paul's, Knightsbridge, on 4th July 1861; the officiating clergyman was the Rev. Robert Liddell; the witnesses were H. Hoverlock and James Smith, her brother. Of the truth of these facts there is, in the familiar words of Don Alhambra del Bolero, "no probable, possible shadow of doubt"—I have seen an extract of the marriage certificate. Mr. Wardle, I understand, was associated later with William Morris and William de Morgan in their artistic pursuits.

It appears, from an article in the *Scotsman* of 4th January 1926, that Madeleine was then alive, at the age of 90, in the United States of America. Her husband, Mr. Wardle, was a man of much distinction, who was not only highly talented, but possessed of a good social position and considerable wealth. " She very soon made for herself a position in the literary and Socialist circles of London in those days, being well known to some still alive, whose reputation is world-wide, and who knew and guarded the tragic secret of her life."

The last word is with *The Times* of 18th April 1928. Madeleine is there stated, on good authority, to have died in America in the preceding week at the ripe age of 92. "Her husband, Mr. Wardle, was one of the first members of the Social Democratic Club in London, and her identity was known to most of the members. When well on in years she went to America, and it was only last year that her identity leaked out. Some cinema promoters suggested the exploiting of the story of the crime by the production of a film drama, in which Madeleine Smith would taking the leading rôle; but she refused. Pressure was brought to bear on her, and a threat made that if she declined to fall in with the suggestion, steps would be taken to have her sent back to Britain as an undesirable alien. As a result of the publicity that ensued, however, more humane counsels prevailed, and Madeleine was permitted to remain. Her death took place last week."

So the long tragedy ended in a farce, and Madeleine, despite her venerable age, was not immune from the ruthless realism of Hollywood. It is pathetic to think of that ancient woman—she was born in 1836, the year before Queen Victoria's accession—coerced into playing again the part of the wondrous girl who had thrilled the susceptibilities of three bygone generations. Surely, those responsible for this grotesque outrage lacked equally a sense of decency and of humour. But the spirit of the age knows neither.

## X

In addition to figuring so largely in the law reports, Madeleine Smith has her niche in polite letters. Miss Emma Robinson, the gifted but neglected author of *Whitefriars* and other historical fictions, told the old tale in novel form: *Madeleine Graham* (London: John Maxwell and Company, 1864). Though marked, or marred, by the flamboyant style then in vogue, the three volumes, charming in format, afford an enthralling study of the facts; the characters of the heroine, of Camille Le Tellier (L'Angelier), and of George Behringbright (Mr. Minnoch), are drawn with much insight and skill— Madeleine herself being uncannily lifelike.

And in our own time a sister-writer, Miss Winifred Duke, has made of the story a grim little play: *Madeleine Smith: A Tragi-Comedy* (Edinburgh: William Hodge and Company,

1928). It is in two acts; the first shews Madeleine at a dinner-party on the day of L'Angelier's death, when the ghost of the miserable Frenchman troubles, like that of Banquo, the peace of the board; the second, the Smiths' drawing-room at Rowaleyn, on the night of the prodigal daughter's return. Here again, her character is drawn with subtlety and effect.

And so we take leave of Madeleine Smith, as she sits alone beside the dying fire—the family having "retired" to rest, after delivering their several opinions on her impropriety; and letting the dead past bury its dead, surveys, rather wearily, the grey vista of the years to come. Had she been able to trace in the embers the tedious course of her pilgrimage, even that indomitable spirit might well have faltered.

# INDEX

Abduction of an heiress, 106

Aberdalgie House, robbery at, 4, 24–7, 32–3, 40

Aberdeen, trial of Mrs. Keith at, 246–54

Adams, Richard, 171, 191

Aitchison, Lord Justice-Clerk, 8, 24–5, 37–42

Alemore, Andrew Pringle, Lord, 214

Allison, Professor, evidence of, 30–1

Anderson, Dr. John, evidence of, 30

Anderson, George, evidence of, 84

Arnott, John, evidence of, 21, 33–4

Atkinson, John, Q.C., 171, 177, 185–7, 193

Auchinleck, Alexander Boswell, Lord, 214

Auchtermuchty, 81–2, 85, 96

Baber, Mr., J.P., evidence of, 123

*Bahr-recht*, ordeal of, 139

Baird, Robert, 285

Balfour, Elizabeth, evidence of, 81

Balfour, Sheriff, 212–13

Banff, 245–6

Barrie, Robert, evidence of, 17–18, 23

Barron, Mary, evidence of, 178, 192

Barrowman, Jean, evidence of, 83

Bartlett, Mrs. Adelaide, 164, 261

Baynton, Sarah, trial of, 105–8, 128–33; and abduction of Mrs. Rawlins, 109–116, 125–6, 130; and marriage of Mrs. Rawlins, 117–18, 121–3, 126, 130; defence of, 131–3; verdict on, 133; sentence on, 134–5

Bell, John, 142–4

Berkeley, Mrs., evidence of, 115

Berry, James, executioner, 195–6

Blake, Miss, evidence of, 122

Blake, Mr. and Mrs., evidence of, 115–16, 123

Blyth, Elizabeth, evidence of, 80

Blyth, Mrs., evidence of, 80–1

Boath, James, evidence of, 251

Borden, Lizzie, 259, 273

Boyle, David (Lord Justice-Clerk), 50, 60, 63–4

Bravo, Florence, 261

Brebner, Isabel, evidence of, 83

Brechin, 205

Bremner, James, 226–7

Brough, John, evidence of, 86

Bruce, Elspeth, 242; evidence of, 237–240, 250

Bulkley, Mr., evidence of, 124

Burke, Peter, *Celebrated Trials* of, 135–6

Burnet, J. R. Wardlaw, 8, 12–14, 18–19, 24–5, 35–7

Busby, Mrs. Sabina, 108–10, 125–6; evidence of, 113–15, 130

Busby, William, 108, 110

Cameron, John (Advocate-Depute), 8

Campbell, Katharine, evidence of, 215

Campbell, Sheriff George, 212–13

Campbeltown, Kintyre, 65–7

Carnegie, Dr. James, 205, 213, 219

Castlehill, Sir John Lockhart, Lord, 146

Caulfield, Captain and Mrs., 168; evidence of, 174–5

Chantrelle, M., 195

Chap, Dr., 234, 241, 243

Charteris, Colonel Francis, 158

Clark, Anne, 202, 219; on poison threats, 203–8; and death of Ogilvy, 209–11; as witness, 214–18, 220

Clerk, John, 50, 60

Clifford, Captain, 106

Coalston, George Brown, Lord, 214

Cockburn, Lord, 43–4, 50–1; *Circuit Jottings* of, 43

Collessie, 78, 85

Colquhoun, Archibald (Lord Advocate), 50, 56, 60

Colthurst, Mr., evidence of, 174

Cotchett, Mrs., evidence of, 121–2

Cream, Dr. Neill, 166

Crippen, Dr., 166

Crooke, Jane, 197–8

Crooke, Simon, inquest on, 197–8

Crosbie, Andrew, 214, 220

Cross, Dr. Philip, trial of, 164, 171 *et seq.*; crime of, 165, 169–71; character of, 166–8; letter of, to the Press, 180–1; obtains arsenic, 181; witnesses against, 174–85; defence of, 185–91; summing up of case of, 191–4; speech of, 194; execution of, 195–7; inquest on, 196

Cross, Henrietta Maria, 169, 175–6, 181, 186; evidence of, 188–91

Cross, Mrs. Laura, 167–9; murder of, 169 *et seq.*

Crowley, Dr. Timothy, evidence of, 183–4, 185, 193, 197

Cuddies Strip, murder in, 3 *et seq.*

Cullen, Robert, 246

Cupar, execution at, 94–5

Dalrymple, Sir David, 214, 216
Dalrymple, Sir John (Lord Advocate), 145–6, 154
Darnell, Mr. Serjeant, 107, 110
Davidson, Inspector, 22, 24, 27
Deas, George, 79–80, 92–3
De Quincey, Thomas, *On Murder*, 97–8
Dickson, Helen, 150–1, 154
Dirom, Sheriff Alexander, 246
Douglas, David, evidence of, 24–6, 33, 40
Douglas, John, advocate, 246
Douglas, John, evidence of, 26, 33, 40
Douglas Cause, 233
Drumcairnie, John Murray, Lord, 146
Drummond, Home (Advocate-Depute), 50
Drummond, James, evidence of, 15–17, 32
Drummond, Mrs., 11, 17
Drury Lane, Star and Garter tavern, 109, 114, 116, 126
Duke, Winifred, *Six Trials* of, 164; *The Laird* of, 228; *Madeleine Smith : A Tragi-Comedy* of, 293–4
Duncan, Detective-Sergeant, 27
Duncan, John, evidence of, 251
Dundas, Henry, 214, 216
Dundas, William, 147
Dunfermline, 76, 80, 84–5, 96

Eastmiln, house of, 216–17
Eastmiln, Lady, 201, 204, 208, 210, 217–218
Edinburgh, Henderson's visit to, 84–5; trial of Stanfield in, 146; World's End Close in, 159; trial of Katharine Nairn in, 214 *et seq.*
Elder, Charles, evidence of, 21
Elliot, Sir Gilbert, of Minto, 214
Elphinstoun, Alexander, 246, 253
Ewan, Dorothy, evidence of, 11, 15, 32

Fenwick, Marjory, 7; and murder of Kerrigan, 3 *et seq.*; assault on, 4–5, 8–9, 29–31; evidence of, 9–15, 36, 38–9; lost clothes of, 11, 28, 35; identifies assailant, 22–3, 39; interview with, 42–3
Fenwick, Mrs., evidence of, 28
Finlay, Dr., 243
Ford, David, evidence of, 82, 96
Forfar, 212
Forgery, in Scots law, 79
Forret, Sir David Balfour, Lord, 146
Fountainhall, Lord, 141, 144, 147, 152, 156

Gelly, George, evidence of, 236
Gibson, J. H., 8

Gibson, John (Attorney-General), 171, 187
Glasgow, case of Madeleine Smith in, 262 *et seq.*
Godfrey, Dr., 181; evidence of, 175
Gordon, Cosmo (Advocate-Depute), 246, 253–4
Gordon, James, of Techmuiry, 244
Gould, Sir Henry, 107
Gow, evidence of, 23–4, 33, 36, 39
Grace, Dr., of Cupar, 89, 101
Green, Mr., evidence of, 124
Greig, Thomas, evidence of, 81
Griffin, Dennis, evidence of, 180

Hammond, Detective-Lieutenant, 27
Handcock, Beatrice, evidence of, 179
Harcarse, Sir Roger Hogg, Lord, 146
Harcourt, Sir Simon, 107
Hartwell, John, 110, 114, 116, 122, 126–127; trial of, 105, 107–8, 129–33; verdict on, 133
Harvey, Judge, 157
Hayes, Rev. Richard, 174–5
Heggie, David, evidence of, 90–1
Heggie, Henry, 88–9, 100
Heggie, Robert, evidence of, 86
Henderson, John, accounts of case of, 73–5, 98–9; early life of, 76–7; trial of, 78 *et seq.*; indictment of, 79, 99; evidence against, 80–8; declarations of, 91–2, 99; verdict and sentence on, 93–4; execution of, 95; confession of, 96–7, 99
Henry, James, "justifiable homicide" by, 65–7
Hepburn, Alexander, evidence of, 239–40
Hermand, Lord, 50, 61
Higgins, Sergeant, evidence of, 181, 190, 194
Hill, Arthur, evidence of, 21
Holborn, Vine tavern in, 116–17, 121, 126–7
Holt, Sir John, 107, 125–8, 132–4
Holt, Thomas, 107–8, 116, 122, 128, 133
Homicide, justifiable, 67
Hope, Lord Justice-Clerk, 267, 271
Hope, Rear-Admiral William Johnstone, 56
Hora, Tudor, 292
Horgan, Mr., Coroner, 196–8
Hume, Sir Patrick, 147
Humphreys, A. L., 291–2
Hyde, Sir Nicholas, 157

Inglis, John, 267, 286–7, 290
Ireland, murder in, 163 *et seq.*
Irvine, Dr. Alexander, evidence of, 251–252
Irvine, James, evidence of, 251

James, Henry, on Madeleine Smith, 274-5

Jameson, Andrew, evidence of, 89-90, 101

Jefferson, Margaret, 172, 175, 181, 186-187; evidence of, 176-7

Johnson, Erasmus, obstinate juror, 132-133

Johnston, Sir John, 106

Johnstoun, Janet, 149-52

Jones, William, murder of, 50-64, 67-9

Juries, curious verdicts of, 41-4, 67; introduction of charge to, 222, 246, 255

Kames, Henry Home, Lord, 214, 246, 250, 253-4; charge to the jury of, 222, 246, 255

Kay, John, 47-9

Keith, Alexander (old Northfield); death of, 234 et seq.; will of, 235; burial of, 242-3

Keith, Anne, 234, 238, 241, 249

Keith, George (young Northfield), 234-235; murder charge made by, 236, 238, 244-5, 252; suspects foul play, 238-40, 242-4

Keith, John, 234, 238, 252

Keith, Mrs., of Northfield, trial of, 233, 238, 246 et seq.; declaration of, 236-238, 240; her relations with her son, 245, 250-1; verdict on, 253-4; pardon for, 254-5

Keith, William, 234, 242; trial of, 233, 238, 246 et seq.; declaration of, 236-237, 240-1; his relations with his mother, 245, 250-1; verdict on, 253-254; pardon for, 254-5

Kennedy, John, Sheriff, 92, 101

Kerrigan, Danny, murder of, 3 et seq.

King, John, evidence of, 239-40

Kirchoffer, Caroline, evidence of, 175

Kirwan, William Burke, 163

Königsmark, Count, 106

Lamson, Dr., 166

Lang, Andrew, on the Madeleine Smith case, 275

L'Angelier, P. E., love affair of, 262-6, 270-1; death of, 264-7, 272; diary of, 264, 266, 272; character of, 290-1

Lawson, Mrs., evidence of, 85

Leahy, Jane, evidence of, 177

Lee, Mrs., abduction of, 106

Leith, murder on pier of, 47 et seq.; firing on vessel entering, 65

Lennox, Margaret, case of, 44

Leven and Melville, Earl of, 78

Levit, John, evidence of, 57-8

Linlithgow, George, Earl of, 146

Lloyd, Henry, 65

Lockhart, Alexander, 214, 220-2

M'Callum, Sergeant, 16-17, 22, 32, 36

M'Carthy, Cornelius, evidence of, 180

M'Dougall, evidence of, 9

M'Grath, Mary, 177; evidence of, 178

M'Guigan, John, 5-6; trial of, 7 et seq.; indictment of, 8; identification of, 12-14, 22-4, 39; gun of, 18-21, 23, 33, 39; verdict and sentence on, 41-3

M'Guigan, Mrs., evidence of, 20, 36

Mackenzie, George, evidence of, 85

Mackenzie, Lord, 79, 94

Mackenzie, Ronald, advocate, 149

Mackenzie, Ronald, evidence of, 19-20, 33-4, 39

Mackenzie, Sir George, 146, 152-4

M'Lachlan, Mrs., case of, 80 n., 93, 195, 261

Maconochie, Alexander (Solicitor-General), 50

Macpherson, Chief Constable, 23

Madras, Mrs., evidence of, 181-2

Mair, John, evidence of, 242

Malcolm, Dr., of Letham, 89, 101

Mark, Anna, evidence of, 150-2

Marriott, Humphrey, 173; evidence of, 184-5

Martin, Alexander, evidence of, 28-9

Maybrick, Mrs., 195, 261

Meadowbank, Lord, and trial of Thomas Whyte, 50, 56, 61; and trial of John Henderson, 78-9, 93-4

Meik, Dr., of Alyth, 209-11, 217

Melvil, Andrew, 146

Millam, James, 210-11, 218-19

Miller, Thomas (Lord Advocate), 214, 220-1

Millie, Catherine, evidence of, 87

Millie, James, murder of, 73 et seq.; forged signature of, 84, 92; discovery of body of, 88-91, 99-102

Millie, Jean, evidence of, 88

Minnoch, William, 263, 265-6, 284, 287-9; letter to, 269

Moffat, Dr., 16; evidence of, 29-30

Moncreiff, Lord Advocate, 267, 271

Moniepenny, William, 147

Monimail, 78, 81

Monro, Dr. Alexander, 94

Monson, A. J., acquittal of, 286-7

Montague, Mr., 107

Montgomery, James (Solicitor-General), 214

Muir of Achindrane, trial of, 156

Muirhead, James, evidence of, 148

Murphy, Mr. Justice, 171, 191-5

Nairn, Katharine (Mrs. Ogilvy, marriage of, 201–2; procurance of poison by, 203, 205–8, 212; her relations with Patrick Ogilvy, 203–6; death of husband of, 208–11; arrest of, 211; letters of, 213, 220; trial of, 214–22, 253; criticisms of trial of, 221–3; escape of, 225–7, 233

Nairn, Sir Thomas, 201

Nairn, William, 226

New Mills, Haddington, 139–42, 158–9

Nightingale, Mrs., 108–9; evidence of, 110–13, 129–30

Norkott, Joan, murder of, 156–8

Ogilvy, Alexander, 201–3, 211–13, 217, 224, 228

Ogilvy, Dr., of Forfar, 207, 211, 217–19

Ogilvy, Lieutenant Patrick, 201–3; quarrels with brother, 204–5; and the poison, 205–7, 210, 212–13, 219; arrest of, 211–13; trial of, 214–22; sentence and execution of, 222–4

Ogilvy, Thomas (Eastmiln), marriage of, 201–2; threats to life of, 203, 205–208; death of, 208 et seq.; health of, 218–19

Palmer, Dr., poisoner, 166

Parry, Dr. Leonard, Some Famous Medical Trials of, 164

Pearson, Dr. Charles Yelverton, medical evidence of, 182–3, 187, 191, 193

Pearson, Edmund, Studies in Murder of, 259

Peddie, John, evidence of, 18–20, 33, 36–7, 39

Perry, Mary, 260, 263–5, 273, 284

Perth, murder at, 3 et seq.; trial of Henderson at, 74, 78 et seq.; trial of Margaret Tindal at, 93 n.

Perth, James Drummond, Earl of, 154–5

Pitfour, James Ferguson, Lord, 214

Pitheavlis, Hill Farm of, 9

Pitmilly, Lord, 50, 62

Poole, William, evidence of, 179

Porteous, Captain John, 65

Powell, Sir John, 107, 134

Powis, Sir Littleton, 107

Prain, A. M., advocate, 8

Pritchard, Dr., 165, 170 n., 185

Ptolmey, P.C., 16

Pugh, Mr., 118–20, 131

Rae, David, 214, 220

Ramsay, Dr., 211, 217

Ramsay, John, of Ochtertyre, 220, 255

Rawlins, Pleasant, abduction of, 105 et seq.; arrest of, 109, 114, 126; evidence of, 116–18, 130; marriage of, 117–18, 120–8, 130

Robertson, Isobel, evidence of, 251

Robinson, Emma, Madeleine Graham of, 293

Rollo, Christian, evidence of, 83

Ronan, Stephen, 171

Row, James, 146

Rushforth, John, 88–90

Russell, Albert, K.C., 8, 24, 27, 31–4

St. John, Mrs., 109, 129

Sampson, Anne, evidence of, 215, 219

Scoreman, Mr., evidence of, 119–20

Scott, James, of Bristo, 158

Scott, Sir Walter, on Stanfield murder, 156

Shandy Hall, murder in, 163 et seq.

Shepherd, James, evidence of, 21–2

Shiells, Mrs., 222, 226

Skinner, Miss, 168–70, 172–4, 177, 180, 186, 197

Smethurst, Dr., poisoner, 166

Smith, Dr., of St. Fergus, 166, 271

Smith, Dr. John, evidence of, 55

Smith, Madeleine, 259 et seq.; love affair of, 262–6, 270; obtains poison, 265–6, 272–3; letters of, 265–6, 268–70, 273, 279–80, 285, 290; trial of, 266–7, 271, 283–6; portraits of, 273–6; Press-cuttings on, 276–8, 289–291; appearance of, 281–2; subsequent adventures of, 291–3

Smythe, George (Advocate-Depute), 79, 92

Spalding, Mr., of Glenkilry, 202, 205, 209–10, 218

Speedie, evidence of, 18

Speedy, Matthew, evidence of, 84

Spence, John, evidence of, 11, 15–16, 32

Spurr, John, 114, 116; trial of, 105, 107–8, 129–33

Spurway, Umphray, evidence of, 144–146

Stanfield, John, 142, 158

Stanfield, Lady, 140, 149–50, 156

Stanfield, Philip, ordeal by touch of, 139, 146, 153; trial of, 139, 146 et seq.; character and conduct of, 140–1; and death of his father, 143–5; indictment of, 147; evidence against, 147–152; verdict on and execution of, 154–5

Stanfield, Sir James, murder of, 139 et seq.; attempted murders of, 141, 153; discovery of body of, 143–4; burials and exhumation of, 145–6; bleeding of body of, 146, 153; cursed by his son, 148, 152; estate of, 158–9

Stewart, Andrew, 205–9, 218

Stewart, Robert, evidence of, 17–18

Strachan, John, evidence of, 239–40

# INDEX

Sturrock, Elizabeth, 206, 208, 210, 212, 215, 220

Swendsen, Haagen, trial of, 105 *et seq.*; indictment of, 107–8; "brother" of Mrs. Baynton, 109, 111–13, 115, 125, 129–30; evidence against, 110–18; defence of, 118–25; verdict on, 128, 132–3; sentence on, 134; execution of, 135

Taylor, Robert, evidence of, 84

Taylor, William, evidence of, 235, 239–240, 242–3, 250

Tennyson Jesse, Miss, on Madeleine Smith, 259–60, 270, 272, 279

Thoirs, Sir David, 147

Thomson, George, 150–1, 153–4

Thomson, James, evidence of, 150–1, 153

Thomson, John Comrie, 287

Tindal, Margaret, case of, 93 *n.*

Topping, John, evidence of, 143

Touch, ordeal by, 139, 146, 153, 156–7

Trotter, Dr., 30

Tyacke, District-Inspector, 180

Tyndall, William, evidence of, 184

Wakefield, Edward Gibbon, 106–7

Wakeman, bailiff, evidence of, 116

Walker, N. M. L. (Advocate-Depute), 8

Walker, Sarah, evidence of, 122

Wallace, William, evidence of, 81

Walpole, Hugh, on Madeleine Smith, 267–8

Wardle, George, 292

Watt, James, evidence of, 84–5

Watt, Janet, evidence of, 251

Webster, Dr., 166

Welsh, John, 140

Wharton, Miss, abduction of, 106

Whinny Park, 77–8, 82, 86–91, 96

Whyte, Thomas, portrait of, 47; trial of, 50 *et seq.*; witnesses against, 51–6; witnesses for defence of, 56–9; sentence on, 60–4; Hume on, 67–8

Wight, Alexander, 246, 253

Wilkie, evidence of, 9

Wilson, Andrew, evidence of, 83–4

Wilson, Rev. James, evidence of, 235, 242–3

Witnesses, inaudibility of, 26–7

Woodley, Captain, evidence of, 179

Wright, George, Q.C., 171, 191

Wright, Robert Houghton, evidence of, 53, 57